REGGIE YATES UNSEEN

MY JOURNEY

BBC
BOOKS

1 3 5 7 9 10 8 6 4 2

BBC Books, an imprint of Ebury Publishing
20 Vauxhall Bridge Road,
London SW1V 2SA

BBC Books is part of the Penguin Random House group of companies
whose addresses can be found at global.penguinrandomhouse.com

Penguin
Random House
UK

First published by BBC Books in 2017

www.penguin.co.uk

A CIP catalogue record for this book is available from the British Library

ISBN 9781785942785

Text design by Seagull Design Ltd.
Typeset in 11.5/19.5 pt Georgia Pro by Jouve (UK), Milton Keynes

Printed and bound in Great Britain by Clays Ltd, St Ives PLC

Penguin Random House is committed to a sustainable future
for our business, our readers and our planet. This book is made
from Forest Stewardship Council® certified paper.

MIX
Paper from
responsible sources
FSC® C018179

For Anna Scher.

Thank you

CONTENTS

INTRODUCTION

8am, summer 1992. The dull hum of cheap strip lights owning the silence struck fear into my pounding nine-year-old heart. An offensively floral-scented make-up artist edged closer. Between her colossal barnet and cherry red lipstick peeped a pair of piercing blue eyes that still haunt me to this day. Her brush powdered with brown make-up (a whole two shades too dark) finally connected with my face. Suddenly and officially, there was no turning back.

This was it. The minute Kieran Buckley and Aaron Burn found out, I wouldn't be able to show my face on the football pitch ever again. The minute Uncle George, who took huge pleasure in referring to me as a *thesssspian*, found out, I'd never live it down. For the first time in my life, I was wearing make-up. I was officially a working actor.

When you think child actor, the first thing that comes to mind is a pre-pubescent millionaire divorcing their parents before riding the cocaine train to bankruptcy. For me, being a child actor was a social education. The people and challenges I experienced have helped to shape my career and to make me the man I am today.

Growing up in north London, I was consistently faced with the realities of class and wealth. Sandwiched between tourist-heavy, upwardly mobile Camden and rough-around-the-edges Hackney, Islington was the London borough I called home.

My mother always joked about the people living behind the huge panelled doors of perfect million-pound properties on our road. She'd laugh because they had no choice but to walk past our dirty council estate. Weirdly, for some reason I was never embarrassed or ashamed by the block.

As young as five while walking to school I remember being fascinated by the people and stories that existed as close as a few hundred yards from my own front door. Even at that age I was aware that, though they lived close by, they existed in an entirely different world.

❦ Different is good and authenticity is invaluable ❧

After escaping the unavoidable cloud of floral perfume during my first make-up chair experience, I found myself in the costume truck staring in awe at established cast members who were floating in and out, howling with laughter while throwing around dirty West Indian jokes. This was my bizarre but brilliant introduction to the world of TV.

I was to be sharing screen time with fictional characters my family had loved from the minute they burst onto British TV. My first gig was to play a tiny role on Channel 4's longest-running sitcom at the time, *Desmond's*.

Desmond's was special. A sitcom about a black family who ran a successful business in Peckham, south-east London began its seventy-one-episode run in 1989. It wasn't just special for me as a new actor and fan of the show; it was unique in TV full stop. The fact the show even existed was beyond a triumph, it was a miracle. This was the only long-running series on prime-time British TV with a cast made up almost exclusively of West Indian and African performers. The show was inclusive and at its core about family; more importantly, it was positive.

Any feelings of intimidation or nerves were quashed as I realised I was surrounded by men and women who looked and sounded like my family and the people I grew up around. Who they were off camera served as a huge driver for their on-screen personas, and what made them unique as people bolstered the show with a legitimacy and point of difference that was not only refreshing, but authentic.

Now at this point, we're talking about me being a natty-haired, big-toothed, newbie child actor who wasn't even in double figures yet. My mother had handcrafted my haircut with a pair of safety scissors complete with orange handles, and I'd probably eaten my body weight in make-up truck sherbet lemons. Age, bad haircut and sugar high aside, I quickly learned a valuable lesson.

Desmond's resonated with all audiences not just because it was entertaining, but also because it was different. The black south-east London take on family life was a huge hit with mainstream audiences as it offered a voice unheard on a platform of that scale. From the calypso theme tune to the West Indian banter, and not forgetting those old African sayings, new eyes and ears were won over as the show delivered an exciting and fresh world for the majority.

Desmond's was different and, for my perceptive younger self, the penny dropped. Different is good and authenticity is invaluable.

Television was never something I'd pined over; in fact performing wasn't something I'd realised I was drawn to. Keeping myself entertained was always the motivation for my moments of showing off for friends, mum or anyone that would pay attention. If it wasn't me filling the silence, it was music or TV and when it wasn't my turn to talk I listened. Closely.

Obsessing over the words used by Q-Tip from A Tribe Called Quest saw pre-teen me desperately trying to understand why Bonita had an apple bum. I spent hours reciting raps I was far too young to understand, but listening to what my mother and her friends spoke about fascinated me on a whole other level.

INTRODUCTION

Even as a child there was always something I found incredibly captivating about the fantastic hidden within the familiar. From the double meanings hurled bar after bar in the raps I immersed myself in, to eavesdropping on adult conversations heard through doors and walls, people and their truest experiences were the stories I gravitated toward.

The journey from actor to presenter in my teens saw the demands on me change radically. I'd learned early on that the best and most successful actors lose themselves within a character; they become someone else, forgoing the foundations of their own uniqueness and embodying whatever role they've been chosen to play. As a presenter, I was given direction and advice that was quite literally the polar opposite.

In 2012, I was fortunate enough to front my own radio documentary for BBC Radio 5 Live called *Is Mum Enough?* about growing up with a single parent. I spoke to friends, family and my role models, talking intimately about key moments in my life. It became a deeply personal and edifying experience, even though I had to venture into testing territory. The subject matter meant that I had to investigate my own role models, and in one part of the documentary I was on mic with a man I describe as my TV dad, Billy Macqueen.

I began working with Billy when I was twelve, during his time as an exec at Disney, and my first long-running presenting role was as one of a gang of child presenters fronting *The Disney Club* for ITV. It wasn't even close to its American equivalent, *The Mickey Mouse Club*, where hosts would sing and dance and go on to huge careers in music and film, including alumni Justin Timberlake, Ryan Gosling and Britney Spears. Sadly, we couldn't dance and were brilliantly British in our hooligan-like singing, so we stuck to just being kids on screen. Somehow, it worked. Billy wasn't on set but occasionally came into the office or studio bringing his own brand of profanity and chaos, which I was instantly drawn to. Our relationship grew closer over the years as we worked together on several other projects, most notably the Sunday morning children's entertainment series for the BBC called *Smile*.

You often see it written in leadership or self-help books that the culture of any company is built from the top down, and Billy's brand of leadership was and still is incredible. Alongside long-term business partner Maddy Darrell – who directed and produced *The Disney Club* and now runs an award-winning production company with Billy – they created the type of environment that encouraged a style of presentation that played a huge role in my eventual fronting of documentaries.

TV was a different place at the time. There was a party for every occasion and a seemingly endless budget for cabs, treats, gifts and whatever we the cast wanted. In hindsight, I can't even begin to imagine what it must have been like working with a pack of pre-teen children's TV presenters. All horny, emotional, spotty and awkward, we must have been a nightmare. Between dousing myself with Lynx Africa deodorant and bathing in Oxy Clean spot cream, I somehow learned my lines and got the job done. To this day I'm not sure how, but I remember as clear as my now spot-free face the advice given by Billy.

His delivery was refreshingly honest and unmistakable. It was a style best described as a relentless machine gun, peppering people with assertions presented as jokes. Unfortunately, they were the kind that cut dangerously close to the bone. 'Be you,' he'd say, quickly followed by, 'We're paying you to be you so don't fuck it up.'

Some of the folks in positions of power viewed us, the bright-eyed bushy-tailed newbies as a flock just waiting to be fleeced. Billy not only wanted us to win, but to do so being ourselves.

As a teenage presenter there seemed to be a strange reaction to what I brought to the table. With years of experience as an actor, I could switch my delivery tonally without really trying and would always embellish on scripts desperately trying to put Billy's advice into practice.

However, outside of working with people like Billy, being me didn't always go down so well. At the time, there was a desire by the industry for the crop of young BBC faces in which I now found myself a permanent fixture, to be . . . well, mayonnaise. Flavourless, colourless and devoid of any individuality. Even as a teenager, that made no sense to me.

At the age of fifteen, I was fronting bits for the BBC as a presenter but also performing as a cast regular in long-running children's drama *Grange Hill* and in Channel Five's soap *Family Affairs*. Acting still felt fun, but with my beak well and truly wet as a presenter, the desire to find work that allowed the personal stamp encouraged by Billy outweighed the opportunities to do so.

In any African home that enjoys television as a family, programme choice is usually placed firmly in the hands of the ranking family member. Growing up in a Ghanaian home right down to the doilies and fridge full of Tupperware, my stepfather reigned supreme over the remote control. That sought-after piece of kit invariably sat submissively on the arm of his favourite chair. For us kids, his dominance of the sole screen in the house usually worked against us, but occasionally he'd pick moments on the box that were brilliant.

It was at this point in my teens that the presenters I looked at with admiration shifted. I was drawn to those that no longer felt like hosts, but far more like versions of their true self only without the profanity . . . in some cases.

The unapologetically loud Chris Evans on *Don't Forget Your Toothbrush* was the commander of every second committed to tape. Regardless of his shoulder-pad-heavy purple suits, somehow I felt that I knew who he was as a bloke. That connective sleight of hand was incredible to watch and inspiring.

Terry Christian on *The Word*, Davina McCall on *Streetmate* and even Jonathan Ross's late-night persona all shared elements of getting the job done in the most traditional way. What made them special to me was their ability to find a moment to inject that little twinkle making the mundane come alive. The one thing all of these fantastic presenters had in common wasn't their likeable personalities or cheeky tone; who they were on screen was fundamentally bound by the style of TV they were fronting.

It was at this stage that what I wanted to do hadn't shown itself yet, but, in the shape of a terrible haircut and offensively loud bowling shirt, it was about to.

❛ *A horrible Hawaiian shirt* ❜

Entertainment has and will always be a slave to format, and so long as the idea is strong enough, every episode commissioned will feel and sometimes even look practically the same. This is never the case for documentary.

On one of the many nights at the mercy of my stepfather's questionable TV taste, as a family we found ourselves watching BBC2. After a fluffy iteration of the channel's distinctive numbered logo did a few back flips, something I'd never seen on screen unfolded.

A handheld camera followed a floppy, friendly young guy in a horrible Hawaiian shirt with huge glasses and bad hair. The sequence clearly wasn't planned, polished or scripted but instantly we were silenced and glued to it. This was the first time I'd come into contact with the work of Louis Theroux and I was flummoxed. Up until this point, in my mind the man in front of camera was a certain type of alpha male, with a particular type of confidence and he never allowed anyone else to best him in a conversation.

That wasn't what was at work on any episode of *Weird Weekends*. This was a young, likeable guy who happily threw himself into every situation, playing the fool, appearing naïve or allowing someone to laugh at his expense. His manner on screen served his intention to cut through the bullshit, arriving at the candid core of a subject's outlook or belief system. I was in full fan boy mode instantly.

After just one episode of watching Theroux at work it became immediately clear to me that this was a lane I would kill to operate within. But given my fluffy list of credits and age this could never happen to someone like me. Right?

I'm a person who has been described as many things. Namely: meddlesome, snoopy, interfering, prying and, occasionally, 'fucking nosy'. I prefer 'interested in people'. The reason I feel the films I make even begin to resonate or trigger healthy conversation at dinner tables and in living rooms across the country is because I don't put myself on the outside of a situation when the camera is on, I throw myself into it.

In some films I've immersed myself in the subject matter by living as the people I intend to understand. Sometimes the way to the core of an issue has been by opening up and sharing my own story with the people I meet. Learning from getting it wrong and making sure I keep in mind what was done when it felt right, I've finally begun to understand that who I am makes my films what they are.

As a black British man with a career spanning twenty-six years in the business, I can honestly say I've nearly walked away several times. As a minority in British TV you're constantly made to feel odd in your outlook, because culturally you're an abnormality, and by the numbers you're an anomaly. Retaining a sense of self is sometimes tougher than the job itself. The feelings of not being understood or a desperation to be heard can breed resentment or, as in my case, a decline in self-belief.

Growing up a stone's throw from wealth but surrounded by poverty as an experience was mirrored later in my life, but in an entirely different way.

In my early twenties I was working full time in TV and earning good money. For the first time I felt like the public knew my face. I had a popular show on national radio and was introducing the biggest international names weekly on the world's longest-running music show, *Top of the Pops*.

I owned two London properties and was calm in my financial position and comfortable in my career. Without realising, I was a world apart from the friends I'd grown up with. Suddenly, the owners of those million-pound properties were my neighbours.

Conflicts of guilt, success and frustration started the rumblings of self-doubt. My progress may have been slowed as, finally, I was offered a role I never believed could come my way. Fronting a documentary was something I'd always wanted but up until now I'd been sure I was the last person an audience would take seriously leading any film of any weight or importance.

By this point I'd established myself as a presenter in the worlds of music and entertainment. The profile I'd achieved with the audience that had grown up with me from children's TV made me the perfect young face to join a group of established personalities in Kenya. The project was an immersive documentary for charitable organisation Comic Relief and I was besides myself to be asked.

Upon returning home after living and working in the Kenyan slum of Kibera for seven days, I was faced with the typical and expected questions from friends, work colleagues and family. 'How was it?' and 'how did you survive?' were the openers, which garnered the stock response, 'how long have you got?'.

This was my first time in this world. It wasn't my show, my name wasn't in the title, but it was the first time I was consistently being asked to be me. Completely. On this occasion I was neither presenter nor contributor, I was somewhere in between. As one of four 'faces' fronting the two-part special aiming to raise money for the slum, I was allocated my own self-shooting director. As both the director and cameraman, his job was to ask questions from behind the camera, but he also insisted on making eye contact below the viewfinder, going back and forth with me in conversation about what I thought, felt and was learning.

His name was Sam Wilkinson, and he's a director I've subsequently been around the world with. We've since found ourselves in every situation imaginable, but this red dirt hillside in Kenya was where we first met. His pasty legs and short shorts left me with no option but to take the piss. It would have been rude not to. The geezer was wearing tight blue gym shorts with a yellow trim for god's sakes. To make matters worse, he had on matching long socks and a T-shirt.

My inevitable anxiety due to our surroundings and my total ignorance as to what lay ahead was quickly killed as we laughed. A lot. I laughed at his outfits mostly, but instantly I was relaxed and something new started to happen on camera. This was the first time anyone had asked me deeply personal questions while rolling and, to begin with, I didn't get it.

And yet, in conversation with Sam, I began to forget the camera was there. We were getting to the heart of a situation and allowing any frustration or anger I felt, motivated by the poverty or illness I was faced with, to show on screen. I'd never before had the opportunity to explore my reaction to very serious issues in this way. That, and having my director's pale beanpole legs to laugh at in the toughest of moments, made for a totally new feeling. I had to do it again.

Crying on camera for the first time and allowing myself to open up about family, and my own journey in relation to the young men I was living with challenged me in a way I had never experienced in my personal life, let alone on camera. I saw myself in the people I met and was able to truly share how that made me feel.

This experience unlocked a desire to push for further challenges and opportunities to make factual TV. I was hungry for situations that could only lead to something positive for the millions watching at home. But when faced with the next opportunity to do so, my old friend self-doubt paid me a visit, and that bastard brought a suitcase determined to stay a while.

That opportunity came around a lot quicker than I could have imagined, in the shape of an offer to front a factual series unpacking autism through the prism of musical talent. It had been literally a matter of months since returning home fried and heartbroken after my time in Kibera. What I'd seen and experienced had taken a personal toll and I hadn't quite worked out how to understand or make sense of my experience and subsequent feelings.

Having had enough time to find some level of normality after what was – as dramatic as it sounds – a life-altering trip, the idea of diving head first into another area I wasn't familiar with just felt wrong.

Sat opposite the then-controller of BBC Three, Danny Cohen, I was adamant he didn't know what he was on about. The film I had just made was telling an African story. I had felt connected to Kenya. As the child of Ghanaian immigrant parents I understood the concept of missed versus seized opportunity first-hand, just by looking at the journey of my grandparents and their desire to make a better life for themselves and their children. But now, as a follow-up, he wanted me to explore autism?

Autism was a word I didn't even know how to spell. I'd had no connection with the condition, no first-hand experience of it and saw the series as nothing more than an opportunity to get it wrong publicly. How could I front a factual series on a subject I knew nothing about?

Yep, self-doubt had really made himself at home. With my monologue as to why the experienced channel controller knew absolutely nothing finished and out of the way, I finally shut up to hear the most simple and silence-inducing response; one I'll never forget. 'That is exactly why you're perfect to do this film.'

His point was that the reality of living with autism is something families around the world deal with quietly and behind closed doors. Simply put, if you're not affected by it, you'll never truly know about it. With that being the case, me fronting the film would instantly make me fresh eyes to the condition and a mouthpiece for the audience.

He knows his onions that Cohen bloke. There really isn't a lot you can say to that level of clarity, so applying that perspective to my role, the conundrum of host, reporter, journalist or presenter all went out of the window, and I placed all my chips on attacking any subject matter as myself. This felt incredibly exposing yet freeing at the same time.

It was 2010 and my career was about to make a huge shift I hadn't seen coming. The best thing about this moment was none of it had been planned. I was about to start a whole new stage of my career but had no idea what it would entail.

The series on autism saw me experience the realities of living with the condition while preparing the contributors for a musical performance with a live band in front of a studio audience. The series was a challenge, but the fact I was learning about both myself and the condition on screen caused the industry and the audience to take notice.

As a result, in 2011 I was nominated for my first Royal Television Society award in the category Best Presenter. It was a huge wake-up call. I'd pushed myself and been rewarded for it. For the record, when I say rewarded I mean nominated. I got me suit, went to the big night and watched Professor Brian Cox walk away with the award. Thankfully my 'It's fine, it's fine, he's great isn't he' face had been well rehearsed, so I was smiling while crying inside, but no one knew.

Off the back of the exceptionally well-received documentary on autism, another series presented itself pushing me in a direction that I, at the time, believed I would now be more than prepared for. How wrong I was. That series was *Tourettes: Let Me Entertain You*.

The first two films were straight documentaries (much like the autism series), exploring the realities of the condition while preparing the singers to perform with a live band in front of a studio audience. The series culminated in a final episode where the now trained singers, all sufferers of the condition, made it on stage and performed.

In shooting the factual episodes with my director Sam (minus the short shorts), I got to know the cast, their families and see first-hand the challenges Tourette's inflicted on their daily lives. On some level, the word 'challenges' doesn't even begin to explain the reality of what I became frequent witness to. For some of the parents, the stresses of medicating their children into a state of numbness left them with no choice but to go without the relief offered by the drugs.

The unfortunate result would be a constant stream of physical or verbal ticks causing all manner of social and educational challenges for the child they were desperately trying to protect. This real-life predicament stirred up all manner of emotions within me, while I desperately tried to retain a level of impartiality. Throughout filming, the encouragement I received from Sam – who was once again on directorial duties – was to engage and verbalise those feelings no matter how uncomfortable displaying my frustrations on camera might feel.

Initially, the idea of behaving this way on camera didn't sit well with me, as my history and training had been to not only deliver someone else's scripted speeches – albeit personalised ones – but to remain in control at all times while sticking to the script. Room for emotion or the requirement to connect with a subject matter wasn't ever discussed in the years spent as a regular face on mainstream entertainment, or during the thousands of hours fronting live children's TV.

This was me finally understanding the role Danny Cohen had twisted my arm to originally fill. This was me for the first time, speaking on behalf of the people just like me sat at home watching, and truly becoming a mouthpiece for my audience in all of its shouty, questioning, inquisitive glory.

In making this series, for the first time I truly found myself fully unaware of the camera falling into a position of protector toward contributor Ruth. To be clear, as a fully independent and socially active woman, Ruth has and will never need protecting, but due to some of the reactions she was getting while shooting in public I went on to totally forget myself. Ruth, to this day stands as one of the most interesting people I've met due to her incredible lust for life, regardless of her impediment.

Living with severe motor and physical tics, Ruth was unable to contain sudden movements of her arms and sometimes legs as well, while the verbal element of the condition showed itself by triggering her to scream the offensive or inappropriate. Sam and I met Ruth in Camden Town to go shopping and walk the famous market while getting to know each other, but the pressure of the camera unavoidably sent her tics into overdrive.

As teenagers flocked upon the camera's arrival, Ruth's tics received the predictable reaction of laughter and ridicule. As a response, I jumped to her unwanted defence. I hissed and snapped at the sweaty teens, calling for sensitivity and respect, much to Ruth's amusement. This was the typical reception she receives on a normal day out and, on her part at least, heartbreakingly expected.

Much to Sam's pleasure, the skirmish unfolded on camera, causing me to confront my reaction to Ruth's reality. It was in that moment that I had no option but to stare directly into the barrel of the unavoidable. This wasn't just the contributor opening up about their life and the stories behind their behaviour. These films were grounded in my own process of self-evaluation and discovery, leading to a level of understanding gained through the eyes of their experiences. By discussing the issue at hand in the most genuine and immediate way possible, I was learning on screen with my audience.

Sam smiled that massive cat-got-the-cream smile directors only pull when they know they've shot a moment that won't end up on the cutting room floor. He smiled that director grin not just because the film suddenly came alive, but because he knew I was hooked.

Earning incredible reviews and praise, the Tourette's series opened the door to further explore a new lane in factual programming as, finally, I had begun to believe what I'd been told years prior by the channel controller. My role had in one series jumped from being primarily about presenting to unexpectedly being much more about letting go.

When I was first offered the opportunity to make documentaries, I was initially convinced my point of view as a young black working-class man with a history in music, drama, children's TV and entertainment would not make my films remotely credible. But through the understanding gained from conflict and challenges on screen, the very things once seen as a weakness would become my strength on camera, as I represented the eyes of the everyman and voice of the audience.

Sat opposite several production companies, the meetings

all opened with versions of the same question. 'What is it you'd like to do next?' By shedding everything I'd learned as a TV host, and opening up to a new relationship with the camera, contributors, content and – most importantly – the audience, the next step had begun to show itself.

With the challenges of the Tourette's and autism series still fresh in my mind, I knew that bringing my own history and relationships to any subject matter could only make for something the viewer could relate to. In my limited history with the documentary genre, I'd already experienced a myriad of people and situations to last a lifetime all causing me to challenge my own convictions and, at times, restraint.

With a newfound confidence in my journey and the value of my honest perspective, learning with the audience on camera became a priority. Finding a personal connection to a subject matter, which could then lead to the scab of any issue being picked in the most balanced way possible, was my motivation to push for a project that would allow me to immerse myself in surroundings I was very keen to explore.

It was 2013 and I decided to put out a very clear message in every meeting I went to. My focus and sights were placed firmly on the continent that not only is referred to as home by my mother and father, but is the home of so many unanswered questions. A few months later, my journey as a factual film-maker would truly begin when BBC Three commissioned the series *Reggie Yates: Extreme South Africa.*

CHAPTER 1
HOPE FOR HIRE

religion

rɪˈlɪdʒ(ə)n

noun: religion

The belief in a god or gods and the activities that are connected with this belief, such as praying or worshipping in a building such as church or temple.

In my limited experience, the recently religious can shift the dynamic of a solid relationship by pulling every chat into a conversational cul-de-sac using variations of the following: 'And that's why you need to give yourself to Christ bro'.

❝ Dude, my car broke down, my dog just died and I'm pretty sure this bump is a corn on my little toe.'
'Well if I were you, I'd give myself to Christ bro. ❞

To be clear, I'm not saying I have anything against religious people. What I am saying is ten-a-penny preachers have a particular talent for getting under my skin.

I have a strange and long relationship with faith and organised religion as, like many people, worship was introduced into my life and quickly normalised as a child. I say normalised, but I still remember being no more than seven and totally fascinated by the idea of holy water. I struggled to understand why I was the only person who found it kind of strange that tap water waved over by a pastor now held spiritual value.

My north London start wasn't that dissimilar to my classmates. It was working class, Arsenal supporting and driven by a hunger for a better quality of life. This was, of course, while I was at school. At home, life was very different.

Behind the yellow door on the second floor, 17 Birkenhead House was a West African bubble. What we ate, the language used and, more importantly, how we prayed was all Ghana. In this way, the home I grew up in was very different to that of my classmates; in our house a perfectly blurred line connected culture and religion. Church was what we did as a family. Some families went bowling, some flew kites – we, on the other hand, would go to church on a Sunday morning and leave at dinnertime.

We were Pentecostal Christians who attended all-day church and I had the squeaky cheap church shoes to prove it.

Now, don't get me wrong, the Ghanaian Pentecostal church we attended ran long, but it was anything but boring. West Africans as a whole aren't known for our timid nature or delicate patter, so with our church made up almost entirely of new-to-the-country men and women, worship was always carried out just as it was back home. Loudly.

My first visit is still clear as day. Walking into the packed and makeshift place of praise was an assault on the senses. The overpowering smell of anointing oil filled my nose. My shiny church shoes squeezed my toes while a live band accompanying the wails of prayer filled my ears. With clear direction by the all-powerful pastor, the jammed room swayed, waved white hankies and stamped the ground in unison in an effort to push satan further down.

As the room reached fever pitch, headwrap-wearing aunties head to toe in their now sweaty finest begun to hit the ground one by one. The Holy Ghost had struck and possession coupled with loud speaking in tongues filled the room. My first experience of 'the Spirit' was when it chose to take Aunty Linda. Now Aunty Linda wasn't the smallest in voice or stature, so when the spirit took her, it also took her plastic chair with a loud snap. With broken seat pieces either side of her convulsing body, Aunty Linda was possessed and the whole church knew about it.

To go from this unapologetic world of Pentecostal worship as a kid, to being steered exclusively by the values of Islam in my early teens was a culture shock and huge left turn.

The short version of the story is my mother got remarried to a Muslim man when I was eleven and, as a household, we became Muslim overnight. The sausages, bottles of Baby Cham and deli paté suddenly vanished from the fridge as a whole new set of rules quickly established themselves, changing my relationship with god again.

Who was this new god and why didn't he speak English? Pray how many times a day? Wear what on a Friday? Confusion doesn't even begin to describe my tiny mind exploding with the information overload. Unsurprisingly, this led me to a change of lane. The moment I moved out at eighteen, I decided that religion in whatever form it might take would be something I'd give myself to when, and only if, it felt right.

With my big sister becoming a born-again Christian and younger siblings identifying as Muslim, you could say I'm the raggedy, godless black sheep of the family. Having this title hanging like an unusually dark cloud above my head, my connection with faith or lack thereof had always niggled away at me.

For my Muslim mother, me finding my path spiritually and embracing a faith (preferably hers of course) has consistently been the unspoken want bubbling beneath the surface.

Funnily enough, my own desire to connect with something bigger than me had been increasingly taking up more and more of my headspace, when the opportunity to look at religion in South Africa landed in my lap.

Was this chance to explore faith and religion on screen fate, or the lord working in mysterious ways? I was game either way as a very personal set of questions could potentially find an answer in a professional opportunity. Stars aligned, or, as my big sister would say, 'Look at God'.

It's rare to be challenged on the fundamentals of what makes you who you are spiritually, let alone on camera. So making the *Millionaire Preacher* film for the *Extreme South Africa* series was a baptism of fire. Pun most definitely intended.

Given my religious history and minimal connection to any organised religion, I was apprehensive but willing to explore religious themes on screen. This would be the first time in my career I'd be openly speaking about faith, Christianity, Islam and everything in between. The sensitivities associated were endless, as this project could only truly connect with the audience successfully if I were to totally give myself to the process. The only way this film could actually come close to its true potential was by me not only discussing what I encountered on camera, but also speaking openly about my own history and connection to the theme.

At this stage of my career in factual filmmaking I was green. This was the first series of the 'Extreme' strand and I felt the weight of responsibility in terms of getting the series right.

I was in Africa, I was fronting the first series with my name in the title and I couldn't fuck it up. In hindsight, there is without doubt so much that could have been done differently and an endless stream of lessons learned from the mistakes I feel I made on screen.

This would be my first time in South Africa. Unfortunately, I didn't step off the flight anywhere near as objective as I'd have liked. I was quietly riddled with preconceptions of a divided country still weighed down by post-Apartheid hang-ups. I was convinced this would overshadow my experience, but then my race-related fears lost all importance as I was instantly confronted with a whole other juggernaut.

After the obligatory post-flight rest day, I was chomping at the bit to get out and shoot. The first sequence scheduled to film seemed, on face value, simple. My director Sam had called for a walk through the town centre, which confused me, as I was unsure as to what a walk and observe on camera would deliver. I quickly found out exactly what Sam was after.

Every street was filled with the sound of worship as various churches pumped their message out into the busy street via huge speakers. With statements as names, churches in Johannesburg aren't shy in declaring their importance. Names like Christ The Solution, With God Anything Is Possible and Amen Tabernacle made clear how seriously they took themselves.

With a different church every few hundred yards, lunchtime prayer was so popular I found the the huge congregations of the more successful pastors literally spilling into the street.

My stroll quickly became an education on the scale of South African faith as hundreds of people stood silently praying on the pavement via PA system. Desperate to take it all in and somehow understand, this inside/outside service became increasingly unusual to my virgin eyes. Suited business types and mums with kids skipped between the crowds without even batting an eyelid. Here, this was normal.

As I continued my amble, now open-mouthed, every street offered its own church and speaker system sharing with passing pedestrians and traffic a new relentless and shouted sermon. With a different international Ministry of this or God's Chosen Place of that on every corner, picking one tailor-made for you wouldn't be that difficult a task, considering every kind of Evangelical pastor imaginable had their own building big or small and a following to match.

What struck me instantly was something I hadn't considered. The live band, the type of people worshipping, and most importantly the message and its delivery, weren't that dissimilar to the church I once attended with my own family in London.

At the time we made the documentary, South Africa had more people living with HIV than anywhere else in the world, while 70 per cent of young people in the country were unemployed. The need for something to believe in and an insatiable appetite for miracles wasn't only understandable, it made sense.

❝ Touch the screen and receive your miracle ❞

The intention of the episode was to unpack faith in young South Africans through the mega church Incredible Happenings and its incredibly popular pastor. Not only was its congregation well into the tens of thousands, it was almost exclusively made up of township people, some of whom had travelled for days to attend and receive their blessing. Its gregarious leader and undeniable force of nature, self-proclaimed Prophet Mboro was a man I had so many questions for.

This multi-millionaire holy man is known to own seven houses, have over thirty cars and wear only the most expensive suits. Hitting the headlines continuously for the wildest of religious claims or practices, Mboro is a regular on the front page of every Johannesburg tabloid.

Shortly before my trip, the prophet was not only connected to a zombie resurrection but accused of waving a gun around at a radio station. At the time of writing this chapter, Mboro was making international news for selling photos he took on his smartphone while in heaven, for 5,000 rand. The man is a true one-off.

Proud of and continuously flaunting his wealth, Mboro dressed, lived and was treated like a rock star. Somehow his lifestyle and behaviour didn't raise an eyebrow in his congregation and I needed to know why.

Seeing first-hand the number of people coming through the door every Sunday to hear Mboro speak, I can't stress enough just how popular the man is. He has a daily TV show and a daily radio show with over 200,000 listeners – for him, its simply outreach. The live call-ins both on TV and radio produced some of the more surprising ideas on how to heal. Touching the screen or the speaker was a regular instruction, and for every one person who fobbed it off as ridiculous, two would turn up at Incredible Happenings the following Sunday.

A huge number of his parishioners are young, so my earliest confusion was how? For the smartphone-tapping, pop culture-consuming millennials, what was it about his message that resonated, and why didn't they see the same things I did? I was dealing not just with a religious leader, Prophet Mboro was a celebrity.

❮ Bad criticism I'm happy for that, they made me famous ❯

In the churches I'd attended as a child, the pastors didn't have time for kids; they were far too busy sweating at the podium speaking in tongues. I'd never met a religious leader who not only had the love and adoration of thousands but a congregation who all felt they had a personal relationship with the man.

On my way in, I met a group of young choir members in the car park all buzzing and excited for the service that was about to begin. Their enthusiasm was infectious and driven by their love for the prophet and his powers. One of the group claimed to have been healed by Mboro in a service weeks before. Apparently she couldn't walk, and with his healing hands, she now could. With the prophet proudly admitting that criticism made him famous, my plan was to observe and judge the man only on what I saw and nothing else. But based on what I'd just heard, I knew that would be difficult.

After the conversation, Sam and I took a break in the car park. He smoked; I fiddled with the car stereo. It's at this stage I should probably come clean about my poker face. Bear with me. My ability to hide my true feelings in situations this foreign is at best minimal, which is probably why my inner cynic took control of all facial expressions and I had no say in the matter.

With the inevitable bad jokes out of the way, how to manage the following service without spending the entire time taking the piss was a genuine concern. I'd just spoken to someone who believed the prophet had granted her the ability to walk! There was too high a chance of more unreal shenanigans ahead for me not to be concerned that the film could descend into a piss-taking ignorance safari.

Being snarky or know-it-all has never been a motivation for any of my work, as that role is well covered by many other filmmakers. So how would I navigate this shoot day while being respectful regardless of the constant stream of crazy? At this point, I had no idea.

Opposite the main hall was a small store selling Mboro merchandise. T-shirts with the prophet's face on colourful logos filled the stands, while a queue to pay went on for miles. Parishioners waited quietly holding onto their blessed items, proud to own something bearing the man's likeness, and it was this that slowly started to pull the humour from the situation. I was beginning to see for myself the scale of influence and, more importantly, the scale of belief.

These blessed Mboro branded items included everything from water and salt to sanitary towels. Men were buying menstrual pads as well as the women due to their apparent powers to heal aches and pains anywhere on the body. How much belief did this huge congregation actually have in their chosen prophet, and how far could that go? I was about to find out.

When Mboro arrived in the church his entrance was flanked by a team of burly security guards all holding automatic weapons. I'm not going to pretend I knew what kind they were carrying; the detail I ask you to focus on here is that they were holding firearms. Big ones. The loaded kind that need two hands to hold.

A standing ovation met his entrance as the thousands in attendance reached new heights of excitement amid his presence. This was real rock star stuff, and the minute he hit the stage everything changed. Jumping, screaming and performing, songs and jokes fell from his mouth effortlessly. In no time at all, everyone was in the palm of his manicured hand.

With cheers followed by laughter broken up by songs, a

clear rhythm was established. The room was enthralled and entertained. The sick came forward and the prophet stepped up to heal all ailments, be they physical, mental or spiritual.

As a non-believer not wanting to pray, my awkwardness was clear and the prophet was on it straight away. As a man not practising any religion, faking prayer felt like the height of disrespect. But with my seat in the front row giving me literally nowhere to hide, I was rumbled and firmly on the prophet's radar for all the wrong reasons. At this stage I hasten to add, we hadn't even spoken yet.

Screaming women and crying men lined up in their hundreds, spinning a noticeable shift in mood. The band dropped their level, the prophet changed his tone and one by one he worked his way through the long queue of believers. The singing, live band and prayer hadn't felt a million miles away from some of the things I'd seen or experienced in my old church back in London. But that was until the prophet began to heal.

A twenty-two-year-old woman stepped up to complain on mic of a painful vagina. She spoke of a recent failed suicide attempt due to the decline in all areas of her life as she believed she'd been raped by a spiritual beast. The prophet attempted to tend to her vaginal pain by pushing down on her genitalia with a pointed patent shoe while speaking in tongues.

During his on-stage and on-mic healing in front of the entire congregation, he referred to spiritual husbands and possessed vaginas. Any humour to be found in the situation had left the room. I'd never seen anything like this and, given the fact that any scepticism in this hall of thousands was limited to my chair alone, I knew that the next week might have one or two conflicts of opinion.

After a seven-hour service, the collection began. Huge pink boxes were filled with sealed envelopes as people waited in line to give what they could. In a room of this size and with so many happy to wait, I'd never seen this many people willingly give up money, especially money they didn't have to give. With a million pounds a year earned via donations and purchase of merchandise, Incredible Happenings was big business, and I was about to meet the CEO.

Post-service I was granted an audience with Mboro. I was made to wait a short while before he emerged from a back room flanked by armed guards. Standing at no more than 5'2" in his patent Cuban heels, he schooled me on possession, witchcraft and talking cats during a crash course on what I'd just witnessed during his healing session.

The prophet could smell the sceptic on me and looked me square in the eye while letting me know that, here, things are different. He made it very clear that, in Africa, people have faith and that African faith is placed in different things from the faith in my Western world.

His tone was staunch but inclusive, warm but firm. This was a man who knew how to work the camera while letting me know exactly who was in charge.

My intention to carry myself with a consistency in

demeanour, tone and respect has served me well throughout my career. The first meeting with anyone – be they punter, pop star or politician – is always important. With that being said, I had a feeling I hadn't won over the prophet just yet.

The following day I found myself invited to join the prophet on a shopping trip. But after waiting for over three hours, it finally dawned on me. Culturally, the longer you're willing to, or in my case made to, wait for somebody, the more important they are. Sat twiddling my thumbs, I knew that Mboro was making sure I was aware of just how important he was.

When he finally arrived, he was entourage-heavy and ready to shop. We walked through the shiny mall to a boutique dripping in expensive gear. The shop owner greeted him like an old friend as they pulled armfuls from the rails. With the majority of suits on sale selling at £3,000 a time, the clientele was almost exclusively sports stars and rappers. Proudly announcing that his regular shopping trips usually totalled over £7,000 a time, Mboro doubled down on his status ensuring I knew who was superior. My choice of dirty Vans, shorts and a hoodie was hard for the prophet to hide his distaste for as, unfortunately, this was once again seen as a sign of disrespect.

I'd offended the man. Again. Unintentional or not, I could feel his patience slipping and that he felt the BBC sending what looked like a man-child for someone clearly so important had begun to get his goat. Two days in and I'd already lost the person I was supposed to spend a hell of a lot longer with.

Stood to one side watching the prophet jump from one loud suit to another, that crap poker face I mentioned began to once again reveal my true feelings about what I was playing a role in. This was a wealthy man, well within his rights and ability to splash the cash. The problem I felt so deeply that my anger forced me to leave the shop, was where that money had actually come from.

With a bank balance powered by his congregation, Mboro continued to spend while pushing me to join him in splashing out. I flatly refused to buckle and he wasn't happy at all.

Sensing my distaste, the prophet explained that he sees himself as an inspiration. He believes that him spending gives the guy at the bottom of the ladder something to aspire to. In theory it made sense, but to me felt like a well thought-out excuse to be as frivolous and lavish as his financial equivalents – sports stars and entertainers.

Tipped off by his head of security that my decision not to buy a suit and the line of questioning had rubbed the prophet up the wrong way, I pushed for another meeting to clear the air.

❝ *Touch your biscuit, touch your Vuvuzela. I will heal you* ❞

Along with his popular TV show, Mboro's radio show attracted huge audiences. During the broadcast he encouraged his audience to attend Sunday's service with underwear so he could heal the entire room en masse. This request was followed by an on-air blessing of the audience's genitalia, where touching ones biscuit (vagina) or vuvuzela (penis) was encouraged.

Outside of doing everything in my power not to laugh at the use of the word 'biscuit', I had no choice but to challenge him on this as, for me, religious or not, the blessing, cleansing and stamping of private parts was coming up far too often.

The stock response that I didn't understand his world ended the conversation and my frustration began to build. How was I to understand his world if he wouldn't let me in?

It was clear that a decision had been made and my disbelief rendered my intentions as cynical. To begin to understand how his world worked I needed him to give me more. No matter how many jokes I cracked or compliments I made about his ill-fitting suits or shoes clearly two sizes two big, Mboro was having none of it.

Possibly my efforts were let down by my feelings as I honestly couldn't have been further from liking the man. What he was doing and how he lived his life was a genuine problem for me.

Starting in TV as a kid and coming home to a council estate gave me a heightened awareness of class, status and wealth at a very young age. My default has and will always be a level of embarrassment in seeing those who don't have much, killing themselves to appear as if they do. Equally, the wealthy flaunting their money via garish purchases is simply bad taste. This man was showing none.

How the head of a church could live the life of a millionaire on the backs of the poor truly fucked with me. The prophet had no issue in spending and justified this, meaning no guilt was allowed to even raise its head. Mboro saw himself as providing a service and therefore should be paid for it. He's a man selling hope and faith as interchangeable products and for him that's exactly how it should be done.

This was the first time I'd truly challenged the prophet to his face yet he engaged in the conversation. It was frank and honest but clearly not what he wanted, especially on camera.

My time on his turf had begun to go sour and I was summoned by his legal team. It was explained that my disrespect had gone too far. I was expected to treat him as a leader and not an equal. Clearly my informal tone and line of questioning were unwelcome to the prophet, as this was a man sat at the very top of his world. Financially and in the eyes of the Almighty, this man was convinced he had no equal. Then I showed up in shorts refusing to pray and calling him mate every two minutes. I could see why I'd pissed him off.

My learning curve as a documentary filmmaker has been steep at the best of times and during this experience, every day was a lesson. My feelings were getting in the way of the film, rather than helping it and that was a first. I had no choice but to swallow all pride and do whatever was necessary to get back into the room with Mboro. It was time to go shopping.

After a day of grovelling I was allowed to follow the prophet as he visited a small township. I had a shave and bought a white shirt in an effort to present something consistent with the appearance he seemed to expect from a journalist. As I buttoned up the shirt in the mirror, I had to keep telling myself that I just had to play along. 'This is just for the film, you're not selling it bruv.' I was.

This was without doubt the first time I found myself bending to accommodate on camera and it cut like a knife. I'd promised myself to always be me no matter the circumstance and as I left the hotel, I knew this was a test in my ability to do so.

❝ Rising from nothing to having anything he wants ❞

With over twelve million people still living in shacks, South Africa is riddled with those in need. My Johannesburg hotel nestled among the wealthy was a world away from where I was being taken. Joining the huge convoy of cars rammed with assistants and security, Mboro led me to a township called Barcelona. Predominantly made up of shacks and small brick-built houses, it was one of the many townships in which – it was explained to me – the prophet supported families and visited to give blessings.

Stopping for snacks en route, Mboro was mobbed. Literally. The gas station came to a standstill as people flocked for photos and selfies. The man was a star. As he embraced every screaming fan and stopped to talk with anyone who approached, I could easily have been with David Beckham. A giddy shop assistant explained to me that simply by touching his arm she might receive some blessings. Thank all that is good he never kissed her on the cheek. She probably would have wet herself, then spontaneously combusted.

There was something about the outpouring of adoration that caused the prophet to soften. His approval of my clean shave and fresh shirt definitely helped, as out of nowhere he opened up. Sharing with me his humble beginnings as a kid living in poverty selling fruit on the roadside, Mboro spoke softly and passionately about his belief. He was obviously a gifted entertainer, the crowds alone were very real proof of that, but his belief was that his greatness came from god.

Rising from nothing to having anything he wants was for him a sign that he was chosen. For the first time we agreed on something. This was definitely a man who was gifted and blessed with the ability to command attention, but more importantly lead. Where our opinions split was on what that ability should have been used for.

At the time of making the film, 45 per cent of black South Africans were living in poverty and the hope that rose in the fall of Apartheid was now in short supply. As we walked through the township of Barcelona, Mboro inspired and lifted everyone he met; his mere presence was a shot in the arm for everyone he touched. From blessing people in the street, to praying for a family who had had one relative murder another, I saw first-hand how this tiny man was a giant in this environment. He had undeniable power and it was palpable.

In prayer with the family, even I felt uplifted. Motivational daggers, reminding everyone in attendance of their blackness, their power and their pride, bolstered his requests of god. One of his comments has stayed with me to this day. We were stood in a cramped, low tin-roofed home, which was the site of a murder days before. The grieving family were told, 'You will succeed if the shack you stand in is not inside of you.' I found it hard not to love everything he gave that family. It wasn't financial, it was spiritual.

On our trip to Barcelona, Prophet Mboro charmed me just as much as he left me conflicted and frustrated. Those huge and packed collection boxes fund his lifestyle, but clearly the giving is a choice. In my confusion, speaking to younger parishioners felt like the best way to find some clarity. The ensuing conversations only threw up more questions as balance and logic was clear in their assessment of the church and its finances.

'It is a personal choice for somebody to give,' said twenty-three-year-old Tooli. She was adamant she wouldn't want to be led by a pastor who doesn't seem to be progressing in life. As far as she was concerned, it was the job of the church to maintain his lifestyle.

The prophet is taken care of by his congregation, so the logic goes, while their lives are a reflection of how the church is taking care of them. The better he looks the more blessed they all can be. I didn't argue with Tooli, but it still didn't sit well.

❛ We have white people here, but you're whiter than white people ❜

Respect is and will always be of great importance to African men of a certain age. I knew this going in. This speaks to why there wasn't one meeting where I didn't wait at least an hour. Mboro felt that I didn't respect him or his world and, in fighting to gain a level of understanding, his expectations were on collision course with my ignorance from day one.

On some level, the rub between Mboro and I was down to cultural expectations on both sides. This was a man who expected behaviour totally foreign to me and, in hindsight, I was exactly the same. The prophet felt I didn't give the level of respect he demanded and interpreted it as arrogance and pride. The majority of his frustration came from my cynicism and the lesson was clear. Maybe I wasn't as objective and balanced as I thought?

It was the last day of the shoot and I was back at Incredible Happenings. It was a Sunday and the building was packed as usual but Mboro didn't want me inside. He called for me to humble myself in his world, I had my blackness questioned and, with my most recent lesson still fresh in my mind, I decided not to react.

He barked at me, 'We have white people here, but you're whiter than white people,' which lit a fire inside I did everything to extinguish. At this stage of the project I'd learned a valuable lesson, one that would go on to serve me well in my future career, particularly while shooting in Russia.

Mboro was the classic difficult contributor. He was a man who needed to be handled with care at all times and only challenged or pushed when it best served the film. My ego and emotions would have to come second to the greater purpose: the documentary. My earlier missteps nearly lost us our fascinating central character. To truly get under the skin of who this man was and more importantly to tell a full and objective story, I needed to shake my vanity.

Wrestling with a contributor simply to win an argument or make a point would deliver a great sequence. But how would it serve the greater story? I'd learnt by nearly losing the prophet that needing to be right rather than listening would stand in the way of the film. A lesson I'd never forget.

Eventually allowed in, the entire sermon was aimed at me. It was bloody awful. I could feel the eyes of thousands burning tiny holes in the back of my head. Mboro sat me front row and enjoyed making me squirm and watched every uncomfortable shift in my chair with glee.

Calling me on stage and handing me a mic, Mboro quizzed me in front of his audience as I silently shit my pants. He squared up and grilled me on my experience, pushing randomly to see if he could find a button to expose me as judgemental, disrespectful or dismissive. I was none of the above as I'd finally begun to get it.

I'd seen the man as a charlatan and didn't understand the importance of the faith he instills in thousands daily. The man is brash, badly dressed and with an unbelievably high opinion of himself, but the part he plays in the happiness, optimism and mental health of his following appeared to be vital. I can say with complete confidence that his brand of religion isn't what I want or need in my life but in his world, I totally understand how it fits, and on some level respect it.

On stage we made our peace, the crowd cheered and the prophet couldn't help but smile. I'd escaped unscathed and won him and the crowd over with a huge roar as I unbuttoned my shirt to reveal his face on my Prophet Mboro T-shirt.

Then, something extraordinary happened. I honestly felt I was stood in front of someone I could actually see eye to eye with. That was until he asked the entire congregation to pull out and wave their underwear for blessings.

Whatever age I live until, that will forever be one of the strangest moments of my life. In an instant I was surrounded by thousands of pairs of pants being swung in the air like helicopter blades, in a church, by men, women and children of all ages. Final prayers were carried out as the entire congregation held their private parts and, whatever the level of weirdness you're imagining right now, times that by a million and you're still not even close to how it felt in that room.

The wealthy and congregation-funded Prophet PFP Motsoeneng Mboro challenged my motivations, beliefs, authenticity and at times made me ask myself the question *who am I really?* In a strange way, he had made me question my relationship with faith, and more specifically patriarchy, in the context of poverty. It had been a fascinating, and at times humbling, adventure – but I couldn't help feeling I flew home from South Africa with more questions than answers.

CHAPTER 2
FAR RIGHT OR WRONG?

From the very beginning, when I started out as a child, forging a career in TV has been strange and consistently challenging. Not that I really knew back then that there was such a thing as a 'TV career'. For a start, there were very few black British faces who'd managed to maintain a long-term presence on our screens. This was always an issue for my parents, knowing what it was I wanted to do. The examples of long-term TV success for anyone who looked like me were few and far between.

For a lot longer than I should have, I would play a game with journalists, much to the amusement of my publicist at the time, Sara Lee. She and I would always laugh long and hard at the squirms of red-top writers as I'd challenge them to name five black faces regularly seen on British TV. The only rule given was that they weren't allowed to count me, Lenny Henry or Sir Trevor McDonald. It was amazing to watch.

Sara Lee's laugh is still just as husky and amazing, but thankfully playing that game isn't as called for now due to things moving in the overdue direction of diverse representation. It's a slow shift, but thank the lord I'm not on me tod anymore.

Despite my parents' very understandable fears for me, I went from a child actor just starting out to an adult secure in long-term TV and radio contracts, and by my mid-twenties I was in a place of job stability. As my appearances presenting documentaries became less of a surprise to viewers and more of a regular occurrence, something shifted and I achieved a personal and professional milestone.

It's only really in hindsight that I understand the significance of having a show on the BBC with my name in the title. As a viewer, it's just a tiny detail telling you who's fronting what you're about to watch. As a programme-maker, to have the channel insist your name comes before the specifics of the film in question makes a bold statement. It meant that, from a professional perspective, it was a new day. What I represented, the audience I'd built and who I was as an individual had become a brand my employers wanted to shout about.

This marked the beginnings of my name alone actually standing for something. Looking back, I only now understand just how fragile that is. I was proud my name was associated with empathy, learning and programming of scale, and I wanted to ensure that the next series I made showed growth. With so many lessons learned during *Extreme South Africa*, I knew that there needed to be some changes.

Extreme Russia was the second series commissioned by the BBC in the 'Extreme' strand. For this particular film I would be working with an entirely new team. *Far Right and Proud* was our title and we were out to make a film unpacking Russian nationalism and its rise in popularity with young men and women.

It ended up being some of the most demanding but honest work I've ever done. The challenges we faced both on and off camera, alongside my willingness to put myself in uncomfortable situations for the good of the film, led to what I consider to be one of my strongest projects to date.

In the making of *Far Right and Proud*, my Russian experience took a decidedly dark turn as I found myself beginning to understand my role on camera as a complicit contributor. I was credited as a presenter but I wasn't presenting. I was fronting the show, but I wasn't the host. Walking into this series I understood that my role sat somewhere between the contributors I'd meet and the host walking the audience through an environment acting as their eyes and ears. This would often demand that my own dislikes or frustrations should be put firmly aside. I had to participate fully, regardless of the company. Listening to and truly engaging even in the presence of abhorrent views and at times people was the only rule. And this would be put to the test in a way I'd never experienced.

Growing up in the late 1980s, some of my early formative years were steered by the idiot box. Television was a mate, one who taught me lots of what I needed to know but so much more than I was ready for. Between the scathing political views on ITV's *Spitting Image* and the occasional boob on Channel 4's *The Word*, I was up past my bedtime and loving the baptism of fire.

Until my journey to Moscow to shoot *Extreme Russia*, my opinions of Russia would still be tied to that Gorbachev puppet on *Spitting Image* and the bad guy in *Rocky II*. Television had taught me well. My entire feelings towards the biggest country on the planet were bound to a pre-teen understanding of the satirical and stereotypical created in TV and film. Great.

Half expecting the first person I met to mumble, 'If he dies, he dies,' like the guy who killed Apollo Creed in the ring, I'd arrived in Moscow and had never felt cold like it. A clock on the street flipping between the time and the temperature showed me it was currently minus twenty-eight degrees. Shit had just got real. This wasn't going to look or feel like anything I'd shot before.

Thanks to that Stallone movie, I assumed the pleasantries might be minimal, particularly given the project's subject matter. Pushing my childhood fears of a spiky super power with nuclear capabilities to one side, it was time to grow up and see for myself what the city had to offer.

My team was totally new, but I found myself bonding quickly with my producer, who to my surprise was both younger and louder than me. Diana Aroutiounova met me at the airport and proved just as entertaining as my attempts to pronounce her surname. With jet-black hair cut into a razor-sharp bob, she wasn't happy about my early observation of her likeness to Dora the Explorer. Regardless, we got on.

The role of a producer is a difficult one in documentary. When you're working in small teams with even tinier budgets, your producer and their relationship with the fixer decide just how strong your film is likely to be before even a frame has been shot. But any fears that the nationalists we were set to meet could be an impossible nut to crack were alleviated as soon as I found out about Diana's incredible talent to charm the pants off anyone – including knife-wielding nationalists. This would become our secret weapon.

Our timing couldn't be more apt as we were making the series of films at a time when anti-Western feeling was high. Russian pride had taken on new meaning and president Vladimir Putin continued to speak to the 'us against the world' belief held by so many Russians. With the policies and cultural belief to support his 'Russia First' narrative, it's no wonder his approval rating was 90 per cent. This unwavering belief makes Putin (still in power at the time of writing, having served a combined total of eighteen years as prime minister and president) one of the most popular leaders in the world.

On my first day in Moscow a visit to the famous Kremlin and Red Square was unavoidable. After an hour and with literally no feeling in my fingers or toes, it dawned on me. From the airport to the hotel, to now, stood in the centre of a busy and tourist-heavy Red Square, the only person of colour to be seen anywhere, was me.

Being the only black guy in any environment had never intimidated me. I've spent years in TV surrounded by all-white crews and I'd never allowed race to get in the way of my interactions with anyone. That being said, at this point my time in Russia was at around the three-hour mark. My presence was getting looks – not because of my spectacular sneaker choice (VisVim FBT for the sneaker geeks), but because of my skin colour.

I was a long way from home and I felt it. But then, strange looks aside, I was in Red bloody Square. I'd only ever seen the Kremlin on the news and suddenly it was right in front of me. It was a tourist hub and groups from around the world busied themselves with cameras and awful fuzzy hats bought from street vendors. On closer inspection, I was thrown by some of the other items for sale on those market stalls. T-shirts, mugs and, yes, even Russian dolls were all branded with one recurring theme: Putin. You'd think the man was royalty or a pop star the way he was literally everywhere. Either Vladimir Putin's profile was beyond that of the presidential and had ventured into the world of folk hero, or he was doing a damn good job of ensuring that's how he was seen.

❝ *The animals love Putin* ❞

Making a play to cut through the unsubtle steers from Vladimir, I attended of all things a fashion show. Bear with me. I'll raise my hand here to openly admit I'm one of those blokes. A lover of clobber, a tart for tailoring – call it what you will, I bloody love fashion. Wherever I travel in the world I always come home with a slightly heavier suitcase because there was a pair of trousers I had to own or a hat that would smash it with that shirt I bought. Yeah, it's pathetic, get over it.

I figured a fashion event showcasing new designers could be a way into a young crowd of forward-thinking creatives. It was, but it also delivered its fair share of surprises.

I was seated awkwardly in the front row facing a woman with sunglasses way too big for her face. I couldn't see her eyes, eyebrows or cheekbones but I could feel her judging my messy demeanour from behind the tinted glass. Hair gel man on my left and hair spray girl on my right threw up a gumbo of smells my poor stubby nose nearly crumbled beneath. I was sandwiched between abrasive power dressing (and smelling) fashion types and they were everywhere.

The lights went down and the DJ stopped playing house music your dad would approve of, replacing it with the really loud dubstep teenagers play in Ford Fiestas. The lights went up. The music was sour milk for my ears, but models were trotting out and the show had begun.

Being as this was a group show, the work just kept coming out. It ran for a lot longer than I was expecting. The other slightly surprising thing about the clothes on display was virtually every garment had some iteration of Putin's face on it. I shit you not – dresses, T-shirts, handbags, hoodies, the lot. It was one of the more surreal moments in my life, so much so at one point I thought my drink had been spiked. By the seventh pair of Putin pum-pum shorts I thought it was a wind-up. Sadly it wasn't, and unfortunately there were still several more designers to come.

When the show finally finished I worked my way through the crowd, trying to make sense of what I'd just endured. I cornered a trendy, Janet-Jackson-braid-wearing fashionista who told me she was there for politics as well as fashion. 'We want something that is ours, something truly Russian.'

The event was put together by SET, an organisation run by young men and women rallying around the president in an effort to fight back against the West. SET believes they use their unique talents to showcase Russia on the world stage. Was their propaganda making politics cool?

I was invited to join SET in their plush offices. Piling out of the lift weighed down with tripods and sound equipment, the crew and I arrived to be met by the immaculate Anna. Her gentle voice and pleasant tone soundtracked a walk around the vast space filled with young people. With every turn there were young men and women having what looked like really important meetings in glass-walled rooms. Those who weren't in meetings were huddled around computers having meetings or stood at the coffee machine . . . having meetings.

Anna was every bit the helpful host as she explained the history of the organisation and the need for its existence considering the current state of the country. Now, there were LOTS I could have spoken to Anna about but I was entirely thrown by the most ridiculous thing I think I've ever seen: the wallpaper.

As Anna walked and talked me through the workplace, my attention was caught by the floor-to-ceiling photographs wrapping every inch of wall. Every photograph was of President Vladimir Putin. Nothing odd about that Reg, stop being dramatic Reg. OK, would you call it dramatic if I told you that every photo was of Putin canoodling with an animal? Smiling while cuddling a dolphin, riding horseback shirtless, giggling with baby chicks and lost in the fuzz of an impossibly furry dog were just some of the highlights. A heavy-set man bashing away at a keyboard stopped to educate me as to how animals are able to feel that Putin is true and real. I turned to Anna for something resembling sense. Her take? 'The animals love Putin.'

SET had eleven offices across Russia and thousands of young people have been recruited to their cause. Anna believes people like her keep coming through the door because they are galvanised by their president and inspired by dreams of a new Russia. Anna went on to laud good old Vlad by saying, 'He is not a political construction unlike Obama,' leading me to believe that, in Russia, loving your president and country are almost one and the same thing.

In a time when it seemed as though the entire world was against Russia, it's easy to see how the patriotic rally behind a man like their president. Putin comes across as more than just a politician, but a concept primed to promote Russian strength.

So who is paying for all of these edit suites, computers and glass-walled meeting rooms? Well, according to Anna, SET is about creating world leaders. By investing in creative minds, that next generation of forward thinkers will have the necessary 'Russia First' mentality.

Leaving what felt like a strange alternative dimension, I feared what politicised creativity could actually lead to. Art and propaganda have always gone hand in hand in post-revolutionary Russia, and I walked away feeling like I'd been on a tour of a farm for Putin support and successors.

As Anna led me out I was told who was paying for everything and suddenly it all made sense. SET is an organisation funded by the state.

❛ Whether you're a man or a woman, the motherland is calling ❜

Russians are more active on social media than any other country in the world. They even have their own Facebook. No really, it's called VK and everyone has an account. Now, to be clear, it's not Facebook but it's blue. It's not Facebook but you can share photos. You get a wall, update your status and everyone has annoying relatives posting cupcake recipes. But it's definitely not Facebook. The only real difference here is that it's all in Russian and has zero rules. People share illegal movie streams and music downloads for free. It's the wild west of social networks, but if you're not Russian, you've probably never heard of it.

This addiction to social media makes targeting millions of potential eyeballs for the purposes of political propaganda easy and commonplace in Russian politics. At a time when online is overtaking TV, internet celebrities are everywhere and I was about to meet one of them.

Nineteen-year-old Macha works for Putin's party and believes traditional values are under threat. Blond, pretty and immaculately turned out, you'd be forgiven for assuming her online success came from make-up tutorials. Yet in her spare time Macha makes videos supporting the president. In promoting her ideas of a stronger Russia to a worldwide audience, she's become an online star.

One of the more popular videos in her arsenal has Macha all in white, complete with a huge fur hat to match. Speaking directly to camera and soundtracked by a stirring string section, she goads the viewer to be more patriotic: 'Whether you're a man or a woman, the motherland is calling.'

I was invited to join Macha as she shot some new photos for her various social media platforms. I arrived at the studio to find a full-on production of lights, wardrobe, the lot. It's probably best I spell out the fact that her wardrobe wasn't made up of the frilly or sexy options you'd expect. Macha had a rail populated with military and traditional Russian outfits. She also had a box of props including axes and machine guns. So . . . yeah.

Obviously my initial reaction was to laugh, as I'm a true professional. Look, I had to crack a smile as everything she was doing was so . . . cheesy. I even got up there and took a few pouty shots myself. (I probably should look into what's happened to those images.) Cheesy or not, her online content was consumed globally and made her voice one of weight in the eyes of a growing audience.

It wasn't lost on me that the pretty blond nineteen-year-old with a political message had a talent at cutting through her digital competition. What was a surprise was the type of content she was producing. In her videos, Macha made no apologies for her opinion. What looked like softcore for horny dads with internet history paranoia quickly revealed itself to be propaganda the moment Macha and I stopped posing and started chatting.

Her steely stare was nothing short of focused. My Mr TV Man ego took a solid squishing the moment I realised the pretty girl wasn't there to meet my black ass, she had a message and was determined to get it out.

In her videos, Macha likes to make declarations like, 'The enemy will be defeated and victory will be ours, if we lose, we will destroy the whole world.' Her tone online didn't really differ in face-to-face conversation. It wasn't one of my warmest chats on camera but she was fascinating.

She believed the West ruined Russia and broke apart a huge country, a super power. She wanted to show that it's not shameful to be Russian. Considering herself a nationalist, Macha explained her main aim was to start a movement. She believed her videos would be the precursor to reuniting all former republics of the Soviet Union as one country again.

I was blown back by her rapid-fire monologues – she definitely wasn't a short-for-words interviewee. I spent the majority of our chat trying not to get distracted by the box of props while stood in polite silence listening. Macha continued to make it clear that Putin would be the man to take the country back to its former glory.

When the Soviet Union was dissolved in 1991, one country became fifteen separate states. Russia remained the strongest financially, and people from the smaller and poorer surrounding countries flooded in.

At the time we were making *Extreme Russia*, there were a round eleven million immigrants living there and, just like in every other stable country (the UK included), those immigrants quickly become an easy scapegoat for any of the country's problems. The saddest thing about this happening in Russia is that many of the immigrants in question once lived in what was seen as the same nation.

I left the photo shoot with a mild headache and a slight

shift in my expectations. As naïve as this may make me sound, my preconceived version of the Russian nationalists I was due to meet didn't look like Macha. I'd prepared myself for a constant stream of hooded men with bad breath and offensive style choices. Macha was every bit the opposite, meaning whoever I was going to meet next could also be a fascinating surprise.

One all-inclusive breakfast demolished, a few deep breaths taken and the next day we were back at it. It was a crisp morning and the extreme cold was again my tormenter. Three pairs of socks on and several T-shirts later and I was out on the street walking to the metro. I promise you it is no exaggeration when I say the Russian subway is incredible. If you haven't already, Google it. I'll wait.

Even your favourite Turkish meze restaurant doesn't pack that much marble into one location. Moscow's underground is really special, and I'm not just saying that because it's so much warmer than on the street.

We ambled to the station, cameras fired up, and were met at the station entrance by flashing blue lights.

With so many Russians holding anti-immigration views, Russian police tend to keep tabs on faces that don't fit. Being fully aware that my African nose doesn't exactly align with the traditional Russian bone structure, I was a little on edge stood feet from the flashing meat wagon.

As men and women exploded out of the station doors,

power-walking their way through the cold for the morning commute, it wasn't long before some were stopped. Minutes later, every officer on the street and station steps had a handful of civilian IDs checking details via radio with the station. The one common theme? Every man and woman stopped was non-white.

Men and women who just minutes prior had been on their way to work, promptly became criminals in the back of the meat wagon. For whatever reason, their paperwork didn't satisfy the officers and they were taken in. My excitement over heated trains and marble now felt trivial in the face of the cold reality experienced by so many in modern Russia. With a bad taste in my mouth all I could think was, 'Is this what it feels like to be an immigrant here?'

As a child of immigrant parents, my life in the UK has always been affected by the reality of being different. In my school days, I found myself going home to a totally different world, culturally, to my classmates. Being born in the UK but raised by parents with a very different start in life, I've always been aware of those difficult first years they spent in the UK. To know the intimate details of their struggle means my reaction to new families on my street, regardless of origin, has always been the same – to embrace. Seeing first-hand what it means to be other in Russia shocked me.

❝ *The whole of Russian Twitter is talking about you* ❞

After the Soviet Union collapsed, numerous-ultra nationalist groups sprung up to protect their country against what they saw as a foreign invasion. At their centre was a group known as the Slavic Union, led by a man called Dmitry Demushkin. Made up of over 25,000 neo-Nazis, the Union was subsequently shut down by Putin for being too extreme.

When Putin thinks you're too extreme, you probably stand a great chance of gold in the racist Olympics.

To paint a slightly more vivid picture, this was a group known for bearing flags branded with swastikas while masked in balaclavas and wearing army fatigues. Being totally blunt, footage of the Slavic Union throwing Nazi hand salutes and generally being all-round intimidating as fuck didn't fill me with joy. This was made worse as I had the pleasure of knowing it had been agreed for me to get to meet Demushkin face to face.

No longer connected to the defunct Slavic Union, Demushkin was now leading a new nationalist group called The Russians. With a growing membership and an increasing level of awareness through social media, Demushkin was as popular as ever and building on his followers daily. Our meet was scheduled for a Moscow-based march, one of ten scheduled country-wide for the same day.

The ironically titled National Day of Unity is a day where Russians up and down the country make their voices heard on any number of issues. Every kind of flag and Russian cause seemed to be represented. The march had been started ten years prior by President Vladimir Putin to encourage Russian unity. Nationalists hijacked the day and made 4 November a very different beast. This was an opportunity for some to support the maintaining of and investment in traditional Russian values. Unfortunately, an unhealthy number of others took the opportunity to chant about keeping Russia white.

Driving in, I couldn't help but wonder what I was getting myself into. I had no idea what to expect and definitely hadn't prepared myself for the number of people arriving in large noisy groups, piling out of an endless queue of buses, watched by police officers and dog units. In nearby streets, groups of men congregated drinking as they prepared to join the march. In previous years, the march had been known to turn violent and this time it looked as if the police were making their presence felt.

Decamping from the crew vehicle, we joined massive queues and made our way in through huge metal detectors. It took a while, as I'm sure you can imagine, considering we had bags and bags of sound and camera gear. The fact that every over-packed kit bag looked like a backpack bomb probably didn't help.

After a few intimate and rough lover-like pat-downs we were in. Mildly molested, but in. As hundreds filtered in behind us you could feel the excitement. Jumping on each other's backs, young guys in groups shouted and cheered as they bounded past. This was clearly thrilling for so many, but what this actually was, I wasn't sure yet.

Before meeting Demushkin, I was introduced to Vadim. Standing at just over six feet with a tuft of chin hair you could call a goatee in the right light, his slight frame was bolstered by layer upon layer of sportswear. He greeted me with a huge smile, which was a total betrayal of the version of Vadim I'd seen online.

Promoting the march in a video uploaded to YouTube, his squinty dark eyes fixed on the camera were accompanied by a deep Russian voice instructing viewers to show up. Encouraging the support for Russian nationals, a hooded Vadim barked his directions while stood in the woods. He challenged his audience of anonymous internet screen names to finally show their faces and to be vocal about their beliefs on the day.

It seemed to have worked, as excited friends and fans continually interrupted Vadim while we spoke. He was known, popular and attracting attention. The march was getting busier and a lot louder by the minute, and as we continued to talk, it began to feel as though my presence might have begun to attract just as much attention as Vadim's.

Filming on location always presents the same issues, whether you're making drama, entertainment or factual TV. Attention. In the case of entertainment, there's nothing better than a crowd forming while you get some random to sing in the middle of a shopping centre. With drama, there's nothing worse than a gawping passer-by while you shoot a heavy dramatic sequence outside.

Factual on the other hand lives and dies in the moment.

Sometimes a crowd forming while you interview someone on the street only adds to the sequence. The disagreeing random piping up in the crowd can deliver an unexpected perfect interruption, forcing your contributor to react in a way you could never have planned. The downside is that sometimes it can go completely the other way. The crowd that might have been beneficial on a good day can be nothing more than a distraction or, even worse, actively try to be disruptive.

It was obvious to the crowd that was forming now that we were press and even more obvious we weren't Russian. Standing out as a black guy with a camera crew worried me. To my detriment I began to try and imagine what the thousands of passers-by thought.

What could possibly be my reason for being there? Having a camera crew with me in the eyes of these young Russian men and women could mean I was either there looking for a reaction or out to catch them being all of the negative things they've been painted as in the press. I began to feel that the camera and my appearance in this environment did only one thing. Put a target on my back.

Falling inside myself in a downward spiral of paranoia, Diana did everything in her power to keep me smiling. I clocked we'd lost Vadim and I think it was at this point that Diana started body popping. Yes, dancing to distract me. Definitely a first and totally hilarious, it made no sense until the reason for her awful performance became clear. Even Diana was worried.

We were in Lublinov, a working-class suburb in the south of the city and a nationalist heartland. We had our own crew but, for some reason, we'd begun to attract other cameras. Every time I'd turn my back, there was a new stills photographer or news crew covering my attendance. A young journalist pulled me aside to explain why. Apparently, I was all over Russian social media. 'The whole of Russian Twitter is talking about you.' I was laughing on the outside but knew what that meant. The photos, tweets and status updates could potentially make my day all the more difficult, or worse, actually dangerous.

Chances were I'd suddenly been blasted onto the radar of every undesirable for miles. I could only imagine what was beginning to fill the walls of VK. The young journalist was concerned and confused at my desire to attend. He referred to the majority of men on the march as real Nazis who kill people. He claimed I'd put myself in the presence of men who openly admit to cutting off the heads of their enemies and keeping them in their fridges.

Let's let that one brew for a minute, shall we? What would you think in this situation? I'm definitely not in the business of putting myself in the line of danger so I laughed waiting for him to join in. He didn't.

Although pretty extreme, his claim felt increasingly possible due to his visible fear as the men he was referencing were now stood literally feet away. Those lighter moments of laughter and silliness I can't help but allow into my life on and off camera had run for the hills. He was deadly serious that I was in danger.

These days, whenever I'm stopped on the street, the film that's most commonly referenced is this one. People continually talk about my bravery in putting myself in that march but I've never seen it as being brave. To me it's always been about getting to the heart of the issue and staring into the eyes of the people I'm trying to understand.

The saddest thing for me about the march wasn't what was being said, it was who was saying it. For so many of the men marching to be so young yet so adamant in their nationalistic and in most cases outright racist views was heartbreaking. It wasn't the amount of people that showed up to chant offensive things or the people that went out of their way to intimidate me; it was the age of those who chose to behave in that way. In a digital age, it's always a surprise to meet a millennial who isn't taking advantage of the thing I never had access to in my teens. Namely the internet. Being online allows anyone anywhere in the world to socially educate themselves. To hold racist or offensive views in the age of information literally makes no sense as the excuse of not knowing how similar we all are has evaporated.

Now, my Russian was hardly fluent, but being able to pick out the continual use of the word *Ruski*, or Russian, in the relentless chanting made the message of the march undeniable. Pride was at the core of every word bellowed, but when I asked Diana to translate some of the more specific detail, I was shocked.

The march attracted thousands of people from many different groups. Their flags might have been different colours or displaying different symbols, but their message was consistent. Russian supremacy. The passion of the protest was at its peak and in my colour and bumbling unashamed Britishness, I represented everything they despised.

As knowledge of our camera and my attendance spread, faces began to be covered and the louder, braver few came forward to ensure I knew I wasn't welcome. I had lost Vadim at this point, and it was becoming increasingly obvious that I needed his co-sign to ensure some sort of explanation and more pertinently, a safe passage out.

When I eventually found Vadim again, I couldn't help but laugh at who had become my safety blanket. This was the man who'd professed online just how much Russia needs to go back in time to a place before the immigrants. This was also the man who was suddenly responsible for helping me feel safe. I stood out and needed reassurance that things wouldn't take a violent turn. He assured me there wouldn't be any problems, all the while totally ignoring the small pack of photographers and cameramen who began to capture our conversation.

He admitted the level of attention surprised even him. As the march went on, voices became louder and chants grew in their intensity. The mood was shifting and I was right in the centre of it all. Vadim walked me deeper into the march, to the frustration of Diana, who was doubling up as a translator. Hardly a shrinking wallflower, she wasted no time in telling off the contributor she'd found and needed to keep on side. We were right in the middle of the march, Diana was furious and the chants here were louder than ever.

The mass of flags and hoods momentarily parted allowing a small pack of men to stride through led by an army-boot-wearing, walkie-talkie-waving man with a smile almost as huge as his ginger beard. I was being pointed at. He'd finally arrived. This was Demushkin, a man I'd heard so much about but didn't expect to meet with such warmth. He seemed almost excited.

Instantly, he joked about my safety and made a point of saying just how many nationalists I was surrounded by. His point was to highlight that, according to mainstream media, a black man wouldn't survive in this environment.

The irony of his words delivered with a smile while skinheads smirked and scowled at me from behind his back wasn't lost on me at all. I knew in that moment that Demushkin saw my presence as an opportunity for his message. Keen to find his way into mainstream politics, his invitation to me was nothing more than a play for the inevitable media attention. Demushkin hijacked our meeting with his own agenda and, judging by the number of cameras on us while we spoke, felt like it was a job well done.

In one five-minute meeting, I'd become a propaganda tool for Demushkin's social media assault. Living online and growing a huge fan base through videos and written posts, the endless stream of content created by our conversation played perfectly into the illusion of tolerance.

Vadim confirmed all suspicions of an ulterior motive by announcing the message that my safety and tolerated presence would deliver for his cause online. What he neglected to consider was the contradiction of our conversation happening while chants of 'Smash the migrants' fucking faces' could be heard from the passing crowds.

With the march running through rows and rows of tower blocks, the residents lined their balconies to watch. What could be going through the heads of the young immigrants who called the area home? What do you do when you need to start again in a country that offers all the trappings of opportunity, yet you're constantly made to feel unwanted? How could you realistically feel safe?

As the demonstrations continued, some of the marching men grew in confidence and switched their attention back to me. Now, Diana and I had become fast friends but were still getting to know each other. That being said, I could see just how reluctant she was to share what was being shouted.

With every random bellow in Russian, I asked Diana for an English translation. Her responses became less and less wordy and she got quieter and quieter, with her head dropped. It was only when I watched the final cut when the film actually went out on TV, that the subtitles revealed just how many horrific racist things were being shouted. When Diana and I finally got around to talking about what was said months after the fact, she explained that what she'd heard not only upset her but made her angry. She didn't want me to know what she was hearing so I could continue to do my job on the day.

As the march closed out, the thousands of attendees wandered off in different directions. Around twenty people were arrested for expressing extreme right-wing views, which in any normal scenario would be a high number. Here, it easily could have been five times as many.

A few days passed and Vadim invited me to sit down with him and Dmitry in a small community centre. It was out in the suburbs, miles from the more familiar corners of bustling Moscow. To be clear, the Russian suburbs definitely didn't match my naive British expectation of suburbia. We weren't in the spacious leafy edges of the big city; we were dwarfed by the endless stretches of high-rise blocks and relentless concrete.

The single-story building housed a barbecue, slightly out-of-place pink strip lighting and a yellowing smoke-stained ceiling. Clearly a social club for Demushkin and his friends, he held court in a corner table while chewing a toothpick, flanked by humourless lumps.

With our first encounter being pretty contrived, Demushkin's use of my appearance at the march to make a public political statement had left me frustrated. I suspected my desire to unpack what I experienced could fall secondary to whatever his chosen agenda for today might be.

I'd barely got comfortable in my seat when Demushkin

launched into his mainstream political ambitions, insisting he had changed since his days leading the Slavic Union. Adamant that the more extreme views and offensive language used on the march only hurt his cause, he expressed shock and distaste for the brand of free speech I was subjected to.

With a strong belief that the immigration laws are chaotic and the radical types I witnessed at the march were almost exclusively the young, he seemed considered in his opinions. This was clearly a man who'd invested time and thought to answers that weren't extreme yet appeased his following.

Demushkin understood the power of concise answers and almost felt rehearsed. He wasn't just performing for my camera, we were being filmed by Vadim on his smartphone. Vadim insisted the video was for his own private viewing but Demushkin was quick to speak openly about the benefits of discourse specifically with a black man. He was adamant that the media portray him as a monster and the march as a hub for racists, so my presence did their cause a favour.

As the conversation continued, Demushkin referred to me several times as African-American. I had to explain to him that I wasn't that, or 'Afro-English' (whatever that is) as assumed by Vadim, I was British. My Britishness was by the by as Demushkin's focus was explaining his reasoning behind giving me the strange African-American label. Rather than paraphrase, I'll quote the man himself. 'We don't say nigger here as it's an offensive word and so we say African-American out of habit.' Call me crazy but his use of the N-word during his explanation felt a little counterproductive for his professed desire not to offend.

Several chewed toothpicks later, Demushkin gave me his take on modern nationalism. He believes it's about putting his people first. When pressed, he described his people simply as Russians.

Now, I'm not one for name-calling but Demushkin was definitely a toxic person. He's like the guy in your office who microwaves fish at lunchtime. Yeah, that guy. The one with an incredible talent to poison any environment with their unique brand of crappiness wherever they go. I felt drained whenever we spoke as his distinctive blend of body odour and attitude lingered. The aforementioned toxicity hung on to his unswerving, and at times abhorrent, views, and I wore that stink all day until I showered it away before bed.

❢ *White, healthy and sober* ❢

This film was tough. Between the weather, the language barrier and the people I had to meet I was struggling. Calls home became more frequent and room service comfort food binges of ice cream and cake more regular. I would wake up and dread the day ahead, as well as look that bit chubbier every day.

Far Right and Proud was directed by a man who I'd never worked with before, but we were learning loads about each other with every sequence we'd shoot. It was a shame the process was so tough while we were trying to get to know each other both professionally and personally. Being the person in front of the camera, I've always found working with self-shooting directors a strange dance. The relationship you share can dictate the tone of the film and more importantly its direction.

I felt isolated and was quieter than usual. Diana regularly pulled me out of my funk and made a real effort to keep me engaged. Thankfully, I can say she's gone on to become a real friend.

It was our blossoming friendship that stopped me on several occasions from throwing in the towel, as the process was unlike anything I'd ever experienced. Diana's unshakable energy was responsible for my willingness to continue. On an expectedly icy school night, she found a boxing event for me to attend. But before I went, I jumped online.

With the hard end of the nationalist contingent sharing trophy videos online, attacks on anyone that didn't look Russian became more commonplace. I watched clips but couldn't make it to the end of any. The level of hatred on display told me that there was something much deeper at play than boys being boys.

With most going unreported, there are no reliable figures on migrant attacks. This desire to hurt anyone presenting as other unfortunately went hand in hand with a rise in a particular kind of past-time. The violent kind.

I met up with Alexi, a protein-shake-guzzling twenty-two-year-old gym fiend, and Lisa, a tiny baby-faced seventeen-year-old. Both were members of nationalist group Restruct, and clearly saw their views not only as something they needed to share with me but also as something they'd wear.

Wearing T-shirts covered in nationalist symbolism and nods to Nazism, their wardrobe was almost as offensive as their point of view. I found it scary they'd want to be a part of what they saw as a family. Alexi described his preferred future and the country he loves as becoming three specific things: white, healthy and sober.

Alexi took me to the boxing night at a local venue organised by friends from the same nationalist group. The hall was filled with men in bad tracksuits and women with heavy make-up and neck tattoos. It was lovely.

Walking into a busy room with a large camera and a sound guy can attract the strangest of behaviour at times. I say that as the promoter of the event went out of his way for us. I guess we represented some of the razzmatazz he was trying to evoke with the scantily clad women handing out finger food and drinks.

It was all a bit low rent and smelly. The room had a strange pong, probably due to the mix of aggressive aftershave choices and pickled onions being handed out on trays. The scrappy fight took less and less of my attention as I had to get off my chest what had been bugging me since our earlier conversation.

Alexi started to open up with his take on race and Russia but stopped himself. What was he hiding and why didn't he want to tell me? Finding a quiet corner, I pushed him on how he truly felt. His answers made for fascinating and shocking

TV, but in the moment, I had to use every ounce of strength not to walk away.

Alexi finally let it all hang out and it was stunning. Not the good kind, the road kill smashed into the concrete sort of stunning. He believed a Russian person should only mix with whites as he was strongly against the mixing of bloods. As I explained my mixed-race heritage, Alexi was confused and deferred to Diana who was translating.

He struggled to understand and when it finally made sense to him, his reaction was priceless. 'When you wash clothes, you can't mix whites with colours. It's not right.' As far as Alexi was concerned, mixing bloods in animals produces problems, therefore mixing races in people shouldn't happen. He had the detail on my family background, yet Alexi saw nothing wrong with referring to me as a mongrel. In principle, he said he believed mixed-race relationships were okay, but his worry was that, 'In the next generation, freaks could be born.'

I couldn't spend much more time with Alexi as his level of ignorance was beyond anything I could tolerate any further. The Russia that Alexi and Lisa were fighting for wasn't about lifestyle, it was about colour.

With Demushkin the top of the tree in terms of my Russian nationalist experience, I knew that to get a better understanding of the likes of Alexi, I needed to go back to the man with the ginger beard. Unfortunately for me, that meant playing a game of niceties with Vadim, my way in. Accepting an invite to his apartment, I found myself in the middle of the odd alternate universe he called home.

Vadim loved weapons and proudly walked me through an endless stream of BB guns and knives. On display and filling every shelf and flat surface, weapons were everywhere. He alluded to using his knives in street fights but, with a broad creepy smile, made a point of leaving things ambiguous.

Knives were clearly a huge part of what Vadim saw as his identity. He never left the house without one. Given his array of different-sized weapons, none of which were small, I wondered what he would carry on a normal day. I would go on to learn quickly that, in the case of Vadim and his nationalist friends, what made a knife dangerous wasn't its size, it was knowing how to use it.

Trust back in place and showing off out of the way, Vadim invited me to a knife club run by Demushkin. I was going to see how they trained with their weapons and hopefully find out exactly what they were training for. But first I had to put up with the obvious dislike of his nationalist pals during the world's most awkward train journey.

Demushkin led the class dressed in a pair of dad-like sweatpants. With a guide on how to land a punch and strike without having your knife taken, I was confused as to what this was trying to encourage. The answer I was repeatedly given was self-defence, but this late into my journey that didn't wash.

With kids in the class as young as fourteen, watching a full-on lesson on how to injure, disable or even permanently damage someone with a knife was frightening. Yes, the packed class was swinging rubber knives, but the fact that they all had the real thing in their backpacks and on their belts scared the crap out of me.

As a London boy born and raised, knife crime is something I grew up around and had no choice but to deal with. To see kids being actually *taught* how to use knives in the street combat context left me speechless.

One teenager I spoke to described his reason for attending the class as the dangerous immigrants. Apparently, as I wasn't from the country I wouldn't understand. What he didn't seem to make a connection between was the only time he'd been attacked was by a Russian and his motivations to protect himself had nothing to do with the people he was afraid of.

I met several immigrants who'd been attacked by young nationalists with knives. My fear was that groups like Demushkin's fight club weren't doing anything to fix this recurring problem, only encourage it.

After the class, I found myself back in the metal box of a clubhouse with Demushkin one last time. I raised the amount of immigrant attack videos I'd seen online while he professed no responsibility for such violence. This man was incredibly difficult to engage with as his disgust for anyone non-Russian continually found itself bubbling to the surface.

Fully aware of what he stands for and who his followers truly are, in asking how he sees his future, Demushkin's answer said everything about his beliefs and the true nature of his message. He believed his future was either in the Kremlin or in jail. With his history and steadily growing following, incarceration for someone like Demushkin would always be a possibility. On the other hand, with former KGB goon Putin running the country, maybe his political ambitions weren't that far-fetched.

In interviews, I have often been asked about my final spikey conversation with Demushkin. The chat, albeit it amicable and calm on the surface, had an undertone of disgust from both sides. My level of dislike for the man wouldn't allow me to even shake his hand as I left. He noticed and couldn't let it go.

As I made for the door Demushkin shouted, 'If we don't like the film we'll send a killer to England.' I stopped, he smiled and I left.

CHAPTER 3

THE ENEMY IN THE MIRROR

Something odd happened the other day. Rolling out of bed was followed by the usual slouch into the bathroom, but instead of going for the toothbrush or scraping away the eye bogies, I went to the mirror. I'd had five days of hard workouts buoyed by clean eating and for the first time in forever my stomach was flat yet bumpy in the right way. I'd achieved the ever-elusive six-pack. Sixteen-year-old me would have been so proud. Present-day me smiled for a second, then got right back to work on the eye crust.

I'd made a decision at the beginning of the year to train hard and feel healthier while gaining a body I felt comfortable in. Somehow, I'd done it. Clothes fit better, my energy and self-confidence had sky-rocketed; yet my physical achievement continues to receive the strangest of reactions. I've learnt that the gym and fitness in general can mean many things based entirely on who it is you're talking to.

For some, achieving the perfect physique is the only way to battle insecurity, while at the other end of the spectrum, a weird mix of ambition and narcissism can fuel an addiction. I'm definitely somewhere between those two extremes and have begrudgingly accepted that my commitment to health and fitness doesn't sit well with everyone. The change in my appearance and self-confidence seems to hold up a mirror for other people, encouraging reactions ranging from the supportive to the judgemental. Whatever the case, I'm the happiest I've been with myself in as long as I can remember.

I haven't always been this content. In my early thirties things got weird, but thankfully it wasn't just happening to me. For some reason, my closest male friends and I started carrying around that extra bit of flab that seemingly appeared from nowhere. The fact that we were all in relationships, had good jobs, full fridges and brilliant excuses for smashing an entire packet of Hobnobs during *Match of the Day* had nothing to do with it. Obviously.

At the time, a fashion aesthetic I'd dabbled with via the ridiculously priced designer Rick Owens found its way into the mainstream and became a trend. Suddenly, dropped-crotch pants and oversized T-shirts were affordable and everywhere. All my friends were suddenly wearing bigger T-shirts and more forgiving denim or joggers that brilliantly cloaked the fact we all suddenly had rugby thighs. Outside of how on trend we may have looked, that slouchy look delivered another way to be overweight without anyone knowing.

By the time I'd gotten over wearing trousers that made me look like a toddler with a heavy nappy, nothing in my wardrobe fit. I had to change something and started to work out religiously for the first time in years. What kept me going was making a big deal out of my routine via social media. I'd roped in a few friends and we started a six-week challenge to sort out our fitness and physical appearance for good.

I was eating better and training harder than ever. My followers across social media cheered me on and their awareness of the six-week challenge applied a pressure to keep it up. Small changes began to happen and I was over the moon with the shift in my stomach size but not the time it was taking. I wanted those big results to hurry the hell up so I could take my feet off the gas – or in this case off the damn treadmill.

Thankfully, my career on screen hadn't slowed down as I'd begun shooting the new series of 'Extreme' but this time at home in the UK. The *Extreme UK* series set out to cover British issues skipped by mainstream media. As I finally began to see noticeable progress with my own fitness challenge, fate stepped in with the timely film *Dying for a Six Pack*.

For the film, I set out to establish the moment when self-improvement becomes self-destruction. What I ended up doing was exploring themes in a way relating just as much to myself as to the men I'd meet.

Dying for a Six Pack placed me directly – and unintention-
ally I might add – in a subject matter that mirrored my own
personal journey. I found myself confronting my own motivations to change my physical appearance and asking the
question, why do I want what I want?

There have never been as many gyms in the UK, and young
British men are now far more aware of their physical appearance than ever before. With everyone from schoolboys to white
collar business types packing out weight rooms countrywide,
something has changed. What was once tied to sports stars,
the minimal body fat and six-pack aesthetic was suddenly
much more common in normal guys.

Not only has working out been normalised, it has almost
become expected to share your results. With platforms like
Instagram totally inundated with images of pecs and progress, it's easy to be inspired or intimidated. Knowing this
going in, I started making the film worried about what lane I
truly belonged in. I felt that my motivations were genuinely
about being happier with myself for myself, but were they?

I was in Swansea, south Wales, and was meeting twenty-
four-year-old Kyle, a builder who worked out daily. With a social
media feed made up of shirtless photos and/or clean meals,
this was a man proud of his body and determined to share it.

As Kyle's building site day job was physically demanding,
he made the most of his time on site fighting to do the heaviest

lifting or most demanding tasks. This need to continually move wasn't to gain approval from peers or a promotion from superiors, it was about burning calories. Motivated by a breakup, Kyle's workouts went into overdrive eighteen months before I met him. His hobby had become an obsession and fitness took over his life.

At the time of shooting, I'd been with my then girlfriend for years and hadn't been pushed to change my appearance once. If there were subtle hints to fix my flab, I'd definitely missed them. My appearance was something I cared about but had never been fixated on, as I'd always relied on my personality when it came to women.

The idea that this rejection might be the motivation for a healthier lifestyle didn't sit well. His breakup seemed to have put him in the gym and he sounded obsessed with being healthy, but for unhealthy reasons. I was invited to join him for a workout and gladly accepted, intrigued by what his time in the gym would look like. To get anywhere close to his physique, I knew I had a way to go. Seeing how he did it wasn't going to be brilliant just for the film, I was eager to steal as much as possible for my own regime.

The familiar smell of cheap deodorant and socks filled the male changing room as Kyle and I got our gym gear on. Before I could even pull kit from my duffel, I was floored by a familiar sound I've only ever associated with the kitchen. Kyle had begun to apply what he referred to as 'a cheat' ahead of the workout. This was a trick he'd used before and one I couldn't follow. Stood shirtless in the middle of the room, Kyle wrapped clingfilm around his thighs and torso in an effort to shed more water during exercise. I'd never seen anything like this before and couldn't help but smirk as he finished up and let out a loud creaking noise with every step as he made his way out.

With his 'cheat' hidden beneath a pair of shorts and a vest, the ridiculous nature of the situation fell away the longer we worked out. Kyle was working double hard only to improve what looked to me like the dream shape. I somehow managed to keep up but was totally distracted the entire time as I was training with a man who was desperately trying to sweat out excess water, risking dehydration and heat stroke.

Openly referring to his body as 'shit', Kyle hated what I thought was a near perfect physique. He didn't see enough cuts and pointed out abs that weren't defined enough. Adamant his body was crap, he saw a stomach carrying too much water weight, whereas I saw the flat stomach I was eating rabbit food to achieve.

Desperate to sweat as much as possible and as a result lose more water, Kyle pushed me to speed up. He wanted to complete each set quicker and wasn't acting up for the camera, he was genuinely pissed off that I was slowing him down.

Upon leaving the gym, I became aware of just how much his appearance affects every corner of his life. Kyle micromanages every calorie and had decided that his post-workout meal would be a single bag of beef jerky. The packet of lean meat proudly shouted the fact that its contents were only 140 calories. This to me said snack, but for Kyle, this was lunch.

I'd made a promise to myself to watch my diet but hadn't been paying attention to calories or fallen into the crazy routine of prepping meals in tiny little Tupperware boxes. I wanted to look and feel better at the end of my six-week challenge, not be worse off in terms of my health.

All you have to do is type 'six-pack advice' into Google and everything imaginable comes up. The researched and proven sit side by side with the ill-advised and falsehoods, all presented as equally valid and effective. In figuring out what I needed to do for the results I was after, my building blocks were simple. Diet and training. Call me old fashioned, but going with the safest and most proven route felt like the way to go.

That didn't seem to be the case for Kyle as his 'by any means necessary' attitude towards results seemed to also define his drive. Unfortunately, Kyle wasn't an anomaly. Young men up and down the country have shifted their ideals and what is being deemed as the new normal ironically isn't.

While my wardrobe had played a huge part in letting me ignore and maybe even hide a decline in physical fitness, what younger guys wear today is becoming part of showing off what they've grafted for in the gym.

Online retailer Reem directly markets clothes at that younger male audience obsessed with not just dressing like their idols, but also emulating their physicality. I attended one of their open casting calls attracting a load of normal guys. Business owner Simon was scouting for new models for his newest collections; only he wasn't looking for new faces, he was far more preoccupied with their bodies.

Only two of the men that turned up were models, the other twenty or so were average Joes and you couldn't pick out who was who. These weren't the lean, sharp-cheekboned, high fashion models that come to mind when you think 'model'. These were commercial models that didn't look too dissimilar to the inexperienced new jacks. Everyone was in shape and everyone fit a specific look. Simon was totally open about which looks and body shapes sold better to his audience of young fashion-conscious men. They wanted clothes that made them look better or showed off their best attributes. Based on Simon's customers' buying habits, the bicep size and type of tattoos on the models were key factors in which products sold.

One by one the guys were called up for their own little test shoot. With their competition in full view, each young guy had to strut his stuff, and the presence of my inquisitive eye (and let's not forget the camera crew) definitely didn't help.

I don't think I've ever seen so many red faces back to back; nonetheless the guys all got through their awkward moment in the spot light. Watching each wannabe go up one after the other, the common theme became obvious. There were two definite, separate looks, and each model fit into one or the other. There was the clean-cut look where a sharp side parting or cropped haircut was accompanied by ice white teeth. Then there was a heavily tattooed and fuzzy faced dude who had the piercings and grimace to match.

It was almost like watching two different McFlurrys being served on a McDonalds counter. One with this topping and the other with that. Both served on an ordinary and apparently commonplace base that in this case was toned physique and the obligatory six-pack.

When I spoke to the guys during a short break, they were open about their chosen look and just how much it had been influenced by the content they consume. Some talked about the men's magazine fitness models they'd grown up learning workouts from. Some spoke about the reality TV stars seen on shows like *Geordie Shore* and *Ex on the Beach*, who are all shoulders and plucked eyebrows.

The conversation got awkward as I realised I was definitely the old geezer in the room as I didn't know any of the people they were referencing. The shows they watched were on my radar, but I generally struggled to watch them because of the shit show of on-screen behaviour featured in them. That being said, the minutes of TV I'd subjected my poor eyes to did leave me thinking, blimey, those blokes are bloody ripped. And they literally went out in tight tops having a great time while getting all the attention from the women in whatever bar they'd chosen to gyrate in that night. As one of the wannabe models explained, 'Lads these days are seeing that and want a piece of it.'

As most of the men I spoke to repeated the same thoughts, I began to see the motivation. It wasn't just about feeling better, it was about the reaction those hours in the gym received. 'Changes become lifestyle and a habit, then you're set for life,' claimed another of the wannabe models. Set for life? I had no idea pulsating triceps could cover your council tax.

Either way I had a lot to learn. For this generation of younger gym addicts, their toned bodies were more than just the visible results of hard work; they'd become a status symbol.

Leaving the shoot, my belief in what young men were striving for in the gym had been totally knocked off centre. I'd spent the day surrounded by a load of blokes with no shirt on, which was odd for a start. I'd also left the casting call with a completely new set of references as to what the new normal had become. With modern icons like footballer Cristiano Ronaldo and (as much as it pains me to type) the cast of reality TV tripe having a huge influence over this generation of men in their late teens and early twenties, how built you are and how masculine you are has become more important than ever.

I've never seen surgery as an option in terms of getting my body closer to my ideals. That isn't me turning my nose up at anyone who chooses otherwise, that's me being sure about only going under the knife when I know it's for something I can't fix myself. But as the science improves and cosmetic surgery continues to drop in price, the stigma it's carried for so long is falling. Increasingly, men are finding new ways to change their bodies. For some, the gym just isn't enough to achieve the results they're after; the amount of time required for perfection (whatever that is) is just too high. That's when the scale of your bank balance comes into play.

Some men are going further afield in their pursuit of the perfect six-pack. Turkey is fast becoming a go-to destination for British men desperate to achieve their dream appearance. I hopped on a flight and attended an abdominal etching surgery where Lee from Leeds (no, really) underwent a procedure to change the visibility of his abdominal muscles.

Spending six days a week at the gym just wasn't enough for Lee, so he had decided on the £3,500 procedure. The minute Lee took his shirt off in preparation for his operation, I had to say how confused I was, as the man was clearly in shape. We went back and forth, but what became obvious quite quickly was that his issue wasn't with what others saw, it was almost entirely about how he felt.

The etching process saw a doctor melt the little fat Lee had using ultrasound, which was then sucked out strategically to accentuate his muscles. Lee lost the count-to-ten game under the spell of anaesthetic and he was taken down to theatre. I changed into scrubs so I could get a front-row seat.

I've never liked hospitals. I think it's the unavoidable stink of sickness in competition with nose-burning hand sanitiser I've always seen as an assault to the senses. Walking into the operating room was a strange place to be, considering my main aim was to stay out of the doctors' way and try not to throw up at the sight of things going in and out of Lee's body.

A long steel pole I can only describe as the lypo thingy poked its way around Lee's chest area just below the skin. It hummed loudly and spat bits of fat into a jumbo-sized glass beaker making me go a little green – and I can confirm that it wasn't with envy.

Watching the procedure come to a close, I was amazed at just how quickly the difference was visible. Lee was away with the fairies and had no idea that his abs already looked like he'd been training a lot harder for a lot longer. I caught myself while watching the surgery touching my soft bits suddenly more conscious of my own flaws.

Thinking about the operation, I tried to take a step back. In one short procedure, Lee had put himself in a position where he'd never have to do a sit-up again. Did he have the right idea while I was totally wasting my time? This gave rise to a whole range of thoughts and feelings in me that I couldn't really make sense of as I felt suddenly hyper aware of how much more work I had to do on myself to be fully satisfied with my own results. It also made me instantly paranoid that my journey to being happier with my body could become a losing battle for perfection.

My addictive personality has led me to some real positives in my life. I've conquered things I'd never dreamed of, from completing Super Mario on the hardest setting (impressive, I know) to putting myself in therapy in an effort to become a better man. With all the positive results of my ability to focus combined with my addictive traits, could I ever find myself doing something as extreme as Lee should I not achieve my physical goals naturally?

I wasn't born this way, I made myself this way

With all this in mind, I decided to meet a man who made Lee look like a total beginner in the surgery game. If Lee's surgery, though intrusive, seemed doable and had incredible results, then I wanted to speak to someone who'd gone all the way.

I found myself in a super-posh London hotel that smelt as good as it looked; it was the type of place you'd regret not stealing from. Directed upstairs to one of the bigger suites, I was greeted at the door by Rodrigo. At thirty-two, Rodrigo was a flight attendant with dreams of a glamorous life played out with fantastic flare on his Instagram page.

This was a man who knew how to have a good time, or at least he looked like he did online. With a relentless stream of glamorous locations and designer outfits, Rodrigo bombarded his followers with images of opulence. The strangest thing was that I found with every image, regardless of the location, what demanded my attention wasn't the opulent setting or his flamboyant wardrobe; it was his face and physique.

At just thirty-two years old, Rodrigo has had thirty-five cosmetic procedures and finally feels he's achieved his goal.

If I were to list his page-filling surgical breakdown, you'd think that he should look every bit the image of perfection. In my humble opinion, he was quite the opposite.

When Rodrigo welcomed me at the door, his arms were open and his face was bright. He was warm, friendly and polite. Every bit the coiffured gentleman, Rodrigo was by all accounts lovely. What was hard to ignore was the obvious surgery he wore with pride. He had that Hollywood face thing you'd usually associate with rich older women who have spent a fortune on their cheekbones and handbag dog.

His work was very specific in its ambition to be noticed. He had surgery that looked like surgery and it didn't stop at his face.

Rodrigo slipped into a nearly there silk robe for an in-room massage and I didn't know where to look. He'd had the same abdominal etching surgery as Lee and his chest area looked as if it had been carved in marble. I was so glad I hadn't met Rodrigo with Lee as his work didn't stop at his abs. His open silk robe placed his sculpted silicone pectorals front and centre.

Wearing a body men fight to achieve, Rodrigo saw himself as reinvented through plastic surgery. With silicone fillers in his biceps, triceps and shoulders he looked broad and pumped. He talked me through the lypo he'd had in his back and waist as well as countless other procedures, amounting to a grand total of £210,000.

Where the budget to actualise his physical goals actually came from was never explained and I'm annoyed to this day that I never asked. As a card-carrying cheapo, whenever I hear talk of large sums of money spent on things that bear no fruit nor return, I struggle not to turn my nose up. Desperately trying to bite my tongue, his reasoning shut me up. This was more about acceptance than attention.

Convinced of a version of the world I'd never experienced, Rodrigo believed who he was simply wasn't good enough and attaining beauty was his way out. 'Some people are born blessed with natural beauty, I wasn't. I wasn't born this way, I made myself this way in order to be accepted by society.'

Rodrigo was adamant the surgery was right for him; even the life-threatening infection he'd battled in a botched arm filler operation hadn't stopped him from going under the knife again. As soon as he pulled out the photo album, pictures of his former self were exactly that. A different person entirely and one he referred to as someone else. Describing his pre-operation self as 'this guy', Rodrigo pointed out flaws I couldn't see. Who he was simply wasn't good enough, and diet and exercise apparently wouldn't have been enough to amend the imperfections he took issue with.

At this point I was a month into my six-week challenge and my friends were well on their way to better bodies. I was happy with my progress but couldn't help but go harder in an effort not to be the lazy one with the worst results come reveal day. With Rodrigo still fresh in my mind, the idea of finding a quick fix still felt wrong but much more understandable. I'd never had his level of dissatisfaction with my appearance, but as things started to change for the better during the six-week push, finding a way to speed things up crossed my mind, even if I knew it was a cop-out.

My routine had changed, my diet had changed, my wardrobe had way more spandex than I'd ever owned. Okay, maybe spandex is a slight exaggeration but I was suddenly wearing tight T-shirts, shorts and man tights to work out. I'd become that gym guy you see with headphones on silently blasting through a workout. I found myself sitting up for hours online trawling the net for tips on diet or new workouts to try in my next session.

At this point I found comfort in knowing I wasn't getting surgery any time soon, but had my intensity stepped up for the right reasons?

Catching myself checking my reflection for that little bit too long after a workout one morning, I knew something had changed. I was focused on tiny details I wanted to tweak. My mate Manny was suddenly lifting heavier than I could and I was trying to catch up. What the fuck was going on? Was this about feeling better or had it become about looking better than the next guy? That fine line between controlling the results and the results controlling me had begun to blur and I couldn't believe what was happening. I was hardly Mr Muscle by any means, but I had definitely improved and was visibly in better shape. But how far would this go?

❛ *Thirty? I'd be lucky to get there* ❜

I went back to Wales to meet up with Kyle for a second time. The last time we had trained together, he admitted he was striving for perfection. A couple of weeks had passed and being that bit further into my own transition, I'd started to see how I could snowball into Kyle's continued pursuit for faultlessness.

As before, Kyle wrapped himself in cling film before his workout. Only this time, he wasn't planning to lift in the gym; he was headed to the sauna. The eighty-two-degree heated room offered Kyle the chance to burn even more calories as he curled dumbbells.

This wasn't fitness, this was punishment. My concern was that his body wouldn't be able to endure this level of abuse forever. At twenty-four years old, like Kyle I'd felt invincible. Now, being that bit older and seeing things start to slow down, I questioned his thought process. I asked, 'What's your body going to be like at thirty?' he replied, 'Thirty? I'd be lucky to get there.'

Kyle was aware of what he could be doing to his health but accepted it as the small print in his quest for the perfect body. This was a workout I couldn't join as I was deflated and upset at what he'd become.

Body dysmorphia is unfortunately commonly associated with younger women. Even with my limited knowledge of the condition, this felt like everything I knew it to be. Kyle was addicted to the results of training and I couldn't see much difference between his addiction and that of someone bound to a class-A drug. He knew what he was doing was bad but he wouldn't stop even if it killed him.

When Kyle returned from his heated weight lifting, he knew I wasn't impressed and explained his hunger for tougher physical challenges as being down to pressure. Kyle believed his appearance made him a different person. He saw his fitness as being a large part of his popularity. Apparently, his abs gave him friends.

That night I was invited to meet him at his second job. As I had no idea what he did outside of the gym and building site, I was intrigued. Arriving at a bar I thought I was going to see Kyle pulling pints.

Once I'd made it past the burly bouncer and crossed the sticky dance floor, I was directed upstairs to see him at work. Passing loud and rowdy packs of women on the staircase I should have known what I was walking into. It was only when I turned the corner into the bar's entertainment space dominated by cackling hen parties and flashing lights that I got it.

A lady in a shiny bodycon dress and sparkly heels purred into the mic with a broad Swansea accent. Camera phones flashed and women cheered as she introduced 'The one, the only . . . Cowboy!' and on walked Kyle.

Plaid shirt, jeans, boots and, of course, a massive cowboy hat adorned Kyle as he strutted out to huge screams. Sliding and grinding about the stage, Kyle shed items of clothing to the beat with a huge grin. Pulling an excitable woman from the front row, he sat her on a chair and gyrated on top of her while removing his shirt. Kyle's evening job was stripping and he clearly loved it.

Taking a deep breath, I slipped out and cornered a few women in the stairwell to try and understand what it was about the stripper physique that they loved so much. The common theme was that the half-naked dancing boys fulfilled a fantasy. But the three women I spoke to who'd dated men with bodies just like the oiled-up ones on stage said they wouldn't do it again. All three – now single women – saw their muscle-bound ex partners as too high maintenance. 'You can't be more interested in yourself than your partner.'

Kyle's big finish was to strip down to his man thong, which was unlike anything I'd ever seen before. The pouch bit that cradles the man bits (I don't bloody know the correct terminology, I've never bloody bought one!) was a small turkey complete with wings and a yellow beak. Popping his rear end to make the Turkey wings flap was possibly the most horrific thing I've ever seen in my life.

Horror show over and the flappy turkey image forever burnt into my mind, we grabbed a drink and had a chat on the side of the stage. Kyle admitted that none of what I had just watched was for the women in the audience, it was more about him feeling more confident in himself. The attention he wanted wasn't from the women that were queuing up to lick whipped cream off his hairless chest; it was more about impressing his fellow stripper mates. Apparently, the men who gave Kyle praise for his body were more of a motivator than the women who wanted to touch it. Kyle was taking his clothes off for a room full of people he didn't even think about.

The more time I spent with Kyle the more his unhealthy obsession worried me that I wasn't getting the full story. He didn't come across as someone who would go under the knife to achieve the results he desired, but I'd seen him employ a dangerous technique that he saw as a short cut. How far would he go?

As a kid, the only guys I knew that went to the gym were the beefhead doormen who drank down the pub with my uncle George, or wannabe tough guys on my estate. Muscles generally meant meathead, as at that time it was the Hulk Hogans of this world who were bronzed and buff.

Things have definitely changed. The gym isn't a boys' club anymore and the spit and sawdust style muscle factories are few and far between. As well as working out being associated with a particular sort of man, the bigger you are, the more it's understood that steroids are a necessary evil. Anabolic steroids are a synthetic form of testosterone taken to increase stamina and improve muscle growth. Legal for personal use whether injected or taken as tablets, their popularity was far greater than I'd assumed.

I visited Turning Point, a central London charity offering clean needle exchange mainly for heroin and crack users. But three years ago, they added a drop-in for steroid users too. Shown around by team leader Roy, he talked about the huge change in who was coming through the door.

The steroid drop-in had gone from predominantly men in their late thirties who'd been training for decades, to young men in their early twenties. Most disturbingly, some of those young men weren't even gym users, these were naïve guys chasing the physical results associated with injecting.

At the time of filming, estimates put the number of steroid users in the UK at around half a million, and Roy was candid in his explanation of what he dealt with daily. He reckoned that only 10 per cent of users he helped were people who knew how to inject properly. The rest wouldn't even know what to do with the needles they'd receive. Some would inject the parts of their bodies they wanted to grow bigger thinking local administration worked.

With continued abuse, steroids put users on a hormonal rollercoaster causing testicles to shrink. With the wrong combination of chemicals, a user's sex drive could be obliterated entirely.

❝ It's always been a women's problem ❞

Travelling north, I visited a gym in Huddersfield with a reputation for its hardcore clientele. This was every bit the grunt-filled machismo pit you're thinking of. Bellows of a personal best being broken were matched by the sound of metal smashing against metal. This was a real gym for real men and I regretted my choice to wear a pink Acne topcoat the minute I walked in.

The changing room was cold, dirty and basic. It didn't have

a sauna, Jacuzzi or any of the additionals I was used to at my local, but it did have needle bins. A sign on the wall indicated a zero-tolerance policy for usage, but the contradictory bins indicated the owners knew they couldn't stop what clearly appeared to be the inevitable.

I walked into the gym itself to meet Dave or, as he's known by his friends, the Freak. On his back, Dave was lifting with his legs while cradling his bald head in his hands. Bright red and shaking, he was pushing his body to the limit and, after noticing his arms, I was glad he wasn't pushing me.

I shit you not when I say the man had arms the size of my head. They looked like lion legs and even his little muscles had muscles of their own. As he squeezed out his last rep, a blood vessel on the top of his head burst and blood made its way across his scalp. I didn't know what to do so, as usual, I did what I always do when I'm nervous. I talked to the guy.

Nonchalantly wiping the blood away, Dave fobbed the bleeding off as being a blood pressure thing. It had happened before and wasn't even a concern. From the age of nineteen, Dave had spent his life in the gym. Now in his mid-forties, his only break had been a twelve-year hiatus due to an injury.

What Dave referred to as an 'injury' sounded to me like a reason to never return to a gym ever. Dave was forced to take a twelve-year break from working out as he tore his right pectoral muscle clean off.

Formally a champion body builder, Dave used steroids regularly and is now a counsellor teaching younger athletes about their safety. Referring to himself as pro education rather than pro use, Dave believes they're not the demon they're made out to be. He saw social media as the main culprit for the rise in usage among younger guys. 'Men have never had to deal with image issues, it's always been a women's problem.'

Dave introduced me to Craig who'd started training at nine years old. Lifting weights as a child, Craig developed a need for better results in his teens. Joining the army at nineteen and up to his eyeballs in testosterone, Craig started using steroids. With the dangerous mix of natural teenage hormones, adrenaline and aggression as a result of the job and steroids, Craig blew his top and ended up spending twelve months behind bars for fighting.

With everything he'd experienced, Craig still used and he put it down to the addictive nature of the results. Pulling out his smartphone, Dave showed me just how easy it was to buy steroids online. Within seconds he had hundreds of sites to choose from and without any real effort found boxes of the stuff for sale at a price cheaper than protein powder from your average high-street chain.

Steroids had always been taboo in my eyes as a teenager, but that would have been smashed had I been living my teenage years now. The information and access available now makes it almost too easy to buckle under the pressure to use.

While steroids are legal to possess for personal use, it's illegal to sell or supply to users. So how are there so many sites selling online? When I meet people who are operating outside of the law producing an illegal substance, I've always wondered just how much they care about the quality of product and more importantly the user.

At the time of filming, three illegal labs had been shut down that year alone. If caught, the self-styled chemists can get up to fourteen years in prison. I visited one such 'lab' that was actually a suburban garage set up to look like a high-school chemistry lab.

The baseball caps and tracksuits confirmed my suspicion that the 'chemists' responsible for the product were kids. The ease of production was mindblowing. This group of young men who clearly had no qualifications to produce this level of chemical for public consumption was turning out batches by the boatload. With a customer base of over 50,000, this group of wannabe Walter Whites were making a lot of money mixing chemicals in a garage. With the negatives to steroid use so public, this group of chemists saw themselves as only responsible for producing a safe product. What the users do with it, they believed, was up to them.

So where did this leave the vulnerable or easily influenced young men who just wanted results? If the makers weren't responsible, how long would it be before someone as obsessed as Kyle started using? I decided to meet up with Kyle one last time as his desperation to be better felt as though it could only really lead him in one direction.

After watching him work out in the most unbelievable ways, I knew I had to be upfront about my worries and, surprisingly,

Kyle was honest with me. He admitted to injecting in the past. I shouldn't have been surprised but I was. What was worse was that he was currently using a course of steroids in tablet form. His reasoning was the tablets would help him strip fat and excess water. I had to ask what the pills were actually for and as soon as he answered I could see a flash in his eyes that even he wasn't sure if it was a good idea.

Kyle claimed to be using a type of tablet intended for asthmatics that in some cases would be used for livestock. Kyle had the pills in his bag and I asked him to show me the packet. The pills he'd bought were covered in Chinese lettering and nothing on the packet was English. With no idea of recommended dosage or an expiry date, he had literally no idea what he was putting in his body.

The perfect mix of annoyed and frustrated, I had no right to tell this grown man what to do but I desperately wanted to scream in his face 'WAKE UP'. After an uncomfortable silence, he managed to drag me from my funk with an announcement I never saw coming.

Kyle told me to keep the pills as he'd decided he wouldn't use them anymore. Having had family berate him for years about, in his words, his obsessive behaviour, my questioning of him as an outsider made him think twice about what he'd been doing with his life. He'd decided after our clash at the sauna to change and not a moment too soon.

There are more and more people pushing for perfection but the problem I have is the reasoning. I started working out wanting to feel better, but as my six-week challenge came to a close I also wanted to look better just as much, if not more. My biggest fear now was losing track of my relationship with fitness, allowing it to ironically become something unhealthy. I didn't want to stop exercising or eating well as what I was drawn to was the change in lifestyle and, as a result, the endless list of positives that came from that.

I only really discovered and fell in love with the gym in my thirties, and given what I'd been exposed to and experienced in the making of *Dying for a Six Pack* I'm relieved it didn't happen fifteen years earlier. Who knows what I might have done.

CHAPTER 4
A SLUM FOR SOME

In July 2016, critic Anna Leszkiewicz wrote a piece in the *New Statesman* with the headline 'Does Reggie Yates have the weirdest career in television?' Thankfully, the thoughtful piece was generous in its praise, charting the broad spectrum of work in my career culminating in my most recent documentaries.

Anna had a good handle on every stage of my varied and eclectic career to date, and how it's shaped who I am on screen today. In reading the piece, even I had to take a moment. There were so many lessons learned with every turn and none more pertinent to my more recent work than *Famous, Rich and in the Slums*.

In September 2010, the project was shot as part of Comic Relief, the BBC's biennial comedy-driven fundraising night. Spending a week living and working in the sprawling Kenyan slum of Kibera, I was made to immerse myself in the issues residents faced daily. The slum was populated entirely by a poverty-struck black community, and seeing as we were in Africa, I couldn't help but see my own family members reflected in the people around me.

Thankful to find myself back home after what was a difficult and testing project, I never thought I'd be shooting in an African slum again. But being the loudmouth I can't help but be, I made the universe-baiting mistake to openly announce, 'I'll never do anything like that ever again.' How wrong was I.

The *Extreme South Africa* series consisted of three films equally challenging in their own unique way. It was 2013 and I was still establishing myself in what was a whole new area for me. I was yet to figure out my rhythm in making documentaries, and was in all honesty running on instinct. I'd go on to find out so much about myself and the filmmaking process predominantly due to the mistakes I'd learn from and never forget.

I realised the importance of having the right team, of challenging contributors on camera, and that putting my thoughts and feelings out there – right or wrong – would only help the film and, in the long term, me as a man. One film in particular brought together the above and so much more. This film would deliver experiences I'd go on to draw from, helping me in the long run to be better on screen. This film was *The White Slums*. It was the first that went to air in the *Extreme South Africa* series and pulled no punches in telling the complicated and heart-breaking history of race relations in South Africa.

One of the things I'm most thankful for is just how much looking inward was required to honestly tackle what I was faced with. This film stirred up some unresolved issues with the realities of poverty I'd only really begun to confront in Kenya. Seen as one of the continent's biggest success stories, South Africa has a recent past that some people would prefer to forget.

I landed in Cape Town and was taken straight to the beach. I'd got off the flight still wearing way too many layers, but I was so excited to see Table Mountain for the first time, I did my best to ignore the heat. Standing beneath one of the continent's most famous landmarks I was in awe of its natural beauty. I stared and smiled like a proper tourist, but probably should have dropped my winter coat and the stupid grin.

Only twenty years prior, my coat would have been the least of my worries. With Apartheid laws in place, my skin colour alone would have made my presence on the beach illegal. Between 1948 and 1994 South Africa was racially segregated; this institutional discrimination that brutally oppressed black people only ended when Nelson Mandela was elected president.

But twenty years on and some people were convinced the country was still governed by racist policies. What I didn't expect to find were some of the loudest voices on this issue saying it wasn't black South Africans who were now oppressed, it was the whites.

Since the African National Congress (ANC) came into

power, they have been accused of replacing one kind of racism with another. Some believed that the new government was openly ensuring all available opportunities were now afforded to black South Africans with a view to give them a greater share of the economy.

With the swing of power taking a recent dramatic turn, I expected those years of hatred to force black and white South Africa towards reconciliation. That was the picture painted to my naïve British eyes during the 2010 World Cup. South Africa played host nation and didn't shy away from the country's history; it embraced its progress as strength and presented a united country.

Within hours of arriving in Johannesburg it was obvious this wasn't the case. As we drove into the city, the large plastic screens either side of the motorway did a poor job of masking the endless townships that seemed to go on as far as my eyes could see. Then, getting closer to downtown Jo'burg, the townships disappeared and visible wealth was everywhere.

That was until I arrived at Coronation Park. On the edge of the city sat a place where some of the hardest-hit white South Africans had made their home.

❝ You're one pay cheque away from this place ❞

Worried about how they might receive me, I was forced to consider who I might be in their eyes. It hadn't occurred to me until I laid eyes on their living conditions that I appeared to be everything they were battling with. On appearance alone, I probably typified the kind of privileged twenty-first-century young black man they felt was robbing them of valuable opportunities in life.

During Apartheid, the park had been a picnic place exclusively for white middle-class families. I pulled in to the now empty and unkempt public space, and it was obvious Coronation Park had become something totally different. Garden sheds and tents were smashed up against ramshackle single-storey buildings; rows of small wooden boxes were surrounded by a chain link fence clearly marking a huge chunk of the park as living quarters.

This was a tiny village of self-built dwellings. This was a slum, but a slum created exclusively for a white underclass.

Barking dogs and litter filled the walkways between houses. Kids covered in mud playing barefoot in the dirt seemed to be doing so without any supervision. This was poverty and a version of it I'd never seen before.

In the UK, the regular televised charity appeals calling for donations for Africa almost leave you desensitised to the plight of those in need. The pictures I'd grown up confronted by were African children who through no fault of their own were subjected to poverty. Those posters, TV appeals and music videos I'd seen since I was a child myself all featured black kids just like me. Now I was looking at kids living in the same conditions, but these children were white.

I felt ashamed that I'd connected poverty and race. My knowledge of white South Africans didn't fit this picture and my mind was racing. What I thought I knew died; I'd never seen what was now in front of me. Poverty is poverty and seeing white people living this way didn't make it any worse than if I'd have found black people in Coronation Park. But the shock of my own expectation, of placing the black experience as synonymous with struggle, upset and embarrassed me and fired me up at the same time.

I met camp leader Irene who'd set up home in the park eight years prior. She believed most people living in the park were there because there just weren't enough jobs for white people any more. 'You're one pay cheque away from this place. Something can happen to you and you'll end up here.'

Described by Irene as a white squatter camp, she explained that residents could build their own homes and didn't need to pay to be there. With 287 residents running their homes on generators and no power in sight, the camp had its fair share of fires. Smoke from wood burners and blackened pots holding stew sat outside most doorways.

The way these people were living made me totally forget that a 200-yard walk in any direction would bring me within view of a major and busy road. We were smack bang in the centre of the city and I'd totally begun to forget. My surroundings were suddenly a world away from life beyond the park.

With no proper sanitation and stray animals everywhere,

health was a real concern. Repeated attempts to shut the camp down had failed as new people arrived constantly. Mainly Afrikaans speaking and white, Coronation Park was unlike the Africa I knew.

Of course, with both my parents having been born and raised in Ghana, I fancied myself well versed in Africa. I'd travelled there for the first time aged four and several times since, giving me what can only be described in hindsight as a rose-tinted view. My experiences in Ghana led me to see the motherland solely in the context of progress. I'd always stay in Accra (Ghana's capital city) and get off on the development I'd see. International investment and a growing multicultural community made my pride for Africa something I'd never hide.

Taking every opportunity to get on my soap box about why it's so special to friends, I became that annoying guy shouting about where everyone should be spending their precious holidays. This broken and segregated version of South Africa wasn't what I knew Africa to be, this wasn't what was presented during the World Cup. This wasn't what I wanted to be exposed to.

❛ *We are not the chosen ones* ❜

I was introduced to twenty-seven-year-old JD who lived in the camp with his pregnant wife, mother and two children. An artist making a living by selling beautiful photo-like pencil portraits, his quiet yet analytical eye made his take on the situation refreshingly objective. With a fading smile, JD explained his reasons for living in the camp as being, 'Hit by life, hit to my knees'. Reflecting that so many white South Africans, through no fault of their own, now find themselves on the back foot, he simply stated, 'We are not the chosen ones.'

With roots in Europe, most white South Africans are called Afrikaners, being direct descendants of the Dutch settlers. During the Apartheid years, this white community separated themselves from the black majority, with many – most – seeing themselves as a superior race. Gaining power and control led to this minority affording themselves only the best education and the best jobs. A super wealthy white elite emerged making the wealth gap synonymous with race.

Then in 1990, the release from prison of Nelson Mandela saw a seismic change. As the leader of the black resistance, alongside his freedom-fighting wife Winnie, the Mandelas changed South Africa forever.

Even with this all being such recent African history, more than 50 per cent of privately owned assets in South Africa are still controlled by the same white minority. The stunning beachfront homes and modern dream mansions I purred over on my drive in, suddenly took on a whole new meaning.

I was working with Sam again as my director, and he and I had found a rhythm. Between knowing when to keep pushing even if we were totally obliterated and when to down tools and rest, we'd previously delivered films we were proud of and had developed a strong shorthand. He still had an unhealthy obsession with pastel colours and short shorts, but by now I'd accepted his fashion choices and he'd accept the insults.

A few days in and my presence in the camp was no longer news; it was common knowledge. Most people didn't bat an eyelid to Sam and I skulking about the place. I say most people; the kids had found something new to play with and it was us.

We fascinated a small group of boys all under fourteen, none more than the super-inquisitive Winston. I found it hilarious that this white Afrikaner kid had the most West Indian name but had no idea. As soon as he shared it with me, I couldn't help but to shout it with a broad Jamaican accent, made funnier by the fact that he and his friends adopted the pronunciation too.

After a lot of thought, I decided to stay on site in a tent. I don't know who I was kidding as I'm definitely not the camping type, but needed to get under the skin of the camp. Showing willing to sleep in Coronation Park I figured could only help gain the trust needed to really understand the place better. To be totally transparent, that willing came with a lot of arm-twisting from Sam, and it worked.

Having only ever camped on screen and never through choice, putting up a tent was like building an entire IKEA kitchen with no instructions. There were poles, forks and things I'd never seen before. It just wasn't going to happen without help, even if Sam was having the best time filming me struggle.

The boys packed in their game of cricket and decided to give me a hand. As the seemingly random pile of materials started to look like somewhere I could sleep, I got chatting with Winston. Affable but shy, Winston was sweet, handsome and full of questions. It was when I started to quiz him that his voice got smaller with every answer.

Representing nearly one-third of the camp's inhabitants, children under sixteen are a huge part of Coronation Park. Winston had started his life in a world unlike his nearest neighbours on the other side of the park gates, but I wasn't sure if he was bothered. As soon as we started speaking, however, he quietly let me know just how aware he was of his lot in life. Totally clear about the way the world saw the camp, Winston was embarrassed about where he lived and said that he wouldn't want kids from the outside world to know where he was from. His main dislike was the issues with addiction he'd been confronted by. Witnessing regular fights and arguments was his biggest gripe and understandably so as I couldn't imagine anyone in a rush to call the police to break up disturbances in what was an illegal settlement.

Irene decided to introduce me to one of the few people living in the park with a regular job to go to. Squelching our way through the wet muddy grounds after a day of light rain, we arrived at a wood-walled shack belonging to her son Gerry.

Stocky, broad and all eyebrows, Gerry worked as a welder and shared his home with a young wife and three children. Gerry was young himself and wore a not quite-there beard, unknowingly showing his age. As one of the few working men living on the camp, he had one of the bigger homes with separate rooms and a big-screen TV. Regardless of his employment, his wage wasn't enough to afford a place outside the park.

The conditions in the 'house' weren't fit for anyone to live in, let alone people trying to raise small children. Gerry and his wife made it as clean and homely as possible, but no matter what they did, the dirt and dust they just couldn't keep out continually made their children ill.

Afrikaner charities believe a new underclass has formed with whites-only settlements just like Coronation Park across the country. Gerry and his family were a great example of people doing everything in their power to progress but unable to, due to a system they saw as racist.

Working since the age of sixteen, Gerry believed he was doing the best he could for his family, but between his qualifications and the opportunities afforded to the white working class, his potential to climb the ladder at work was minimal. With tears in his eyes, Gerry couldn't contain his emotions as he expressed his frustration. His family was suffering and no matter what he did or how hard he worked, he saw no change in their future.

Playing the race card was something I'd only heard people that looked like me be accused of. To hear so many white people blame their quality of life and prospects on their skin colour was a first, but it was a belief I'd hear more and more as the days went on.

It was my first morning waking up in the camp. My cheap tent was sweating and I had a pain in my lower back after spending the night laying on a rock. Schoolboy error. I shouted for Sam, who'd apparently had a great night's sleep. I had a sneaking suspicion he'd snuck off in the middle of the night and had a few hours in a nearby hotel, but he was at least making an effort to make me feel we were in this together.

At the first sign of movement, Winston and the boys rocked my tent. They were like kids on Christmas morning and I was their new toy. It's always nice to feel in demand, but not at 7am while you're swearing at a rock for giving you a bruise.

Shaking off the excitable boys and their offers to join them for a pre-breakfast game of cricket, I helped JD start his morning fire for tea. Months away from his fourth child being born, JD knew that once delivered, his little one would be brought to the camp. With Irene on board and the support of the camp, JD felt as if his new child wouldn't just survive the harsh conditions but be safe in the community it was being welcomed into.

Social housing felt to me like the best way to protect and grow a young family of his size. But with over two million people on the waiting list for rehousing in the city, JD saw a government-assisted roof over their heads as a dream.

❛ Diamond in the rough, in need of some polishing ❜

Heading back to the centre of Johannesburg, I reconnected with an old friend and Jo'burg resident Sizwe. As one of the leading faces on MTV Africa, Sizwe and I met through one of my now best friends, Yemi Bamiro. At the time, Yemi-Bam (as I called him) was the director I'd always be paired with for MTV, and that particular gig saw us covering the European Music Awards in Germany.

We were shooting a crazy sequence with a few hundred dancers having a pillow fight in underwear (it was MTV, don't ask), while Sizwe was doing the grown-up thing asking really smart questions to some of the biggest names in music. Catching up on his corner of the globe was perfect as I couldn't think of a better person to give me a breakdown on what it meant to be young, South African and black.

Gerry and Irene had laid out the way they saw the world, but just how different would Sizwe's take on the country he loves so much be? We hopped into his just-washed Mercedes Benz and I was instantly in a different world. Sizwe was educated, international and successful with a huge job in media. Given his lifestyle, there was no way Sizwe could possibly identify with the lens Gerry viewed the world through. Surely?

As we drove through the shiny apartment buildings and skyscrapers that dominated central Jo'burg, Sizwe pointed out countless developments and the growth of the city. This was a man proud of the changes he saw around him, and an obvious embodiment of the successful black contingent we hear so little about in the West.

Introducing me to the excitement associated with young black success, Sizwe explained how he'd been lumped in with a group now known as the 'Black Diamonds'. Originally coined to reflect a community growing almost as quickly as their spending power, the Black Diamonds were affluent and influential young black South Africans. It evolved from a word thrown around by marketing types carving out a corner with ever-increasing earnings, but 'Black Diamond' is now used almost exclusively as a pejorative term. Laughing off his connection to the label, Sizwe referred to himself as a 'Diamond in the rough in need of some polishing'. He was proud of his hard-earned success, with or without the title.

But despite the growth of a black middle class, the majority of wealth still remained in the hands of the old white masters. Our drive continued and Sizwe pointed out the armed guards and gates protecting mansions and car collections. These were the homes of the white elite hidden behind high walls and barbed wire.

With a huge gap between the haves and have nots, the ANC introduced the affirmative action policy (AA for short) in an attempt to rebalance wealth and opportunity. Quickly transforming the South African courtroom, AA ushered in a shake-up, ensuring over 60 per cent of the most senior judges in the country were now black. According to Sizwe, in this climate you're better off if you're black.

Sizwe believed, as a non-white South African, 'The odds are stacked in your favour.' He was adamant that he'd get chosen over his white equivalent when applying for a job. I was shocked. As far as I was concerned, discrimination is disgusting regardless of the victim's race. South Africa has seen a dramatic change of power and the white minority are now the marginalised.

But was this reverse racism or a long overdue rebalance of a corrupt system? In the current climate, the black population is seeing opportunities in a way they never had done before. Progress is always a positive thing, but I struggle to agree with any progress that is to the detriment of others. I've always believed equality is about treating everyone the same, but things were different here.

Known as 'Boer' people, this Afrikaans word meaning 'farmer' is used to describe the descendants of Dutch settlers. Until the nineties, the ruling Boer treated the black majority as little better than animals. Removing families from their homes by force, the ruling whites created huge ring-fenced compounds with basic buildings to rehouse the black majority. These compounds inevitably grew into what we now know as townships.

The white regime ruthlessly enforced their laws, leaving a stain on the country's history still felt today. The legacy of those settlements is still visible in the never-ending townships; it touches and arguably impacts on the lives of millions of black people to this day.

I met twenty-eight-year-old Colin, an expert on the history of race relations in South Africa. He schooled me on life in the Alexandra Township, which houses many black people living in poverty. He described growing up in an environment where residents were under constant threat from what they called the 'Mellow Yellow vans'. These were government-funded vehicles that appeared and scooped people up who were usually never seen again. Colin explained that when they arrived, men, women and children would run for their lives.

Having been under constant threat of violence from authority, these communities' relations with the powers that be are still incredibly strained. In my mind, segregation was always a word I'd associated with the United States and the fight for equality in the sixties. Colin was educating me on much more recent history. Frightening anecdotes like that of the Mellow Yellow vans were tied to my lifetime as Apartheid didn't end until the 1990s.

Blacks who broke segregation laws were sent to prison. Colin took me to the Old Fort, one such location that has now become a museum. Even with open cells and unlocked gates, the building remained intimidating and contained an unsettling atmosphere that hung in the air. While awaiting trial, Nelson Mandela was incarcerated at the Old Fort.

Colin broke down what went on during the prison's functioning years, and I couldn't help but feel sick. We sat in the central courtyard which was open air and visible from all sides of the prison. This was the area guards used for acts of humiliation. One such degradation was the 'strip search dance'. Inmates were stripped naked, made to spread their legs and arms then jump. They then had to clap their hands above their head, leaping in the air and making a clicking sound. If no objects were seen to fall from the body, officers would insert a finger or torch inside an inmate's rectum to ensure nothing was hidden. This humiliation was assigned to those suspected of smuggling and included both men and women.

The brave people fighting to change the system dreaded being caught by the police, as they would invariably receive brutal and inhumane treatment. Freedom fighters were kept in solitary confinement cells no wider than a single mattress. Walking in and lying down on the concrete floor where inmates would have had to sleep, I couldn't help but feel like I was in a coffin. The tall, thin cells had no furniture and tiny windows.

In one generation, the country had gone from government-sanctioned brutality towards blacks to affirmative action. But being sat in that cell began to weigh on me. The degree of injustice experienced here spoke to the level of anger understandably still fresh in the air. Swimming in the atmosphere of the prison I felt an anger of my own beginning to bubble in me too.

❝ It's a black government, it's a black country, they don't want white people here ❞

Today, black and white South Africans are afforded the same freedoms. Regardless, at the time we were making the film, sixteen million black South Africans were still living in poverty. With that being the case, the leg-up on a systemic level is understandable, but where does that leave the white people living in poverty like those in Coronation Park?

Once part of the privileged minority, Irene, her son Gerry and the rest of the white South Africans living in the camp saw their living conditions as a result of the new system. Nonetheless, Irene believed on some level it was just. Seeing her situation as a direct result of her forefathers' sins, Irene was resolute: 'It's time now for us to pay for what our fathers did.'

When I first met Gerry, I'd got the impression that he was frustrated and felt powerless in the situation he didn't create but was born into. What I didn't realise straightaway was just how deep those frustrations went. Seconds into Gerry joining my conversation with Irene, he slipped into a rant that started calmly but quickly escalated.

'What happened twenty years ago was nothing to do with me,' he barked, as his mother's take on the situation annoyed him. Gerry believed his generation had done nothing to deserve their reality. He was frustrated that black workers doing the same job as him could go on to be promoted or gain better jobs in a way that was apparently denied to him. As he became more emotional, Gerry began to raise his voice, harking back nostalgically to the days of Apartheid, saying he felt segregation had made South Africa a better place. Believing there was a better economy and lifestyle for all under segregation, his total disregard for what Apartheid meant to the country's black population was unfortunately not as surprising to me as I'd have liked it to be.

Wherever I find myself in the world, I try to take people as I find them and focus on the similarities we share rather than the differences. I've always harped on in interviews about the idea that people are the key to any issue at the core of my work. What that really means is that if I can't connect with who I meet, I can't truly know why they hold the views they do.

My desire in meeting Gerry was to paint a picture of who he was and what mattered to him before getting into his feelings on the state of the country. I had suspected his views might differ from his mother's or at the very least be one sided due to the extreme nature of his reality.

As his voice got louder still, I felt disappointed that those niggling suspicions sat at the back of my mind on that very first meeting were all being proven. This was a man who held offensive and racist views, but Gerry was also a man so boxed in by his situation he seemed to need someone to blame.

'But the black people had jobs,' he snapped, and I had to remind him that some may have been given employment, but none had basic human rights. 'I can't say because I wasn't there' was Gerry's way of deflecting the fact that the injustices dealt out during segregation didn't remotely compare to his situation.

'It's a black government, it's a black country, they don't want white people here.' Gerry walked back to his shack cradling his son in his arms. The entire time we went back and forth, he held his child close. Gerry clearly loved his family and the life he held in his arms seemed to be a present and constant reminder of who he was working so hard for. Given his job, his earning power and his prospects, Gerry seemed to have decided that the life he wanted for his children may not happen.

As Gerry stamped off back to his shack, a watching neighbour bumped fists with him in a show of support. It occurred to me in that moment that Gerry might not have been speaking just for himself. Maybe his outlook was more common than I'd realised.

As I stood alone in the aftermath of this conversation, Gerry's hard and unrelenting views felt increasingly like less of a defence and more of a comfort blanket for his position. Gerry wanted better but might have quietly recognised this was his lot.

To say the people of Coronation Park were stuck there sounds like a cop-out, but this was the inescapable reality. The laws in place might have played a part in why progressing was so difficult, namely affirmative action. With fewer opportunities in the workplace given to white applicants, the chances of Coronation Park growing were high. Putting myself in the shoes of a working-class white man like Gerry, I can see how race resentment could fester and grow. Unfortunately, Gerry was one of many in the same position.

In desperate need of some objectivity and a less heated conversation, I pulled up a tree stump and shared a fire with JD and his family. As ever, their corner of the camp was warm, light-hearted and full of considered thought. I shared my conversation with Gerry and my belief in what fuelled his frustrations. JD cracked a wry smile and in his slow and now familiar delivery he hummed, 'I ended up here for a reason, nobody comes in here because the country is screwed up, they come in here because they screwed up.'

JD had a point. Everyone in Coronation Park had a story, everyone had a life before the camp. Something must have gone wrong with their lives to have brought them there, but I hadn't heard anyone speak about their journey. 'You can't blame everything on the system,' JD said, and he was right. This was the first time I'd heard any ownership. Up until this point, nobody I had spoken to had seemed willing to accept the part they'd played in ending up homeless.

The more he spoke the more I needed to know who JD was before he'd arrived at Coronation Park with his family. 'Even a rich guy can find himself here in two weeks.' At one point, that's exactly who JD was. He was in a band he refused to tell me the name of but he was doing well enough to look after his entire family. 'I was a rock star, I used to sign boobs.'

JD told me that he had everything but was selfish and lost it all in a matter of days. When his music career ended, he struggled to find his feet and began to move from place to place. With a baby on the way and the responsibility of his entire family on his back, JD was living with immense pressure but somehow retained a sense of calm and dignity. I was in awe of the man. I'd never met anyone with such balance and objectivity, especially considering what he was dealing with.

If I had to start again literally from nothing, I'm not sure if I could muscle up anywhere near as much resolve. This was the first time I'd seen this kind of strength in the camp, but with so many Afrikaners living in similar conditions, was JD a one-off?

Coronation Park wasn't the only place where whites living on the breadline had created small camps or communities; it was beginning to happen across the country. I hopped in our comically small hire car and hit the road. The ugly car was tiny and slow and made it look like I was taking my driving test and Sam was my instructor. I crunched through the awful five-speed gearbox while Sam's long legs got more and more numb the longer we were in the thing. To this day I have no idea why anyone thought a hatchback would be a good idea.

An hour's crappy driving later, we were out of Johannesburg and had arrived in Pretoria. Once the spiritual heartland of Afrikaner population, the city is now predominantly black. We pulled into an estate made up of several small residential blocks, the biggest of which was no more than three stories tall. The condition of the estate suggested the blocks had been abandoned and recently kicked in and repurposed. They were all in a state of disrepair, but every flat seemed to have signs of life bursting from its windows. Washing lines filled balconies and people sat on short walls talking and smoking, not because they were after a tan, but because they had nowhere to go.

Kids played barefoot in the dirt, but unlike Coronation Park, the kids here were black and white.

The illegal settlement was clearly home to both white Afrikaners and black immigrants from all over the continent. So many languages and dialects could be heard the minute we unfolded our bodies from the tiny car.

Young or old and regardless of colour, the residents all shared the same look. It was a strange mix of aggressive, defensive and helpless. A young white man sat biting his nails flanked by a rolled-up tent and duffel bags. Staring me down as I took it all in, a tone was set. Even the children playing in the flowerbeds watched me closely as I walked by. I was a new face and if tent man was anything to go by, new people seemed to be a regular fixture here. The problem was, in an environment like this where clearly trust was in short supply, new faces were greeted with scrutiny, not warmth.

Anyone who made a home here would be living side by side with his or her neighbours in desperation, whether black or white. The place really did feel like the end of the line.

I walked into the block through a set of double doors both defaced and bending out of the doorway. The smashed windows caused me to watch my step, and in paying attention to where I placed each foot, I couldn't help but notice just how filthy the place was.

Standing at the entrance to a long dark hallway with door after door bolted shut with padlocks and chains, I rapped the wall to the first open flat. A smiling man quickly appeared and introduced himself as Hardis. Gangly and all limbs, the twenty-five-year-old greeted me with a massive boy-like smile and quickly introduced me to his tiny wife Vivian.

I walked into their single-room home and tried to focus on Hardis as my eyes were uncontrollably darting from corner to corner trying to take it all in. The room was rammed with stuff as this was an entire family operating out of a tiny space; the couple shared the space with their two children. The youngest looked no older than one and was flapping about on its back on the bed, the other was a cute little terror who was running about the place. The room showed all the obvious signs of a family who'd outgrown their space. Clothes were overflowing from every corner, while toys, food and all sorts of other stuff took over every surface.

Home for the last four years, the room was safe and all they could afford. What I hadn't considered was their choice of building, as their room wasn't picked randomly. Hardis explained that this was a whites-only building. The other blocks were either mixed or all black.

This self-imposed segregation even in poverty was baffling. With a shared sense of struggle being a constant for every resident, I would have expected people to be drawn closer regardless of race. Hardis claimed, 'They keep to themselves. You leave them alone, they leave you alone.' The only other place I'd heard people speak in that way about living alongside a different racial group was in prison.

Hardis took me on a walk around the block and I wasn't ready for what I was about to see. The shared shower and toilet facilities were filthy. The toilet cubicle doors were all broken with no working lights. Showers were full of mould and only pumped out cold water. His toddler ran ahead of us bare foot and Hardis pulled her close, lifting the child from the ground. He pointed out used needles and broken glass; this was no place for children.

We wondered over to a neighbouring block that was much quieter as it had been abandoned. Hardis explained that two months back, a resident lit a fire in their room to keep warm. Falling asleep with no one to keep watch, the fire eventually set the entire building alight. As we walked through the burnt shell, I looked into most rooms, stopping at one when I noticed a sleeping bag.

On the top floor, several of the rooms still riddled with ash and smoke stains had already been reclaimed by new residents moving in. These rooms had no windows and, in some cases, no roof, but some were willing to call the death trap home.

Desperate to find a way out of the estate, Hardis and Vivian were surviving without employment. The only incoming money they saw was coming from the unlicensed shop they ran out of their room's window selling single cigarettes and sweets. Desperate to find work, Hardis claimed to have handed out over sixty CVs. He believed every job he'd apply for would end up going to his black equivalent due to AA laws.

Feeding the family with whatever was earned via the illegal

shop, the family was living hand to mouth. What they fed their children and themselves came down to what they earned, which on the day of my visit, was nothing. Making do with what they had, a tiny single gas burner served as their cooker. Boiling macaroni in a pan, Vivian poured soup into the pasta from a pint glass.

Dinner was macaroni and soup. I watched Vivian dish the meal into plastic bowls for her husband and kids. Taking in the room, the, children . . . I couldn't help but think this wasn't a life. Like anyone, I struggle to witness poverty, but there and then it was so palpable and I hated it.

Poverty clearly wasn't just a white issue, as at the time of making the film 45 per cent of black South Africans also lived below the breadline. People from both black and white communities were struggling. With the problem being so unavoidable in all corners of the country, why was it not higher on everyone's agenda? I decided to head back to Coronation Park as one question continued to trouble me. How much did race play a part?

❛ You won't get white people here ❜

Not long after arriving, I was given a rude awakening as to how different the South African worlds of the haves and have nots actually are. What I was about to witness would challenge my own prejudices and inadequacies, but this moment of clarity started with a conversation outside JD's tent.

JD and I were chatting as ever and loud music playing from beyond the trees and into the park was unavoidable. Unsure as to who was responsible, he described the music makers as 'the rich people'.

We climbed a small hill and were suddenly able to see out and into the other side of the park. Beside a stunning lake surrounded by trees was a clearing. A small drive where families could park up and picnic held several parked cars huddled around a barbecue. A group of young guys and girls were having the time of their lives dancing and drinking.

I couldn't help but feel embarrassed at the assumption I'd made. I admitted to JD that due to his description of the noise-makers as being 'the rich people' I was expecting to see young privileged white kids. I was wrong, the group dancing and drinking by the lake were black.

According to JD, they were getting what they deserved as their parents wouldn't even have been allowed in the park, let alone been free enough to party in public.

This was a group of middle-class kids from Soweto. The famous township was once a shadow of its current state, as today, Soweto has gentrified and attracted the upwardly mobile blacks, some of whom I was watching chug beer and booty pop on a car bonnet.

Cool boxes and food sat outside every car boot as the group of about twenty milled about with drinks and paper plates. It was a party and they were clearly having fun. They were enjoying (as JD put it) their deserved freedom, but what did they think of the residents in Coronation Park? I followed the noise and joined the group.

Drinks flowed and the music was loud. I asserted myself, cornering the chattiest guy to ask him about the camp. His reaction I didn't see coming at all. He didn't even believe it existed, let alone less than a hundred yards away. 'You won't get white people here.' I pushed but he refused to accept the level of poverty I'd literally slept in the middle of.

Both JD and Hardis had a dream and that was to find work to feed his family. But unlike JD, Hardis wanted desperately to get his family out of South Africa. He felt strongly that, due to laws like AA, there wasn't a future for his family in the country where he had been born and raised.

The voice of poor, young white men was loud and clear: they felt the South African system didn't care. But what did their black equivalent feel about their chances? I took a drive out of town to attend a rally held by a political party known as Economic Freedom Fighters. The EFF were gathering a steady momentum and taking the poor young black contingent by storm.

My squeaky rental car was waved towards a makeshift car park beside a huge field. Men and women in red T-shirts and berets were everywhere. I hopped out of the embarrassing granny car and made my way towards the music and crowds. I jostled my way to the front, where a long strip of tape working as a barrier held the swelling crowd in place as all eyes were on the empty stage while distorted music played loudly.

As I'm sure you can imagine, it didn't take long before the guy with the London accent and the white dude with the camera began to stand out a little. Suspicion swirled from the elders and, as usual, the kids were the first ones to come up and ask about my tattoos. It was a strange set-up as hundreds of people were literally standing around looking at each other and the stage in anticipation, but for what?

A short sweaty black guy in a red beret took to the mic and in no time had the crowd whipped up and in the palm of his hands. From old women right the way through to their grandchildren, everyone was raising fists while stood side by side screaming 'Viva EFF viva!'

The party was growing quickly with support swelling particularly in rural townships. The party believed that affirmative action as a law wasn't doing enough for young poor blacks. Rising up as an alternative to the in-power and well-loved ANC, EFF believed the current government hadn't gone far enough to ensure more black people had a route out of poverty.

The EFF was calling for a total overhaul in societal structure. One of their more controversial policies relates to the sensitive issue of farmland. Intrinsically connected to the wealth of the Boer people, the EFF wanted white-owned farmland to be taken back. Also calling for nationalisation of lucrative natural mineral mines, the party and its leader were ruffling some serious feathers.

The party had become controversial, as they'd been known to sing a famous Apartheid rebellion song 'Shoot the Boer, kill the farmer'. Speaking directly to the anger and frustrations of voters who lived in poor townships, the party and their unapologetic attitude to their former oppressors had become national news.

In the opinion of Gerry, the current government might have served the black South African people better, but poverty for the black majority is still rife. Poor black people were still angry and demanding more to be done.

People had been staring and sizing me up, and inevitably they began asking me questions. I found myself getting into a conversation with a few red berets from the party. A young father and I got into it and quickly; his version of South Africa stood out as a totally different world to Gerry's. He referred to the country's current state as that of so-called independence. 'I may be free to sit next to a white person on a bus, but I've got no income.'

The similarities were uncanny, these people felt just as marginalised and ignored as Hardis. People at the rally wanted change, and the feeling of militancy was in the air. The excitement reached fever pitch as a silver Mercedes arrived.

Kids ran towards the car screaming and people started to jump around in song. This was what the stage was for, the commander in chief had arrived and he was a star. A woman screamed 'I want to touch him with my hands' as she ran by, and I was confused as I thought we were waiting for a politician. We were, but this guy had more than a constituency. He had fans.

Red berets surrounded the man linking arms keeping the crowds back. This was Julius Malema, the leader of the EFF. He'd arrived to give a speech, but it felt like a pop star doing community outreach. If the noise was anything to go by, I'm pretty sure people in the next two towns knew about it. As he made his way to the stage, it was chaos and everyone rushed forward, desperate to touch the man.

He was a hero. The minute Malema touched the mic, the place fell silent. He instructed his followers where to be for the next rally and when he spoke, they listened. As he mused, they cheered. He had his audience in the palm of his hand and had the community galvanised to his cause.

His speech came to a close and, rather than leaving the stage, Malema began to march on the spot. Surrounded by red T-shirts and berets, his team and security did the same. Then it happened, Malema began to sing the song.

This was the first time I'd heard anyone sing the 'Shoot the Boer, kill the farmer' song but this wasn't the version I'd expected. Malema sarcastically sang 'kiss the farmer' not kill. The song in its original form had been banned, so it was being sung but not with its original lyrics. But it might as well have been.

Everyone there had joined in singing the song, but I didn't leave thinking his followers all wanted to kill people they hadn't met, far from it. One supporter I talked to spoke about wanting to win the battle using knowledge not violence, but with such a divisive song still being sung, what message was that sending to detractors? For a political leader to knowingly sing a hate song couldn't be good for his cause, regardless of the new words.

As a former member of the ANC, Julius Malema was once tipped to lead the party but ended up forming a new organisation in his own image. Malema and that song have become famous as a point of contention for his opposition as well as for white South Africans, who see the song not only as hate speech but a direct threat.

Back at Coronation Park, Irene explained to me that she believed all EFF supporters wanted to kill Boer people just like her. Failing to understand why the anger in the townships might be as fresh in the present, Irene was resolute. Reminding her that Apartheid was a long time ago but not a lifetime ago, I urged her to understand how many people still alive lived under segregation laws. That level of hate is hard to forget, but forgetting is exactly what Irene expected black South Africans to do.

'Forgive and forget' was what she kept repeating, expecting the horrors of the black existence under segregation to be forgotten. I was totally confused by her total disregard for what was hell for millions of black South Africans. What was a seemingly conversational back and forth quickly escalated into a loud dressing down.

Irene had stopped listening and decided I was a 'stupid man'. She said so several times. 'That's why the world is how it is, because they can't forgive and forget.' I knew I'd get nowhere so I let her rant. Knowing we'd never agree, I let Irene leave in a huff. To forget the pain of Apartheid would be nothing short of irresponsible as there can only be lessons learned from history. As far as I'm concerned you must never forget, because if you forget, what the hell are you going to learn?

It was time for me to leave the camp for the last time. As I left I gave JD and his mother a hug. As I walked away she called after me and said, 'Always look to the trees and to the sky, remember us there.' I'm not the most sentimental person, I have no idea what she meant, but the surreal, sudden and heartfelt request couldn't have been more perfect.

On this trip to South Africa I didn't see the rainbow nation I'd hoped to find. Essentially, both black and white people had become victims of Apartheid but in very different ways. JD believed his generation was paying a price for the mistakes of their forefathers, while Irene just wanted everyone to move on. Who am I to say who was right, but one thing I did agree with was one of the last things JD said to me: 'Change takes time.'

Surrounded by squalor in a slum populated solely by white South Africans, I was confronted by the results of the political and systemic rebalancing of power and opportunity in the country in the most real world, first-hand way. My initial shock at seeing white faces living in abject poverty made me reassess my own preconceptions.

The poor whites were paying a price after decades of oppressing black people. With hangovers of Apartheid still continuing to affect race relations, my personal hang-ups and desire for equality forced me to confront the question, what do I believe to be fair? Fairness for me will always begin with balance. Unfortunately, with some of the most painful years in the country's history still so recent, that idealistic desire looks a long way off.

Power in South Africa has changed hands from the minority oppressor to the oppressed majority. Ask yourself this question. If you'd watched your family oppressed for generations because of the colour of their skin and suddenly you were in power, what would you do?

CHAPTER 5
NO LOVE LEGISLATION

In the early days of my career, I treated every day at work as a social education. I was surrounded by middle-class, white men and women who were from a whole other planet culturally. Their interests, the way they spoke, even what they ate was new to me. No one cared about football, but everyone understood wine. This wasn't just about the authoritarian African value system I'd been raised in. This was about class.

I was a kid who only knew one type of adult and that was the men and women in my family. The gumbo of working-class grit, mixed with African values and culture made for a financially scrupulous and insular existence. At home, respect, rules and money mattered. We were pinching pennies, shopping at Dalston market in Hackney for our meat and vegetables and Chapel market in Angel for our toiletries. At work, runners were sent out to Sainsbury or Waitrose solely to purchase bags and bags of treats for us, the cast of kids.

Let me put this into context. At home, I'd carefully pick my moment to ask for a biscuit and was never allowed more than two custard creams with my tea. At work, I was encouraged to take huge bags of party-sized chocolate bars that I'd obliterate during the cab ride home.

The bizarre nature of being a working-class kid growing up in a polar opposite world of professional and personal conditions is only really dawning on me as I type. I have to laugh, as the gangly twelve-year-old version of me was about to have the shock of his life.

Working on the ITV Saturday morning kids show *The Disney Club* was the dream. I was cast in a show I'd watched every weekend, and overnight I became one of the kids on the colourful set getting covered in gunge and introducing cartoons. Once the buzz of access to that endless stream of sweets and sugary drinks had died down, I actually started to pay attention to the team that were now my co-workers.

This group of grown-ups were young, smart and liberal. They were unlike my family as for a start they were all white, but also because they all saw the world in such a different way. Yes, they encouraged me to take advantage of what seemed to be an endless budget. Food, cabs and gifts kept coming. But beyond that, their attitude towards sexuality quickly normalised what was an absolute taboo in the world I came from.

We the cast of presenters were all children and were

definitely annoying a solid 80 to 90 per cent of the time I'm sure, but at the time I felt supported and included. I was obsessed by one member of the crew in particular who happened to run the art department; his name was Ant. To this day I can't remember his full name and I'd prefer to never know it as he was this cool, crazy-haired creative, given free rein to build and design the most incredible props.

Ant was the complete and total embodiment of cool to me. He had one name like Prince, Madonna and Seal, and he also signed my birthday card with a drawing of a cartoon Ant not his name. What a dude! To my twelve-year-old self, this guy was the man. That shock of my life I referred to earlier came when things got busy on the show and Ant brought in some support to bolster his department.

A few days in, I remember meeting the new French guy who was helping out with props. The dude had an accent and could paint! I was in awe. I'll never forget the moment I was introduced to Claude, as his name was quickly followed by 'This is Ant's husband.' I'd never knowingly met a gay man in my twelve years. Furthermore, I'd never had to hide shock and confusion before and I'm pretty sure I did a terrible job in that moment.

At the time, gay marriage in the UK wasn't legal so in hindsight, their rings and titles were both a showing of unity and defiance.

Looking back, there's a few bachelor uncles of mine who definitely had an 'alternative lifestyle' the family never spoke about, but that's another book entirely. Who Ant and Claude were wasn't a secret; they were an openly gay couple, married and clearly in love. They were just another two members of the team who weren't treated any differently and that was mind-blowing to me as attitudes towards homosexuality at home, at school and on my estate weren't as accepting.

It was the 1990s and my mother worked for the health authority in HIV and AIDS awareness. Through her work and connection to AIDS, I learnt that the gay community was intrinsically linked to this sad and scary disease. Acceptance and understanding was essential while she was at work, yet culturally and off the clock gay men and women were people you simply didn't mix with.

Thanks to Ant and Claude, my understanding of same-sex relationships was thankfully not influenced by the playground or my uncle George and his laddy beer-swigging mates down the pub. To me, they quickly became just another couple who loved each other and after a few hours, their sexuality wasn't something I'd even think about again.

My life has constantly been coloured with conflict. The things I'd been taught versus the first-hand experiences I'd had since childhood forced me to form my own opinions on so many things from a young age. Working in TV throughout my formative years, I grew up constantly butting against the world view I'd been presented with by my home life. Who Ant and Claude were as people made twelve-year-old me reject what I'd been taught at home.

The documentaries I went on to make have put me in places and with people I'd never have met in my own life. Who I am today is massively informed by that understanding I started to gain as a child, and extends to the way I carry myself both on and off screen. That same understanding would go on to be challenged every day while shooting *Gay and Under Attack*, the second film in the *Extreme Russia* series.

By now I'd spent a decent chunk of time in Russia. No, I hadn't got used to the cold as yet, it still felt bloody freezing but I'd got used to the 'fifteen layers and two pairs of socks' life. That being said, I'd yet to best the constant and relentless draining of energy I'd encounter wherever I went. This film would prove to be a difficult one to make due to the nature of the subject matter and, unfortunately, the kind of people I'd have to engage with to truly get to the core of the issues at hand.

It was 2013 and in Russia it had just become illegal to tell anyone under the age of eighteen that being homosexual was in any way normal. I was in St Petersburg for the first time and the beautiful city totally threw me. The place looked like Venice, with central blocks of the city built around the water, and it felt like Europe with so many people eating and drinking coffee outside.

I was in the city to attend Queer Fest, a festival organised by and for the LGBTQ community. I was collected from the airport by the city's only gay taxi service. The Rainbow Taxi service's driver Alena was behind the wheel and ferried me into the city along with my guide Sergei.

Providing small clues as to who the car service was aimed at, the rainbow radio knob and steering wheel were conservative by British standards but walking a dangerous line for Russian eyes. Alena explained the reason for the service was 'So we'll be safe and protected.' But how unsafe was it to be Russian and gay?

Getting into the city, the beauty of the water and architecture made the final leg feel like a European getaway. Driving in at golden hour didn't hurt either as the sun was staining everything yellow and pink. Bringing me right back down to earth, Sergei reminded me not to be fooled by appearances.

The further we drove the more I noticed the country's history was clearly a big a part of its present. Statues dedicated to Lenin, the leader of the country during the Communist years, were huge and they were everywhere. Up until as recently as 1993, being exposed as gay in Russia would see you behind bars with hard labour for up to five years. Today, to be gay is no longer illegal, but the attitudes that supported such laws have proven harder to abolish.

According to Sergei, when it comes to Russian mentality, 'A boy must be a boy.' To be young and openly gay legally isn't an issue, but one's appearance could lead to violence. If looking gay (whatever that meant) could lead to an attack, did that mean to be gay in St Petersburg meant you'd be living a life under constant threat?

The tiny cab dropped me off at what Sergei called the gay hostel, I thought it was a strange way to define the place I'd lay my head until I noticed the steps painted with rainbow colours. I expressed concern that such an obvious symbol would essentially wave a red flag to any passing homophobic bull, but Sergei reassured me that most Russians didn't know what the rainbow flag actually meant.

Once inside my room, the pride levels displayed by the painted staircase at the entrance paled in comparison to the explosion of fabulousness I'd be staying in. The room was electric pink with a giant exploding heart mural filling a wall. The curtains were (yes you guessed it) rainbow coloured and within a few minutes my eyes had started to hurt.

I've stayed in some strange places throughout my career but this one took the cake. It wasn't the most uncomfortable room I've stayed in by any means, but it was straight up strange. Unsurprisingly, my director Sam loved every minute as he knew me well enough to almost predict my reaction. Pissing his pants, Sam's shots were shaky due to his chuckling. He had the camera right on my face knowing how I'd hate it the minute I walked in.

With the lights down and those aggressive colours numbed, I jumped online. I was due to start my next day at Queer Fest, the largest LGBTQ festival in Russia. Over the course of ten days, a schedule of cultural and social events all leaning towards the gay and lesbian experience had been scheduled and was advertised on their official site. Albeit under a huge graphic almost as big as the festival's logo stating the event would be 18+. I thought of the annual celebration of Gay Pride marches that see men, women and children all involved in the event with every attendee encouraged to be vocal.

With negative attitudes towards homosexuality being a global issue, I was aware of Russia's bad rep for intolerance but hadn't realised the extent of what I'd be walking into. The Anti-Gay Propaganda Law introduced by Putin's party was created to 'protect' young people from the 'moral and public health dangers' of being homosexual. These laws were very real and strictly enforced. Thinking about this, my fears were instantly based on something I couldn't change. Should my attitudes and feelings about any gay issue such as gay marriage for instance be overheard publicly, I technically could be thrown in jail.

It was the first morning of Queer Fest and I returned to the website to get further information on the day ahead. The website detailed everything about the event, but said nothing about where anything actually was. Sergei explained that to be involved with the festival in any way, be that performer or punter, I'd have to call for details, as it would never be advertised publicly.

I hadn't considered the level of fear the people attending and putting on the festival actually felt, until I learned that Queer Fest was a free-to-attend public festival that wouldn't tell you where it was actually being held.

❝ *Homosexuality is disgusting, homophobia is beautiful* ❞

After a few phone calls and some bad Russian from Sam we finally received the address. When we arrived, the venue already had several police vans and officers surrounding the entrance. The police were there to keep the peace, but the minute I noticed just how heavily armed they were, I worried about what they might have known that I didn't?

As ever, the power of the camera attracted a few passers-by to stop and try and figure out who we were or show interest in what we were shooting. Across the street stood two noticeably trendy guys watching us and the festival entrance clearly not wanting to be seen. Obviously, I crossed the street making a beeline right for them. They looked uncomfortable and unsure but Sam had the camera on them and I wasn't going anywhere.

We got talking and it turned out that they had passed by to check out the event but were worried the minute they saw cameras and the police. They introduced themselves as Vanya and Nasrullah and turned out to be a couple who were unsure about going in. They didn't see the officers as attending to protect them; they believed the law was there for another reason.

Without giving me any more, they urged me to go and see what it was like for myself. I noticed that their status as a couple wasn't obvious considering the distance between them as they interacted and they described just how frustrated they felt not being able to publicly show any level of affection or love. Then Vanya and Nasrullah decided to leave and I made my way inside.

I was early and the event was still being set up. I met Alfred, one of the organisers, who pulled himself away from hanging lights and artwork to say hello. Tall and slight, Alfred cut a lean shape but was warm in his greeting and seemed pleased to have me and flamboyant scarf-wearing Sam at the event.

Even though he was expecting homophobic trouble-makers and orthodox activists to turn up and try to cause problems, Alfred seemed flippant about what could become serious conflict. He wasn't fazed, as his attitude was that it was almost inevitable.

Minutes after talking to Alfred, the entire staff started packing away literally everything that had only just been set up. I found another organiser who explained that they'd been kicked out of the venue and were packing up to move to another location. Bearing in mind this was literally an hour before guests were expected to arrive. The building's owner claimed there was a safety issue and had to shut it down.

On the other side of the door stood a pack of undesirables. Shifty and heavyset, the group was led by Vitaly Milonov, the politician behind the anti-gay propaganda law. I had to find a way to engage even if the sweaty man clearly wanted nothing to do with me.

Approaching Milonov and questioning his attendance

initially received zero reaction; he literally refused to acknowledge my existence. After several attempts to start a conversation, he eventually turned and vomited a word salad as to why he was there. His demeanour screamed self-importance while he explained his presence as representing authority. Milonov had taken it upon himself to ensure that no children would be affected by the event and the pro-gay propaganda he believed to be on display.

I hadn't even noticed the main cause of his frustrations as they were doing a great job of not being noticed. Albert and his team had organised security who were guarding the door refusing entry to Milonov and his goons. Becoming increasingly annoyed, he singled out a young gay woman with short hair standing nearby. 'If you are a woman dressed like man, like this one. Dressed like some faggot, you can enter. If you're dressed like a normal person you cannot.'

Milonov described himself and his pack of silent tracksuit-wearing backup as Russians. He saw Albert and his team on the other side of the door as something else. Wondering what it was that made him so against the festival taking place, I asked if he saw Queer Fest as dangerous. Milonov flicked his eyes between me, the gay woman and the floor spitting, 'A piece of shit is not dangerous, but it is quite unpleasant to see on the street.'

It was safe to say that Vitaly Milonov was a different kind of politician. This clearly wasn't a man afraid of being controversial, this was a politician on a mission, openly spouting offensive statements like, 'Homosexuality is disgusting, homo-phobia is beautiful.'

I wondered how difficult this film could become consider-ing this was a man who should be cautious with his messaging. Unapologetic in his views, Milonov represented the hard right of the government. If he was able to speak in such an openly offensive matter, what on earth would his man on the street equivalent be like? Growing up in a country where it's against the law to discriminate against all minorities, I was shocked by the public nature of such an offensive opinion being spewed. To witness a politician and member of the current ruling party operate in such a disgusting manner publicly, without any fear of reprisal was outrageous.

Coping with the bigoted attitudes I knew I'd continue to encounter started to worry me. I didn't want my personal feel-ings to get in the way of the story, but how I felt would give the film the authenticity it required. In the moment, I found a way to silence my disgust and pushed ahead.

While I was busy in the whirlwind that was Milonov, the Queer Fest organisers had snuck out of the building, moving all of their artwork and equipment to a backup venue ten min-utes up the road. Desperate to get to the venue before it was shut down Sam gave me a look that said, 'You're not gonna like this but . . .' and I knew what we'd have to do.

Sprinting along a wide and busy pavement, Sam's camera bounced and smashed against his shoulder repeatedly while I trailed behind desperately trying to catch him up. I had no idea he was so bloody quick, especially with the ridiculous scarf he was wearing at the time. We finally made it to the venue, but somehow Milonov and his goons were there just before us.

The festival was now at the top of a beautiful old building with no lift. After that ten-minute jog in a heavy wool coat, that wasn't the news I needed to hear. Climbing flight after flight we eventually made it to the entrance just behind what looked like an even bigger group of Milonov supporters. Held off by security, the men were denied entry. Tempers and voices grew, then the pushing started.

Milonov shouted and insulted the guards but they held and refused to budge. 'Do you want these gays to rape our kids?' he screamed. Shutting the door, security was able to keep the unruly pack outside. Unfortunately, I was stuck with them.

Frustrated and defeated, the noisy crowd quietened down, all but for one very vocal protester. Chanting alone, he was pasting large stickers bearing statements written in Russian onto the closed door. I asked him to translate the biggest one for me. Looking pleased with himself, he announced loudly, 'Not Queer Fest, it's a festival of sodomy.' He finished pasting his stack of message-heavy stickers and explained his reasoning. This was a man who saw Russia as an orthodox Christian country and saw the lifestyle he believed was being led by the gay community as not acceptable.

A strange and quiet guy in a blue tracksuit was determined to find a way in. This iPad-wielding man seemed to be orchestrating even though the group didn't appear to have a leader. He walked hard and with purpose and the pack trailed. I followed closely through a series of corridors, reaching a second entrance where Milonov led a shouting and pushing match with security a second time.

By the time I'd made it to this second entrance, the man wielding stickers at the other door was now squirting festival attendees with green ink from a syringe. In an instant things became still and something was up. At the doorway, a young woman was desperate to get out of the event. Once the doors opened, she sprinted down the staircase and out, dropping what looked like a small plastic tube that was letting off a strong, eye-watering smell.

Trying to follow her outside, the smell was so bad I began to gag and the air outside suddenly became what I was chasing, not her. Once in the street, the woman who was responsible for what turned out to be the most pungent of stink bombs headed straight to the homophobe I'd met upstairs with the stickers. They'd come together and between them had caused more disruption and chaos then Milonov or any of his followers. From the same Orthodox Christian organisation, the couple had set out to ruin the event and they just might have.

Back upstairs, Mr Blue Tracksuit and the rest of the anti-gay protesters were lingering at the venue entrance unable to bypass security. I spoke to Mikhail, one of the more confident protesters, whose fearless and vocal challenge to security instantly made him stand out. He claimed their purpose was to ensure no kids were in attendance as that would be gay propaganda towards children.

I was pretty confident that the event wasn't aimed at children (not forgetting the huge 18+ sign on the website) so I wanted to get inside myself and see not just who'd actually made it in, but what all the fuss was about.

Passing security and rushed through the doors, the unbearable stench of the stink bomb was instant. It had forced everyone in the venue to huddle around open windows for fresh air. The smell was foul and for those not able to get close to the windows, they were covering their noses and mouths with T-shirts and scarves.

Once I'd got used to the smell, I was finally able to take in the room. It was busy, there were men and women of all ages chatting and enjoying framed artworks and stalls selling T-shirts. This wasn't the edgy temple of gayness I'd been sold. There were free cookies and soft drinks, and stalls selling vintage dresses. The event wasn't even selling alcohol. Defiant and vocal, the organisers announced on the mic that they weren't going anywhere to rapturous applause.

Being gay in Russia isn't illegal so long as you're over sixteen. Many gay people, understandably in the circumstances, choose to keep a low profile for an easier life. Meeting people online has become one of the easiest ways to connect with someone new, but going that route was also riddled with dangers.

I reconnected with Vanya and Nasrullah who I met outside Queer Fest. They met the old-fashioned way, face to face not because they were particularly traditional, but because they both didn't trust online dating. Vanya spoke of many cases where use of gay dating apps like Grindr would lead to robbery, beatings or even public humiliation. To meet someone via one of the apps was to risk being set up.

Staying safe was their priority and Vanya had gone so far as to have a fake girlfriend appear in pictures throughout his Facebook account. However, this situation had become even more complicated as she now had a boyfriend who refused to even shake hands with Vanya and Nasrullah as he had strong homophobic views. What's worse, was her new boyfriend worked as a prosecutor for the police.

Unsure of what could happen, the couple decided to leave their future to fate and, with the laws being what they were, I didn't blame them. Being in a same-sex relationship in Russia apparently wasn't only down to the two people involved. Here, the law had a say.

❝ Those people are God's enemies ❞

Banned in Soviet times, the Russian Orthodox Church had seen a massive resurgence. When we were filming in Russia, three out of four Russians claimed to follow its teachings. One such follower was Dmitry, who I'd met when he was pasting stickers across the doors into Queer Fest. He'd brought with him his friend Mila, who'd dropped the stink bomb in the venue.

Both in their early twenties, their youth clashed with a palpable intensity. When Dmitry spoke, Mila was silent and stared. To begin with, her piercing glare was almost comical, but the longer it went on the weirder it felt. Heading up a religious pressure group known as God's Will, Dmitry was firm and clear. He had a natural leader's air about him and at moments during our conversation his sense of strength would boil over into something much darker.

God's Will took it upon themselves to educate their followers against accepting anything remotely in support of the LGBTQ community. I attempted to share with the staunch and humourless pair just how liberal British attitudes are towards homosexuality, but they quickly made it clear they found my culture as alien as I found theirs. In asking Dmitry's opinion on my family members who happen to be gay, he didn't flinch in informing me 'Those people are God's enemies.'

Dmitry described openly gay people as both disgusting and sick, causing me a silent battle to retain my professionalism. This man was now speaking directly about members of my family and some of my closest friends. These were people I loved.

Regardless, I pushed on. They laughed in describing the stink bomb they left behind at the Queer Fest opening night and saw it as an important thing to do, as in Dmitry's words 'sin stinks'. Seeing as how they were pleased that some of the attendees were so repulsed that they were being sick out of the window, I knew that I wasn't dealing with people who had any empathy. Their cause could have been anything, they seemed more content in feeling superior rather than right.

Another member of God's Will joined us; she spoke better English and was suspicious of me and the camera from the jump. Her name was Leila and her energy was noticeably off with an unwarranted aggression I didn't even feel from the coarse and clipped Dmitry. Describing their actions at Queer Fest as non-violent, Leila explained that should the law have allowed her to throw Molotov cocktails instead of ink, she most certainly would have done.

At this point, I suspected an unhealthy level of hate bubbling just beneath the surface but I wanted to be wrong. I handed Leila the opportunity by asking what Dmitry would have done at Queer Fest should the law have allowed him to? Leila smiled and, with the most monotone delivery, said, 'If the law allowed it, he would kill those people.'

Wandering off behind me and pulling from the grass a rock that filled his right hand, Dmitry announced that he'd kill them all by stoning, just like in the Bible. At that point, the conversation was over for me. I wasn't even angry; I was just disgusted and wanted out.

Couples like Vanya and Nasrullah, who only want to lead normal lives, were living in an environment where people they'd never met wanted them jailed or dead. With groups like God's Will taking it upon themselves to police activities of the LGBTQ community, it became clear just how much the organisers of Queer Fest were battling.

It was only the second day of Queer Fest and I'd had no word about the whereabouts of the next event. I called Albert only to find out they'd lost their venue due to homophobic and Orthodox protesters.

Amnesty International reported that President Putin had introduced thirty new repressive laws to silence opposition; gay or otherwise. This was in the tiny gap of a three-year period.

Some laws had been changed to discourage protesters, and seemed to increasingly enforce the ideals of a bygone era. Challenging authority was not being tolerated. If caught protesting twice in a six-month period, offenders would go to prison.

I joined Kiril, a meek-looking man in his early twenties with a reputation for causing trouble. With a video of his one-man rainbow-flagged protest going viral, he was on the radar of the police and every homophobe in town. Taken down aggressively by the law on camera, Kiril had become well known online. Kiril was defiant and refused to allow new rules to stop him being heard. Freedom of speech laws didn't seem to hold much weight regardless of the issue and for Kiril, he saw his future being one of three things: leaving Russia, going to jail or being killed.

❛ *We don't deal with lesbos here* ❜

Back at the Queer Fest offices, Albert was busy searching for new venues as, after the public and reported clashes on opening night, all of the other secured venues cancelled their contracts with the festival. Unsupported and fighting for themselves, the team battled to get their ten-day festival back on track.

But unbelievably, with hooligans attacking people as they arrived and left on the opening night, nobody had been arrested. The Queer Fest team was frustrated by the level of protection they received from the authorities, which they saw as minimal, and Albert believed fighting back was the only option. He maintained that defiance and perseverance would leave those who'd chosen to ignore the existence of LGBTQ people in Russia no choice but to wake up.

Visibility for the community had its positives, but in a country like Russia there continue to be unavoidable risks associated with it. With several homophobic websites publishing the names and addresses of the most vocal protesters, to use your voice would put you at risk. Albert showed me one such website and images of a young woman called Darya kept coming up. Looking no more than fifteen, the baby-faced twenty-something had moved from the centre of town to the outskirts of St Petersburg after being viciously attacked.

Now living in an entirely new corner of the city, Darya invited me to the flat she shared with her girlfriend and two massive dogs. Cradling a cup of tea, she showed me around their home as I clumsily avoided huge dog toys and laughed at awkward school photos. She was friendly, welcoming and strangely didn't look much older than her framed teenage photographs.

Quietly she shared her story in all of its graphic detail; her undeniably teenage looks making the attack all the more menacing.

A group of men wearing masks and waving knifes confronted Darya outside her flat, their name-calling quickly escalated to violence and she was stabbed in the stomach and left for dead. She spent several days in intensive care but the police didn't look into her statement and no one was charged or arrested for the crime. After recovering, Darya was sent home by the police and told, 'We don't deal with lesbos here.'

Confident the government was doing everything to make things worse, Darya felt unprotected and victimised. Darya believed the recently passed anti-propaganda law encouraged homophobia and I could see why she felt that way . . . and why her pets doubled as protection.

Reconnecting with Kiril I decided to attend a protest. He was meeting with other activist friends at a protest about the war in Ukraine. With police everywhere, tensions would be high as the police, anti-war and LGBTQ activists shared the same space as skinhead nationalists. This was going to be a long afternoon.

The demonstration was illegal, which meant that any obvious protesting would lead to arrests. With so many people in attendance, I had no idea how it would work without everyone being carted off in meat wagons.

It was a short walk from the station to the site of the protest and once Kiril had found his friends and we were on our way, we quickly picked up a shadow of sorts. Either this bloke was the worst secret agent ever or he was obsessed with the likes of Kiril and his protesting friends.

It was the guy in the blue tracksuit from my first day at Queer Fest. His bright blue trackie top and bottoms helped him stand out like a sore thumb. His brilliantly broken nose caused his sunglasses to keep slipping off his face as there was no nose bridge for them to rest on. He carried a tablet and was constantly taking photos and making notes. The geezer was strange and I needed to find out who the hell he was.

Kiril was convinced he was from United Russia, the current ruling political party. I thought he was just another nutjob with too much time on his hands. Walking just behind us the whole time, I dropped back and asked him what he was up to. He quietly avoided any real conversation mumbling monosyllabic answers to everything I threw his way. I was getting nothing out of the weirdo so I left it at that.

When we finally arrived, it might have been the strangest protest I'd ever attended. There were no banners, no chanting but people were everywhere and standing still. As the police were in among the crowd, anything could lead to arrest. Before I'd had any real time to take it in, Mr Blue Tracksuit showed up and he wasn't alone. Ushered through the crowd, the anti-gay politician Milonov made a beeline for Kiril. The two men instantly traded insults. 'Careful of this AIDS-ridden thing,' snapped Milonov. The politician astounded me with his brazen use of hate speech.

Milonov left and Mikhail replaced him, instantly flaring up the group as it emerged he'd attacked them physically a few months prior and hadn't been charged. We were on what was being called a peace march and insults had begun to fly from all angles. Mikhail referred to Kiril and his friends as repulsive scum. The police walked by demanding rules be adhered to as 'violators would be physically harmed'.

I really was a long way from home. I'd never heard the police threaten protesters publicly, let alone through a megaphone. The rules here were different and I definitely didn't want to end up on the wrong side of the law. My desperate attempts to grasp the reasoning behind so many people consumed by hate and totally unwilling to understand left me drained. I was honestly glad my time making the film was coming to a close, as the relentless rollercoaster of fear and anger I saw in the people I'd meet was taking its toll.

❮ *A traditional Russian man is a warrior* ❯

With the collapse of the Soviet Union in the early nineties, suddenly gay life found a confidence and swiftly became visible and decriminalised. But at the time of filming, a recent poll had 72 per cent of people saying being gay was unacceptable. Still confused as to what could be driving this level of homophobia in the average normal Russian, I decided to spend time with Mikhail.

Planning to show me how real Russian men spent their weekend, we were taking a tram out of town. On the way we got chatting and some of the things that came up left me silenced. Telling me he ran a recent referendum against homosexuality, Mikhail proudly announced that, 'If it was decided to burn or hang them, that's what we'd do.'

This was a guy who saw himself as a real man. Mikhail believed in traditional Russian values and he was taking me to meet a friend who felt exactly the same way. We were headed to the beach to do some boxing training and Mikhail's opponent was a lump. Introducing himself with a voice so deep it could have been a joke, Victor looked and sounded like a caricature but was entirely for real.

I genuinely thought he'd been invited down in an effort to cheer me up. He felt like one of Sam's bad jokes, especially as he was head to toe in full traditional Russian gear, right down to the hemp slacks. Wearing with pride the height, frame and icy blond hair of Ivan Drago from *Rocky IV*, this guy couldn't have been more of a man's man if he'd tried.

The 'training' they'd planned was a boxing-led workout on the beach. Taking a seat and sending as many signals as possible that I wasn't even remotely likely to get involved, they got stuck in and it was a total mess. The wild and undisciplined few rounds of boxing were brilliant to watch as they clearly had no idea what they were doing. Thank god they were wearing gloves because, even though their punches were mostly missing by miles, when they connected, it was brutal.

Mikhail started to explain that fighting had always been a huge part of Russian culture, but I was distracted as Victor started to wave a knife. Pulling it from his belt, Victor showed me the blade. Admitting he carried it everywhere, Victor didn't see anything wrong with such a weapon. Victor and I were just as confused by each other and in his efforts to help me understand his world better, his deep voice boomed, 'Above all, a traditional Russian man is a warrior.'

Let the record show I didn't want to get on the wrong side of this warrior. He was a size and a half. Victor continued to explain his way of life in the context of a traditional Russian man, which in his own words demands him to be an 'Extreme homophobe, just like most of the sane Russian population.' Admitting he wouldn't use his knife if approached romantically by a homosexual, Victor preferred to use his hands. 'I would smash his face in.'

As difficult as it was to spend so much time with these guys, the more they spoke, the more their attitudes towards homosexuals revealed themselves to be based on not much more than fear. This strange new community operated in a whole new way and – they thought – endangered what was so dear to them as proud Russian men. Traditional values were at stake and the change represented by the LGBTQ community was seen as a threat, not progress.

With another round of sparring coming to a close, Mikhail stumbled away after taking a few to the face. To be fair to him, he did catch big Victor a few times who was now bleeding from the nose, while I was stood to the side waiting to see when the fun part of their workout would start.

From out of nowhere the police showed up and we were told to stop filming. It was strange and sudden but became less of a surprise as it became clear our friend in the blue tracksuit was leading them over. He was back and for some reason didn't want us shooting. All I could think about was whether he had several of the same outfits on rotation or if he just kept wearing the same set? Either way, he was dedicated to the look, or had lost a bet, one of the two.

Cleared off the beach and with not many options, Victor invited me for some real Russian man time. Led by the man in hemp, we arrived at a dark archway and wandered into an underground men-only sauna. Towels grabbed and quickly undressed, we stepped out of the changing room and I stopped dead. In Victor's hand was what looked like a tree branch wrapped in herbs and dried leaves. He called it a 'sauna whisk'. It was apparently intended for beating the body in the sauna and he wanted to whisk me.

Going to a sauna in the UK with a tree branch to whip other men wouldn't go down particularly well. But we were in Russia and this was apparently what real men did, so I was in. Unfortunately for Sam on the camera, that meant he was in too. Victor wasn't shy or retiring and dropped his towel without batting an eyelid. I, on the other hand, had on swimming shorts that weren't coming off. For some reason, Sam was sweating like a rotter before we even got in the wooden box, and it was only when we'd all stripped down and he was in the biggest pair of dad pants did I realise why.

Victor kept throwing water on the magic hot rocks making the room unbearable. The sauna felt like the devil's waiting room to hell yet we kept shooting. Sam's camera rig was metal and kept burning his arm with a fizz every few seconds. Victor started whipping my back with the branch as it was apparently good for me, but I didn't see the fun nor benefits in the whipping.

There was a moment in that sauna when I stopped, looked around and had one of those internal conversations quietly in my head. I was lying on my stomach while a naked Russian dude called Victor was whipping my back with a tree branch. It was 80 degrees and my director was burning his body every few seconds on his scorching metal camera frame. Just in case I ever questioned the event actually happened, it was all being filmed for national TV. Lots of people would see it. Brilliant.

Bonding out of the way, I'd won Victor's trust (and seen his penis). It was all a bit much in the sauna, but thankfully he called time and we took our leave, diving into the icy cold plunge pool.

I pushed Victor to open up on his dislike of the gay community, and what came out as his reason was surprising. Victor tied homosexuality with depravity; he saw them as one and the same. Believing Western propaganda was the main cause of homosexuality emerging in Russian communities, he believed it was something new that hadn't existed in the days of the

Soviet Union. Victor saw same-sex relationships as undermining the foundations of Russian values and culture.

With culture so important to Victor, he invited me to a night of traditional dancing which he attended regularly. I accepted the offer because anything at this stage wouldn't be weird after what I'd just been through. The club was packed with men, women and children all in traditional dress practising and learning group dances accompanied by live accordion music.

Being roped in, I shook a leg during a couple of the group dances and suitably embarrassed myself but had a giggle while doing it. Victor was over the moon I'd joined him and his dance group and I was too as it was all starting to make sense. Victor was protecting and continuing the values he held dear in every aspect of his life. The LGBTQ community simply didn't fit into that ideal and the values that meant so much to men like Mikhail and Victor had no room for gay rights.

The state-funded dance group was another opportunity for the government to encourage the likes of Victor to invest in traditional values, which connected quite conveniently to the greater message of the ruling party. Traditional values weren't just good for Russian people, they were being encouraged as they were good for politics and spoke to policy.

It was the last night of Queer Fest and the closing party was at the one place that wouldn't get shut down, a lesbian bar. As I approached the door a familiar face appeared surrounded by giddy kids excited at the slim chance of conflict. It was Mr Blue Tracksuit, who'd finally found a red pair of jeans. He was mixing it up but would his behaviour be any different or was tonight another case of linger and intimidate?

I asked directly if he'd ever get tired of behaving in such a way, or if he would ever see his behaviour as juvenile? He started to explain himself but I'd heard it all before and it was bloody freezing.

Cutting the dry conversation short, I left Mr Blue Tracksuit and his mates outside in the cold, making my way into the party as I was over conflict and wanted to enjoy myself. Inside were Darya, her girlfriend and so many other faces I'd met during the week. For Darya, the festival was a success, not because the organisers were able to still throw events regardless of venues pulling out, but because no one was hurt or even worse killed.

I left the party and city with mixed feelings. I hadn't discovered any breakthroughs in progress, as every turn spoke to Russia going backwards when it came to gay rights. That being said, I'd met a gay community that were willing to stay and fight regardless of the conditions or the laws.

CHAPTER 6

KNIVES AND YOUNG LIVES

It's become increasingly rare to find a Londoner born and raised in the capital and I'm proud to be a card-carrying member of the minority. Lauded for the endless list of positives, the big smoke has so much going for it but we all know the city isn't perfect. Knife crime in the capital is one of the many problems that seems to keep rearing its ugly head.

When I was a teenager my school life was dominated by bravado. I attended Central Foundation Boys' School in east London, which was a twenty-minute bus journey from my block of flats in Holloway. With that many teenage boys in one building it's a wonder the testosterone alone didn't blow the roof off the place. Looking and acting tough was essential for survival as gangs dominated the playground.

It was the mid-nineties and gentrification was only just

beginning to hit my area and definitely hadn't swallowed east London yet. Populated by working-class kids from the neighbouring London boroughs of Islington and Hackney, my school sat just behind Old Street roundabout and was full of runts like me from council estates.

In my early teens it was impossible to go a day at school without encountering gang culture, as it was rife in the areas my classmates and I were from. Daily we'd deal with racist gangs like the White Cross boys and the Junior National Front, as well as the expected butting of heads that happened regardless of race.

In my first few years at Central, I saw my journey to and from school as the best and potentially worst part of the day. On my way in, sharing the top deck of the 43 or 271 bus with the burgundy-skirted girls from Elizabeth Garrett Anderson Girls' School was a dream. They smelt better than us boys and occasionally smiled back. Occasionally. The worst part was the journey home. Remember, this was a time before smartphones and iPods so distractions were minimal.

If it wasn't a fight on the bus, it was the emergency alarm being set off. If it wasn't the alarm, it was a window being smashed. I'm definitely guilty of moaning about today's teenagers being obsessed by their smartphones, but for anyone reading this commuting into work on the 43 or 271 bus, be thankful kids today are staring at screens and not smashing bus windows like my mob.

In my first couple of years at school, the thing to carry

making you instantly tougher was a glass hammer. The plastic tool would be clipped to the internal walls of the public bus I'd ride to and from school as a safety measure. Within the first few weeks of term, every bus had theirs stolen. By the time I was thirteen, the thing to carry stopped being a glass hammer and overnight graduated to a knife.

I stayed out of trouble but was always around it as, whether you welcomed it or not, violence was a part of school life. Things were so racially charged that games of blacks v whites football at lunch break became a regular occurrence.

By my mid-teens, knives were increasingly present, as they'd fast become the accessory of choice. This unfortunately wasn't just the case with the harder kids that always seemed to be in some kind of trouble or have some rival hard nut 'after them'. Some of the quieter, normal boys who happened to live on a bad estate would see the weapon as a necessary evil, just in case something happened on the way home.

I never carried a weapon in my teens, but I definitely saw so many that now, with hindsight, I see just how dangerous those times were. Getting older and taking more of an interest in the changing face of the place I call home, to see knife crime as an ongoing problem particularly with teenagers haunts me.

Travelling all the way to South Africa in making the *Knife Crime ER* film, where I was confronted with similar issues of violence but on a whole other level, forced me into an uncomfortable corner. I'd go on to face the actuality that everything

I saw might have happened to me, but the toughest question I'd have to ask myself was, why didn't it?

I was back in Cape Town and the beauty of the city was still able to catch me off guard; Table Mountain still had that magic about it every time it caught my eye. The picture-perfect views, sunsets and beaches led me to make the classic embarrassing Brit abroad statement . . . 'I reckon I could live here'.

But South Africa had an impressive gift of slapping me with a reality check whenever I found myself getting too comfortable. The beauty of Cape Town had my attention for all of five minutes before I was reminded that I was in the country's murder capital. Twelve miles from the city centre sits Khayelitsha, one of the biggest townships occupying a sizable chunk of the Cape Flats. Partially illegal, the predominantly residential township continues to grow, housing millions.

It was my first time driving into the township and I hadn't even realised we were in. My limited experience told me townships were essentially shantytowns. I was expecting rows and rows of badly built walls and corrugated iron roofs. I was quickly corrected as Khayelitsha was not only huge, but it might as well have been a city in its own right. Street lamps lit the route and the perfectly paved roads made getting to our destination a lot easier than I'd expected. Excited to see how people lived while being slightly embarrassed of my naivety, I arrived in this chunk of Cape Town I didn't know, but was desperate to experience.

It was payday weekend and it was buzzing. I was twelve

miles from the centre of the city but the streets here were just as busy. Music seemed to come from every passing car and kids wouldn't take no for an answer washing windscreens at traffic lights. The night had just begun and the taverns were opening. Khayelitsha was clearly a place full of life, but how could somewhere so vibrant carry such a reputation for violence?

My first port of call was the newly built hospital situated right in the heart of the township. At the time of filming, the shiny new facility was only a year old but already had one of the busiest emergency centres in Cape Town.

As a kid I'd spent much more time than any child would ever choose to in a hospital as my mother worked in one. The Whittington Hospital in Archway was and still is an impressive group of buildings overlooking the whole of London. When I was around five or six, my mother worked as a medical secretary in one of the taller buildings. I ended up spending some of my half-term and Easter breaks with mum at work because, well, why would you pay for childcare when there was a fully functioning children's ward? I'd hang out with kids dealing with all manner of conditions, but all I saw was new friends to play with and an endless stream of toys. I'd go on to have health issues of my own as a child, but I'd never dealt with anything that made hospitals a scary place for me.

Walking into this hospital felt strangely familiar. I was on the other side of the planet, but the smell and feeling was instantly recognisable. It was just like being back at work with Mum, even if outside the building was another kind of life entirely.

It was a Saturday night and beyond the colossal car park, you could hear the parties just getting started. Music was in the air and steadily getting louder from the streets of Harare, the nearest residential block just beyond the hospital. Known as one of the most notorious parts of the township, the whistling and cackles coming from the bars and clubs sounded like undeniable fun.

Unfortunately, given its proximity, once those bars and clubs had closed for the night, their tipsy patrons would hang out in the street. Any violence would see their night end right where I was stood. In the hospital.

Over the next few days, I was set to shadow the junior doctors. Being in a hospital I was totally good with, but I hadn't really thought about just how much I'd see in the presence of the medical staff.

❛ *Welcome to Khayelitsha* ❜

The weekend shift staff change was under way and it was busy in the emergency room. There was already someone being stitched up after a fight and another man who'd lost a leg. The staff were from all over the world and predominantly young with a hunger to learn.

I met Lauren, one of the junior doctors who was beginning her shift, and so full of smiles you wouldn't think she was surrounded by blood and bandages. Totally in her element, Lauren grabbed a clear plastic bag and handed me a foot severed at the calf muscle. I stared in a panicked awe as Lauren pulled and twisted the limb exposing tendons and bone talking me through the intricacies of anatomy. She was fascinated and excited from a medical standpoint; I was trying my best not to throw up.

Lauren went on to explain that the inebriated patient had stumbled onto the train tracks and not got away quickly enough as the fast train approached. She described it as a traumatic amputation; all I could think about was the poor bloke arriving at the hospital holding his severed foot.

This was my first two minutes in the ward and Lauren happily chewed gum, describing what I'd just seen as a typical start to the weekend. This was apparently the calm before the storm. The drunken man would wake without a foot, but thanks to the junior doctors he'd be alive.

Lauren worked every patient in the room alongside Amy and François. Buzzing from bed to bed, they were just getting started but had a fantastic shorthand and rhythm. All under the age of thirty, it was all they could do to cope with the frequency and extremity of cases coming through the door.

Amy saw to a young man who'd just come in. She marked a diagram indicating the various wounds he'd received across his entire body from being attacked with a panga blade (a type of machete). The thick and heavy blade had left the back of his skull soft, and Amy injected his scalp and tended to the three-inch gash on the back of his head. Totally nonchalant about the severity of the case, Amy had seen this before and assured me I'd see lots more that very same night. She wasn't wrong.

'Welcome to Khayelitsha' was her dry closer before being called away to help with another patient. I'd been introduced to new parts of the world in so many ways over the years, but for victims of knife crime to act as a fitting introduction was a chilling first.

The shift continued and it wasn't long before the floodgates opened. Quickly, young men covered in stab wounds filled every bed and were queued up side by side in the hallway. The stench of blood began to fill every corridor managing to over-power that strong chemical hospital smell.

A man with bright pink blood pouring from his head sat slumped in a wheelchair while an older man clutched at his chest in pain. It was so much to take in. I was taken aback at how the group of young doctors buzzed from case to case while I watched, totally overwhelmed. In a typical weekend, the emergency ward would see over 100 patients; 90 per cent of those cases would be stab victims. Blunt force trauma was another cause of young men coming through the door and the numbers were astounding. One of the most common causes of death for young men under the age of twenty-five from Khayelitsha is violent crime.

After an hour of blood, stitches and pain-fuelled moans, the room felt less like an emergency ward and increasingly like a chop shop. People were being wheeled in, repaired and rolled out, with a similar case filling their spot as soon as they'd gone. It was incredible to watch but completely understandable given the circumstances. These doctors had to work fast as their speed, or lack thereof, could affect a life for good.

❛ Relax, Booti ❜

At twenty-six, François was an incredibly assured doctor who jumped from patient to patient. Filling the bed in front of him lay a man with internal bleeding in need of immediate treatment. Wiping his sweat away with his elbow, he called me over to help him with a chest drain.

I jumped at the opportunity to help and shrugged off my bomber jacket, throwing on an apron and gloves. I was on camera doing what I always do, and getting stuck in here felt like the best way to bond with the doctors. I figured helping might just stop me from being an annoying, question-asking obstacle and even make me useful.

We were in a hospital surrounded by people in need of serious medical attention and I had absolutely no right to administer any medical help, but François felt differently. I was worried my involvement would create another foot-in-a-bag situation or worse. Given no choice in the matter, I was holding the terrified patient's arms and desperately trying to keep him still while François made a small incision between his ribs. 'Relax, Booti' was said repeatedly in an effort to calm the patient down. Booti, meaning brother, would become a term of endearment I'd hear repeatedly over the next few hours.

Aggressively working the cut open with a steel tool, François needed to drain the chest cavity of blood or air that had built up around the lungs because of the stabbing. Blood trickled out of the new opening and a loud sharp hiss of air spat its way from the gap between the man's ribs. Acting quickly, François snatched up a tube and inserted it into the gap to prevent a lung collapse.

Stood with my eyes impossibly wide, I couldn't believe what was happening right in front of me and totally forgot about my role of holding helper, instantly becoming a gawping idiot. My mouth was wide open but I wasn't even close to my soundman Joe in the race for stupidest facial expression. Joe held a huge boom mic above the entire procedure and every squelch and spit was in loud stereo sound booming into his ears from the huge pair of headphones he had to wear.

Joe looked like he was going to be sick as I decided to focus on the doctor who was making light work of what might have been the scariest thing I'd ever witnessed. François explained that the way he'd gone about the procedure, was neither the best or his preference. It was an unfortunate necessity due to the time pressure of saving the man and being able to get to the next in-need patient. My squirming wasn't helpful, but the incredibly polite doctor found time to thank me before rushing off to save another life only two beds away.

As the night went on, the stream of injured men was

constant and the cause hardly varied. Frustratingly, it was one stab victim followed by another. A knife wound, regardless of its severity, is an awful thing to witness but, after the first few hours of the weekend night shift, those reporting a single stab injury, I began to consider lucky. Many victims had multiple cuts and wounds and, more often than not, huge gashes on the head.

Pulled from a car covered in blood, Lukanio was wheeled into the trauma room. Mugged and stabbed on his way home from a tavern, the 21-year-old didn't look good. Quickly tended to by the pack of international doctors, he was being helped but with the amount he was wailing you'd never think it.

❝ He'll survive . . . to come back next week ❞

At the time we were filming in South Africa, UK statistics recorded around seventy-seven stabbings countrywide in a week. In Khayelitsha, that number would usually be matched if not beaten in a single weekend.

The phrase 'Relax Booti' calmly uttered by François earlier would continue to be said for the rest of the shift, but in the case of Junior Doctor Nicole, it would be shouted. Taking no prisoners, Nicole was broad, stern and an incredible presence in the ward. She didn't suffer fools gladly, and abruptly explained that most of the knife fights arose out of drunken disputes over women.

Sewing up bright red bloody head wounds, Nicole explained

that the scalp bleeds a lot more than most other places in the body so an injury can usually look a lot worse than it actually is. I wasn't desensitised to the blood just yet, but as the night wore on I became so used to seeing bleeding men doubled over drunk I had to check myself. I hated the constant thread in every story being poverty, the release of alcohol-fuelled partying and the inevitable violence as a result.

Nicole had seen it all before – as recently as the previous weekend to be exact – and was in a strange place of acceptance. Working on her patient's prescription, Nicole looked up to watch the man lying unconscious with a head ridded with lumps. 'He'll survive . . . to come back next week.'

The night continued, as did the flow of drunken stab victims. One doctor described the combined smell of blood and alcohol as unbearable and I understood his position. It wasn't an easy environment to be in the middle of and I'd only spent a few hours there. For the junior doctors, this was school and term was far from over.

One of the senior consultants, Dr Henny, arrived to oversee the work of the young team. I followed him into a curtained-off cubicle where he explained the young man lying on his side had been stabbed in the head and his skull might have been fractured in the process.

He injected the man's scalp and began to stitch the wound while talking me through his process of assessment. With no time to waste and lacking specialised, sophisticated medical machinery, he slipped his little finger into the second and bigger gash on the man's head. Sliding it under the skin and rubbing the bone was the quickest and most effective way to rule out an underlying skull fracture.

The man was conscious but pain free due to local anaesthetic. Dr Henny grabbed my hand and launched my finger beneath the skin, guiding it up and down the smooth skull bone. The thickness of the skin was strange and heavy while the skull bone felt like the perfectly smooth stone to skim across water that I'd spend ages searching for at the beach.

It was fascinating but a first I won't be repeating anytime soon. If you catch me fingering some random bloke's skull, pull me aside and have a word. Thanks.

The nine-to-five for these doctors was doing everything in their power to tend to whatever came through the door. They were doing amazing work but they were literally just doing their job. The truth was that the medical staff in Khayelitsha Hospital were the most positive part of a crime cycle. Every young stab victim they patched up was half expected to make a return visit in the not too distant future.

The emergency ward was only one side of the story; what was causing so many young men to end up as victims of shockingly similar knife attacks? I saw so many casualties on my first night that I wanted to see where they were coming from, so the next day I headed into the township.

In Khayelitsha, the scars of a troubled history were everywhere. Built in the late eighties, the township was situated on the fringes of Cape Town during Apartheid. Twenty years on, the place was alive and home to millions. Signs of regeneration were visible as small pockets of houses built to a high standard stood proudly side-by-side. That being said, there was still a 61 per cent unemployment rate and many of the township's residents were still bound by poverty.

I hopped in a local taxi and was ferried around by Zuka. Filling his seat and then some, the mountain of a man pointed out the skinny alley ways that criminals would flee down after altercations. Muggers could hide between buildings and pounce whenever they saw fit, making the atmosphere shift dramatically as soon as night fell. A breeding ground for violence, the living conditions seen in the majority of the township that was home for so many was also the perfect place for a career in crime.

Speaking to Lukanio who I met in the hospital, it was clear that his brutal mugging not only left him covered in stab wounds but also hungry for revenge. Describing the police as inactive, Lukanio explained that many people would take justice into their own hands. He stressed that drugs and alcohol usually lay at the root of any violence.

❝ He's gonna kill our children ❞

While talking on camera to a small group of teenagers, I had no idea I was about to be given a first-hand experience in the effects of substance abuse.

A car roared its way towards us and a small group of children playing in the road. Wild and clearly out of it, the drunk driver was pulled from his car by the quickly forming mob. Local men and women surrounded his car pulling and dragging the man in different directions. The keys from his car were confiscated and what was about to happen to the inebriated driver looked like it was going to be anything but positive.

An angry man screamed, 'He's gonna kill our children,' as things became suddenly more menacing. I feared the mob might take matters into their own hands, exerting what was commonly known as Community Justice.

In an environment where an underfunded police force struggles to get to corners of the sprawling townships across the country, over the years the communities themselves have increasingly become police, judge and jury. Lukanio explained that had the man hit a child or injured someone, the mob might decide to punish him there and then using the most extreme version of force imaginable.

That level of extreme punishment would be the case for his attacker, causing Lukanio to keep his stabbing quiet and manage it without any help from the police or community. One such punishment used in community violence was known as necklacing. The guilty party would be trapped in a stack of tyres, have petrol poured over them and then set alight.

In the twelve months leading up to my arrival in Khayelitsha, there were nine incidents of necklacing. Thankfully community justice doesn't always lead to death. Back at the hospital, the night shift had seen four men turn up accompanied by the police. Stripped naked and beaten, their punishment was humiliation, hammering home the fact that the township was home to so many, but also a world operating within its own brutal rules.

On the night shift, I joined paramedics Ata and Ricardo. The minute a call came in, we dashed for the ambulance and I was made to sit up front with Ata. I did a terrible job of hiding my excitement, as a flashback to a fire station school trip caused immediate regression. The day I wore that fireman's hat and got lifted into the driver's seat of the shiny red truck was happening all over again, only this time it was probably for the best I didn't press all the buttons or pull at every switch.

En route to a call, the sirens wailed as Ata ripped through the streets. Ricardo sat on the patient bed flipping through a battered book of maps trying to figure out where we were going. There was a new sat nav that hadn't yet been completely installed, leaving Ricardo and Ata no option but to go old school.

Scooping patients from every corner of Khayelitsha, each shift saw the two men inundated with young victims of knife crime. Practically on the frontline, ambulance crews were not just the first to respond to an incident, they'd put themselves at risk of attack every shift.

Eventually arriving at the address, a man with a T-shirt wrapped around his head emerged from the doorway. It wasn't until he stood in the red and blue lights of the ambulance that I could see just how much blood was pouring from his face.

I spotted deep stab wounds on his arms, chest and head but couldn't work out why he wasn't doubled over in pain. As he called for his screaming mother I could smell the alcohol on his breath. Between the adrenaline and booze, the pain hadn't hit. Yet.

Appearing from the open doorway to the small house, a boy no more than four stood silently among the chaos. The kid was totally blank faced, not knowing where to go or what to do. I ushered the child inside and regretted doing so as soon as we walked in.

The house was a compact three-room building with concrete walls. Upon entry, the harsh light from a single bulb revealed just how brutal what had happened actually was. The doorway to one of the two bedrooms was covered in blood. There was a small pool of blood in which a bent screwdriver wrapped in bloody fingerprints sat waiting to be collected by the police. Given what I'd been told, chances were they wouldn't be arriving any time soon.

I tried desperately to pick out the story from the noise, but the random faces barking different versions of what went on were just too confusing. What was clear was alcohol had been consumed and a fight ensued. The bleeding guy in the ambulance had been attacked with the screwdriver but to what degree I had no idea. It was impossible to tell exactly how bad his injuries were as his head was so tightly wrapped in the T-shirt that was now sopping wet with blood.

The small boy cowered at my legs holding my hand while shaking uncontrollably. He'd seen everything and was clearly struggling to process it all. I headed back to the ambulance to check on the man in the van as Ata attended to the bleeding. The shaking boy reappeared at my side taking my hand not wanting to be left alone. With no idea who the child was or the severity of what he'd seen, I was in over my head in a situation that continued to provide no answers.

Handing the child over to a neighbour, I said my goodbyes and returned to Ricardo and Ata in the ambulance standing over the now bandaged man. Counting out six stab wounds, who knows what would have happened to the guy had Ricardo's map reading been as awful as mine. Working furiously on his wounds, Ricardo explained he'd been stabbed in the nose and just above his eye hence the relentless flow of blood.

Ata pulled away, dodging potholes, and the rush was on to get him to the trauma unit as quickly as possible. Led by Nicole, the trauma team pounced on the man working furiously as Ata and Ricardo quietly returned to their ambulance to wait for the next call. Suddenly much calmer and quiet, the back of the van felt like an entirely different place.

Nicole got to work removing the bandages and a huge flap of skin fell covering the man's eye. I had to turn away as the stitching began, I flicked my eyes back to the treatment periodically as I couldn't really take it.

For my sound man Joe, not so much. Holding the mic on a long pole, Joe was covering the sound of the stitching but couldn't keep his eyes on the procedure continuously dropping his boom into shot. Shouted at repeatedly, Joe's hilarious squirms ruined a solid 70 per cent of everything shot. To be fair, I was fine, as I could turn away. If I had no choice but to watch an eyelid being stitched closed, I'd probably have been just as much of a mess.

Ata had explained to me that in the past, he himself was no stranger to drunken brawls. Pointing out his own set of scars across his face and body, Ata spoke of a past filled with drunken fights and constant close calls with serious danger. His firsthand understanding of the young men he continuously picked up didn't make his past a hindrance, it in fact made him better placed to do his job.

The loud barks of 'Relax Booti' dragged me back to the trauma room as Nicole tended to bed after bed of drunk and bloody young men. Slumped on his chest, a man coved in deep slices to his back was being stitched up by Nicole. Every time the half-asleep patient roused himself to moan, she loudly told him off.

Growing up nearby, the ten months at the hospital had begun to wear on her. Her bedside manner had become short, sharp and full of tough love. Getting the job done and fast, Nicole hated the constant stream of violence she would see daily, especially as it was so close to home. 'This is the most trauma I've seen, this is frontline stuff.'

Softening, Nicole explained how she used to have nightmares but now blocks what she witnesses out. The more staff I met, the more I heard versions of the same story. The tireless team spending their working hours patching up victims of violence had all found their own ways to deal with what they'd see. Nurses saw their own sons in the men they'd treat, while I was still overwhelmed with it all not quite knowing how I'd process the images now burnt into my retina.

It was Sunday, the last night of the shift for François. Running through the fully stacked trauma room, the patients filling the beds were all there for reasons that had become sadly usual. Pointing as he went, François listed two stab victims, a man with heart issues, an overdose and gunshot victim without even flinching.

A twenty-three-year-old stab victim had sixteen bloody wounds to the back after a mugging. He kicked and moaned during treatment but was happier to have survived and be alive than in pain. The man squeezed my hand as his chest was drained and the doctor repeated the procedure I had previously helped François with. The speedy procedure had saved the man from a collapsed lung. Once the bellows were over, the tears and gripping of my hand were followed with an unexpected and very macho 'I love you, no homo.'

Between the nature of my surroundings and the occasional minutes where even the staff looked like they'd seen enough, there weren't many moments of laughter that night.

But in that silly break in all the seriousness, we all laughed and it was needed.

The night shift ended and Amy and François gave me a lift back to my hotel. Heading home as the sun came up, the quiet roads became busier the closer into town we got. Looking into the passing cars headed into work as we were leaving reminded me of the unreal nature of the junior doctors' work day in comparison to that of the average commuter.

Believing neither him nor any of his work colleagues would survive a day in the township, François saw the majority of the community they served as no different, bar their resilience to endure. Believing the community shared the same values and intolerance for crime, he put their situation down to a lack of support from the police and government.

❝ We're there to kill everyone, rob everyone ❞

Despite being so close to Khayelitsha, the city of Cape Town could have been a new country entirely. This was home to the doctors and a world-class tourist destination, but left me feeling uneasy. With the night's activity still fresh in my mind, a walk around the affluent city made the infrequent black faces I passed stand out as anomalies.

Young black men just like me were earning six times less than their white counterparts. I was walking through what felt like a place overflowing with opportunity, yet the township on its doorstep had generations of people living in a world that had been left behind.

With my time in Khayelitsha nearly over, I knew I needed to confront the issue that continued to come up, but came with so much fear attached. Gangs ran the streets of the townships and, according to the doctors at the hospital, were responsible for a large part of the injuries they'd spend the nights patching up.

At the township's busiest junction, a roadside cluster of stalls selling barbecued meats pumped smoke into the sky. The sun was setting quickly and that inner carnivore demanded I purchased a serving of beef for the team and myself. I talked to the twenty-one-year-old girl manning the grill. The sun was setting and she was scared of gangsters mugging her for the day's take, so she made my order the last of the day. The vibrant and busy pocket of people would go dramatically silent the moment the sun had gone down.

Threatening the women selling food with knives and guns, the gangs would rob and steal while getting a free dinner but this would only ever happen in the dark. As dangerous as it felt, hearing from the men accused themselves felt like the only real way to truly understand their motivations and reasoning for such behaviour in the place they call home.

Five main gangs were responsible for the majority of crime seen in the township and the key reason for the continued bloodshed was a battle for control of the corners. Split by a long bridge, the township was divided into east and west territories. Conveniently carved up and easily claimed, the gangs fought for their own areas but aimed to be the biggest and most powerful. Local papers reported the usual entrance age for new members could be as young as fourteen.

The team made contact with the Vatos Locos, one of the most known and feared gangs in the area. I was due to meet them and told to wait at a staircase by the bridge.

I was on camera while my director collected shots of me waiting and the obvious trepidation I couldn't hide. I had no idea what to expect. Would they be carrying weapons? How many would show? I didn't even have the time to send myself into a panic as the Vatos arrived as if from nowhere, surprisingly punctual and eager to chat. A pack of men bounded toward me confidently introducing themselves, all carrying huge machetes as if it was the most natural thing in the world. I held eye contact and tried to focus on the people, not the rusty blades.

Wearing an electric green baseball cap and walking with a noticeable limp, Mark was one of the first to shake my hand. He was softly spoken but looked me dead in the eye in a way that demanded respect. My plan to keep it all about the eye contact was totally scuppered as a huge greeting from one guy caused his massive blade to catch my knuckle breaking the skin.

In a moment I was right back to noticing all of the weapons and the reality that I was surrounded by gang members who

I probably should stay on the right side of. A new internal briefing was repeated and loudly inside my own head. 'STAY ON THEIR GOOD SIDE REG, DO NOT COCK THIS ONE UP.'

As we spoke, it quickly emerged that Mark was their leader. He held no weapons but had a quiet confidence and was the most intense. As I felt the mood slowly relax, I began to look around and take in the detail. The men I'd just met had suddenly changed in appearance the more I looked at them. They were kids, all baby faced, but their faces were covered in tattoos and scars. All still teenagers, their leader Mark was only eighteen years old.

The gang members pointed towards the area on the other side of the bridge. The boys identified the small cluster of houses as home to their rival gang the Vuras. Calling the area 'Ghostland', Mark explained that when they ventured into their enemy's territory, 'We are like devil in hell.' They had no remorse for anything they did while on the other side of the bridge. Mark was crystal clear, 'We're there to kill everyone, rob everyone.'

What sounded like the most cold-blooded attitude seemed to come from a place of twisted and bloody honour. The boys operated on a reactionary basis and justified their behaviour as retaliation for actions committed on their side of town by their enemies. 'If you kill my brother and I see you walking on the road, I'll never leave you. You must die.' Retaliation was a huge driver for kids hoping to avenge the death of a loved one.

As we spoke, the group of young men began to sound less like a gang and more like kids fighting for honour in the most violent and at times brutal of ways.

The conversation was abruptly interrupted as several members of the gang sprung up, spotting their rivals approaching on the bridge. Weapons were suddenly pulled and everything changed in an instant. Anything I had to say was suddenly a whole lot less interesting as the group of teenagers ran at their enemies. The shouting gangs kept some distance between them, and cars stopped as rocks were thrown and machetes were waved.

The rival Vuras gang suddenly began to swell in size causing the Vatos to retreat. It felt as if things could spill over into something far more serious at any moment but, as it was, the fight happening in front of me was a tad embarrassing. What was unfolding was two groups of shouting teenagers throwing rocks. Yes, they were all armed with knives but for whatever reason, no one was getting close enough to cause any real damage.

Pulling the handbrake for a second, this isn't me making light of an awful situation. These young men were defending their homes and what they saw as the honour of their friends who'd lost their lives. For them, this was a war. Yes, in that moment it was thirty people throwing rocks on a bridge, but later that night it could be one on one with knives in a dark alleyway.

Stood at a distance, I was able to remain calm while

watching the rocks fly. Then out of nowhere, everything jumped up a gear. One of the Vuras pulled what looked like a gun from a blue plastic bag and the Vatos began to run. My nonplussed demeanour went out the window as I made for our nearby crew car and we screeched away as fast as we could.

In a matter of seconds, the kids throwing stones had become men with guns and I wasn't sticking around to find out who might win.

❝ Revenge . . . It's the only thing I think about ❞

They were so young with so little remorse and it was scary. Luckily, the fight had ended with nobody seriously injured, so Mark asked to finish the conversation and I agreed. I met Mark and the Vatos less than an hour later as they walked us through their corner of the township. As we made our way through the streets, kids ran at the boys cheering and waving. Women stopped and patted them on the backs as they passed.

To their neighbours, the Vatos were heroes and I couldn't understand why. Mark beamed proudly. 'Everyone around here knows us, because we protect them, and the things we've done to save them.' Idolised by everyone, the teenage gang were celebrities and they knew it.

Mark wanted us all off the streets as the rival gang had threatened to retaliate in Vatos territory. I followed the boys along a narrow walkway into a small shack as Mark continued to educate me on their world and just how much he'd been through, while cradling a small knife.

With some sort of reprisal imminent, Mark advised me to leave as it wasn't safe for me in the township. I challenged him about his own safety but Mark saw his wellbeing and future as out of his own hands. With no fear of death, the boys saw themselves as soldiers, but the more we spoke, the less convinced I became. Their age started to show and the idea of not backing down in front of the pack was clear. They were scared, just like everyone else, and through a combination of factors out of their control they'd ended up on the frontline tackling the violent end of the darkest of circumstances.

Stripping off his shirt, Mark showed me his tattoos and scars. He had more stab wounds than ink as a victim of twenty-eight stabbings. The severed nerves in his back caused him to limp, but he saw it as part of his journey. He had several scars around his heart as he'd been stabbed in the same area time and again. Believing he'd survived for one reason, Mark looked right into me and said, 'To get my revenge . . . It's the only thing I think about.'

My last night saw me back in the ambulance with Ata. We picked up a young woman in the first stages of labour who'd collapsed on the side of the road. As the ambulance pulled in, I noticed we'd arrived at a different section of the hospital. It was the first time I'd seen the maternity ward. The mood was calm and Ata was in good spirits, laughing and joking as he wrapped up his shift for the night.

Standing in the maternity ward, surrounded by newborn babies, it felt like the first time in days I'd seen anything positive and life-affirming in Khayelitsha. It was a reminder of the beauty that existed in a township that seemed more attuned to pain, fear, violence and death.

CHAPTER 7
MINORS AND MODELLING

Before puberty reared its spotty head, I was acutely aware of a fact that most of my male friends came to realise much later in life. For some, it came when they had their first real relationship, for others it was marriage. For me, I was literally a kid when it became very clear that the people in charge are and always have been women.

With two older sisters and two younger, I still face constant reminders of my place on the sibling totem pole of power. The minute my two younger sisters arrived, I lost all privileges as baby of the family. Overnight I'd become a big brother with a long list of responsibilities that would forever change my relationship with women.

My role as big brother demanded maturity, but my late teens and early twenties saw a flurry of short-term girlfriends and stupid spending contradict the example I was supposed to set. My younger sisters would never question my emotional immaturity, but my big sister Cerisse would take pleasure in calling me on my bullshit and challenging me on my part in any relationship breakups.

Now in my early thirties, with a history of platonic and romantic relationships to reflect on, the ones that didn't work out always came down to the same crap. I seemed to have a talent for ignoring the gulf between what I'd say and what I'd do. As I'm sure you can imagine that went down brilliantly with girls I'd date, but thankfully I'm yet to have the windows on my car smashed in. But there's still time . . .

In my twenties – my first full decade of independence – my location, lifestyle and career constantly put me in the mix with working models. I dated and was in mini relationships with models, and, if I am honest, messed some of them around quite a lot . . . Appearances alone would say their beauty made them members of a super race, but, call it fearlessness or blind stupidity, somehow I wasn't intimidated. From music video girls (the Instagram models of that time) to high fashion models, my inexperience and deliberate distance allowed me to freely jump from one girl to another totally unaware of how my behaviour might hurt.

I understood that the world these girls belonged to was a million miles from my own. Just like the models I dated, I earned a living in front of the camera, but their working world carried pressures bigger than I could even begin to imagine.

As a kid, I saw the camera as my chance to show off; I'd pose for photos and gurn or smile on cue. Unluckily for me, just as my teenage angst and paranoia about my looks kicked in, I found myself front and centre during promotional photo shoots for the TV shows I was in. The zits and bad haircuts seemed to find a way on screen every time. By the way, this isn't a signal for you to go looking for the archived proof. Yes, it does exist and, yes, it is horrendous.

Thankfully, during the earlier years of my career, the photo shoots where I found myself under very specific direction were only a tiny part of the job. And I was never made to change my appearance, unlike some of the young girls I'd act or present with. Changing a hairstyle, minimalising the appearance of curves and softening an accent were just some of the demands I'd hear suggested by thoughtless execs. Considering the fact that I was still trying to figure out who I actually was, had I endured that level of scrutiny, I have no idea how I would have turned out, although I have a sneaking suspicion it wouldn't have been positive. While I was having the time of my life interviewing pop stars and seeing the world with work, the girlfriends I'd come home to would never want to speak about theirs. I always thought I knew why, but I was so wrong.

When my team and I were in discussions about making the follow-up to *Extreme South Africa*, Russia in all its uniqueness was a perfect fit. I was positive about all of the potential episodes and stories we were due to cover, but part of me expected the *Teen Model Factory* film to be the least challenging.

With two of the shows on Russia dealing with nationalism and homophobia, my worry was that a film on young models would be lightweight by comparison. Nationalism and homophobia are global issues that remain firmly in the public's consciousness. The Russian relationship with both is well documented, and it felt like a certainty that we'd deliver a hard-hitting film on either topic.

The Russian connection to modelling was something I was aware of, as so many successful faces had emerged from the country over the years. I'd always wondered what was behind the long list of talent finding its way onto the world stage. That being said, I initially didn't place this film in the same league as the first two. I feared we'd be ending the series on a softer note. I knew there would be a wealth of new information to dissect, but didn't think so much of what I'd encounter would speak to my upbringing and personal relationships with women.

This project didn't start anywhere near what was slowly becoming familiar territory. I'd left the massive cities of Moscow and St Petersburg and was boarding a tall metal train that looked like it went on forever. I was about to ride the Trans-Siberian Express – the famous railway that spans 9,000 km and crosses eight time zones. My destination was Siberia and it was somewhere I had never imagined I'd see in my lifetime.

The train rattled and swayed its way out of the station and

the endless blackness on the other side of the window quickly took hold. We were in the middle of nowhere headed to a place where, at the time we'd be shooting there, the temperature could drop as low as minus sixty degrees. I'd learnt a lot about myself during my time in Russia, but there was one thing I knew going in that only became clearer the longer I was there. I'm crap in the cold.

The thought of sleeping through most of the journey made the prospect of three days on a train tolerable. As the first night wore on, the occasional stretches of well-lit track allowed for moments to take in where I actually was. The flat white expanse we spent hours cutting through appeared endless. At fifty times the size of the UK but with around half the population, Siberia is massive and predominantly untouched.

Given our shooting schedule, the only real choice for travel into our destination was the Express. I passed people from every walk of life in the train's endless hallways, fascinated by the prospect of their stories but unable to do anything about it. No matter where I was in Russia, there was a constant reticence to speak English, even if the person I was desperately trying to connect with understood my every word.

It was like being on holiday in Paris, dealing with a snooty waiter annoyed at your pronunciation, only worse. Maybe it was the cut of my jib, or, given my most recent Russian experience, there was a good chance it might have been the colour of my skin. However, I chose to focus on those who did engage.

There was a pack of men and women from around the

world all headed to Siberia for the same reason. To find models. Packing the cafeteria carriage, a loud and upbeat international crowd of model scouts in search of new Siberian faces chatted up a storm. I met Tako from Tokyo (which sounds like I'm making it up but that was his name and where he was from, promise) who, in his short trip, was looking for girls with strong features and preferably someone young.

As someone who started working as a child, being young and employed has never seemed strange to me, but in the context of the fashion industry, I've never totally seen it as the healthiest world for a kid. Tako was looking for girls as young as thirteen as, according to him, the fact they were still growing was a bonus.

Model scout Kate was looking for young faces too as her Asian clients preferred that look. Their employers and audience clearly had different ideas to my own when it came to beauty. I'd been raised in a culture where the youngest models legally walking the catwalks of London Fashion Week were sixteen. Magazines might employ younger, but Western aspirations associated with beauty were tied to youth, definitely, not childhood.

❮ She can show her beauty, it's part of her job ❯

Political prisoners were sent to Siberia to die during Soviet times, as it was a chunk of the country offering very little beyond endless cold. Decades later, things had moved on and my first impressions completely crushed my expectations. I'd anticipated mountainous snowy nothingness, what I found was a bustling city full of tower blocks and busy streets.

The search for new faces began at our first stop. We were in the mining city of Krasnoyarsk and a large, soulless building played host to a huge open casting call. I walked into a lobby full of excitable girls buzzing around the room all lip gloss and selfies. The slightly older girls in their late teens looked stoic by comparison as they stood quietly, clearly more conscious of the scale of opportunity the day held.

Supermodel Natalia Vodianova had an international modelling career and the bank balance to match. Discovered by the side of a Russian road selling fruit, her rise to fame became a modern Cinderella story and was a tangible example of what could happen to any one of the hundreds that had showed up.

An equal mix of nerves and excitement, the girls stood in a long line for registration while those who had breezed through the process were measured and photographed. The totally awkward thing for me was that they were all stripped down to their underwear. Uncomfortable and desperate to escape, the last time I'd felt this awkward was the moment I saw my younger sister's huge bra for the first time. For some reason, I believed she'd been frozen in time on her ninth birthday, but apparently she'd grown up, had boobs and huge ones judging by the connected tents hanging out to dry on the bathroom heater at my mum's house.

The girls stood shoulder to shoulder in a line holding a piece of paper with their measurements scribbled in marker. Catching the occasional uncomfortable look from the younger, still developing girls it was obvious how hard an experience this was for the younger and less confident. I'd never felt so out of place. It was like being in the ladies' changing room at the local swimming baths with your mum and her mates from work. Everything inside was screaming, 'Get me out!'

Remember the guy on the train who had a name that sounded fake? Well Tako from Tokyo had already told me that he was looking for girls around the age of thirteen. For whatever reason, I'd neglected to really consider the fact until I'd seen it myself. These young girls wore next to no clothes and high heels. Their tiny bodies looked ever more childlike as tiny frame after tiny frame partially covered in bad bras or swimwear gave the impression of a window into teenagers playing dress-up in their mother's closet.

The atmosphere shifted, suddenly chatter died down and all the girls were standing up that bit straighter. Tigran Khachatrian had arrived. Director of Noah Models, he was responsible for putting on the cattle call and clearly had a reputation as a man to impress. One by one, the pack of international model scouts from around the world shook his hand. He was a gatekeeper and everyone in the room knew it.

I turned to see the outstretched hand of the guy in charge. Introducing himself with a softly spoken and warm demeanour, Tigran seemed to be pleased I'd arrived. I was unsure as to why he was so calm, as any camera crew in that room could paint an incredibly dark picture. Either he trusted me without even knowing me, or saw nothing untoward with the hundreds of half-naked kids I was reacting to for the first time.

Of these hundreds who'd turned up, Tigran was expecting to find only ten to fifteen girls that really could stand a chance in the international market. He described the majority as having great potential even though he'd openly admitted a tiny few would actually make it.

'Most Russian girls are like Ferraris with no engine, but when we start working with them, we put those engines in.' The man didn't come across as a creep; there didn't even seem to be an element of wanting the girls for anything other than professional purposes, but even that began to trouble me and change my take on the process as a whole.

There didn't appear to be anything untoward with the casting or the adults taking on bright-eyed children as new employees. My issue was with the commercial expectation dumped on the excited kids who'd never worked a day in their lives. The glamour and money of fashion was an obvious draw, but no time was being given to explaining the realities of the job.

I was growing increasingly uncomfortable. Everyone was there for business and nothing more. The children were told where to stand and when to speak, which they did without barely a mumble out of turn.

It was a room full of children and young teenagers, but the people in charge didn't seem too concerned about any duty of care. The occasional girl in her early twenties didn't soften the blow of my realisation that the day was about business above anything and nobody was there to piss around. I eventually started being less freaked out by the amount of skin on show, but I continued to be shocked at the number of girls fourteen and under that had showed up to be discovered.

The scouts watched quietly, scribbling away in their notebooks and taking pictures. Small two- or three-person teams from Europe, Asia and the US buzzed over Polaroids of their new discoveries. Strange as it sounds, there was a huge desire for the youngest girls from the Asian scouts. In their market, girls could work professionally from as young as twelve. They were entirely in their element, as one thing the room didn't lack was baby-faced teenagers.

Tigran described Asia as a nursery territory for those scouted, Europe as high school and America as the university. Based on how he framed the metaphor, I took the statement to be in reference to earning potential and not about fashion influence or work conditions for the girls. Clear in what he was looking for in terms of face geometry and proportions, Tigran had got selecting the girls who would find good work down to a science.

The room was full of girls trying to get the job and in any other environment they'd be handing out CVs. Here, their bodies were their CVs. Their proportions and confidence gave them a better chance of being scouted and, as the day wore on, I could almost predict what scout would go for what girl.

For the lucky few, every scout wanted them to work in their territory. For Yina, who'd brought her daughter, it was a dream come true. When she was a child, she too had dreams of being like the supermodels she'd see on TV but it never happened for her. She wore a full face of make-up and figure hugging clothes. Yina wasn't shy, but her teenage daughter seemed to be.

Yina believed the high praise her daughter was receiving was not only an achievement, but also an opportunity. I'm not a parent, but I found it difficult to watch the clearly uncomfortable younger girls stand in a room full of strangers wearing just their underwear and a pair of heels. I must have been missing something as Yina beamed with pride. Her daughter beat a room full of competition, but to do so in these conditions I still found a struggle to witness.

I had to ask about her allowing her child to wear so little in public and Yina didn't even flinch. 'She can show her beauty, it's part of her job.'

I met one of the oldest girls in the room, twenty-year-old Anya Sosnovskaya, who'd been cast by two agencies including Tigran's company Noah Models. She'd found a corner with some of the other girls and thrown on a sweater.

Some were beginning to show signs of tiredness, but for the room full of novices, it was just the beginning. Walking the line, Tigran sized up the new row of girls. Stopping the minute he spotted potential, he called forward a thirteen-year-old. Asking her to smile, he pounced on her teeth instructing her to get them fixed. She smiled and nodded but even from a distance I could see her heart breaking and her cheeks reddening with embarrassment as the entire room was watching.

I expected a drill sergeant, but Tigran wasn't barking instructions at the room of hopefuls, his style was gentle and softly spoken. He presented himself as a wise older friend, an adviser not a boss, and it worked as the scared girls softened in the palm of his hand. Explaining he'd got into the business to help young women, Tigran saw himself as some sort of facilitator. He spoke of the spiritual benefits and pride he felt in seeing his girls go on to find success (though he neglected to mention his improved bank balance that came as a result).

Okay, I really sound like the snarky British cynic right now but give me a break. I'd spent the day with a man who was clearly doing well for himself with a business that had become the go-to agency in a climate of minimal competition. His company Noah Models was huge and no other agencies came close to his reputation or ability to launch new girls. It would be remiss of me to ignore the reality of financial gain built on the tiny backs of his selected children. This was a business that worked and one that made good money for Tigran, even if in the long term, the industry as a whole didn't do so for all of the models.

Standing to make thousands in commission, for any of the scouts the signing of a model was a win. For girls like Anya, who I'd met earlier cowering beneath her huge sweater, this was exactly the sort of opportunity she'd fought for, regardless of the cut she'd lose should she make it. Tigran didn't appear to have any intentions for the girls outside of business, but my paranoia couldn't shake the chances of things not being so above board for his chosen girls once they were working alone all over the globe.

❝ If there's an opportunity to earn, why not? ❞

Anya had agreed to show me her life at home, so I ventured just an hour out of town to find snow-covered mountains as far as the eye could see. Anya lived in the vast and snowy version of Siberia I'd expected. Ovsyanka was the tiny village fenced in endless forestland she called home.

Anya had strong opinions on the benefits of her rural upbringing. She believed that living so far from any real opportunities could only strengthen one's character. Fully aware that there were more opportunities abroad, Anya now saw a better future and better life for her family in her travelling for work as a model.

Siberia is a place where doctors would make just over £400 a month, why wouldn't she want to escape and have a better life elsewhere? Anya's true passion was art and her painted canvasses covered her bedroom walls. However, she viewed a life as an artist as a dream that was out of reach. By contrast, modelling was a profession that gave her an opportunity.

'If there's an opportunity to earn, why not?' Fell from practical Anya, as I stood thrown by the sudden cynical take on her future. She'd decided what she truly wanted wasn't possible and I couldn't tell who was more jaded, the idealist in me or pragmatist in Anya?

Anya's mum put on a spread and the small centre table was stacked edge to edge with every kind of cake imaginable. We settled into the couch for my favourite past time of tea and a chat – unfortunately my focus would occasionally drift due to the selection of jams.

Home was a one-bedroom flat where mum slept on the couch and the little money coming in barely covered expenses. Anya's home may have been humble, but she was driven. Seeing her mother make the best of what little they had, I could understand why she wanted to only make the best for her family, as I too had the same oil in my engine when I realised how much my talent could do for my loved ones.

Back on the Siberian Express, I settled in for the next leg of the modelling tour that took me a further 800km to Siberia's capital city, Novosibirsk. My home for the twelve-hour journey was a small brown cabin with a fold-down bed and small nightlight. It was hardly the Ritz but it would do.

Tigran's company Noah Models ran the scouting tour and Anna Yuzhakova was his eyes and ears on the ground at every stop. It was a night train and not long after boarding, almost everyone had locked their doors and I began what was a fruitless pursuit of sleeping on a long-haul train. Running the tour for six years, Anna knew the detail and I wasn't letting her occasional yawns and clunky hints that she was tired get rid of me any time soon.

Fascinated by the idea that Siberia appeared to be the source of an endless stream of beautiful girls, I pushed Anna on what was in the proverbial water. She put it down to roots. The Ukrainian, Baltic states and Asian parts of Siberia all had left their own footprint on every family tree, leading to some of the most interesting features in the world. Anya went on to describe the common thread being height, good skin and incredible hair conditioning. Almost every girl at the first casting call had shiny thick hair down to her waist. Anna saw the mix of ethnicities as responsible.

But who was responsible for these young visions of beauty being unleashed onto the world on their own? My questions were to the point and Anna looked me right in the eye, answering with a smile and confidence the entire time. Anna explained that looking after the girls was a team effort between their company Noah Models and the agencies they'd work with.

With so many people involved, who was being paid and how much would be left for the model doing the heavy lifting? What I'd totally overlooked was the amount laid out by the agency. Anna explained that for every girl they'd send halfway around the world, they'd cover her flights, accommodation and allowances. This money would be later recouped as an advance on earnings. Should the model not make that money back, she wouldn't owe the agency, but they would know she couldn't deliver the return on investment rendering her chances as a model over and done.

The minute I'd met Tigran, I knew I'd have to ask about money, but choosing my moment would be the hardest part. Softening my voice, knowing how sensitive the question could be, I went for it. According to Anna, excluding super-models like Kate Moss and Claudia Schiffer, normal working models could earn up to $20,000 a month. That was a lot of money for any working adult, let alone a teenage girl. But that being said, should her expenses outweigh that lump sum earned, none of that 20,000 would end up in her account.

Ten hours into the train journey and I braved the loo. Surprisingly, the toilet actually wasn't too bad; it was the walk through standard class that was a culture shock. Either side of the aisle was what could only be described as bunk beds on crack. Rather than the expected bed above a bed, each side saw people sleeping in what could only be described as racks.

Four, maybe five bunks from floor to ceiling held coughing, farting and sweaty bodies. I fell about the place trying to get through the carriage on my way back to my section. Naked feet hung from every other bunk and I couldn't get out of the cheese festival quickly enough.

Waking up in the capital of Siberia, I felt as far away from the fashion and glamour of Paris as humanly possible, but glamour was exactly what was on the lips of everyone I was about to meet. Fashion had found a home here in the shape of what seemed to be an endless stream of beauty. With twenty-four model agencies and schools in Novosibirsk alone, this small city had a modelling industry, and business was good.

I met Olga, director of the Kids Modelling School, Global Russian Models. Resisting the temptation to suggest a snappier company name, I wandered in to see exactly what it was they did and what kind of girl was being taught.

The agency wasn't short of hopefuls as the posing class I walked in on had girls of all ages, the youngest being four. These girls were being taught how to walk, pose, apply make-up and diet. The endless corridors had unmarked doors all with people flying in and out, hinting at just how busy the place was. Me being the nosy clown I try my very best to be, I found what looked like their on-site studio and wandered in on a portfolio shoot for a six-year-old.

Just a generation ago this would never have happened. In Soviet times, there was no modelling industry as attitudes then saw it as anything but a respectable profession. With mindsets shifting dramatically, the shoot I was now at the back of (watching with the young model's parents) couldn't have exemplified that change better.

The girl's father said he used to see models as 'women of

easy virtue' until his wife brought him along to see what the school and industry was all about. Wanting her young daughter to have a shot, the mother had sold it to her husband as a healthy physical challenge – all about stretches and choreography classes. This sounded quite wide of the mark to me, but I was keeping schtum. The heavily made-up mum went on to explain that the stigma came from Soviet propaganda comparing it to prostitution, and that attitudes have undergone a total reversal in the minds of the majority.

Sofia and her mother were next in the studio and I watched quietly as the twelve-year-old demonstrated that she knew exactly how to work the camera. Her mother was beautiful and a former model herself. Seemingly disillusioned by the industry – contradicting Anna's strong beliefs – Sofia's mum didn't enjoy her time as a model. Unable to achieve anything like the earnings I'd been told were common, she didn't want her daughter to be in the business and struggle. But clearly buckling to the desires of her own child, the young mum was giving her kid what she so badly wanted. The young performer had asked for a birthday gift of a red Ferrari at seven and today was telling me she wanted a jeep covered in crystals. This child clearly had a very different attitude to modelling and the world of fashion when compared with her mother. For Sofia, a fashion model personified glamour, had a real career and lots of money.

It was fascinating to see the bright eye of an excited child talking about the fashion industry when only one generation ago, the country was Communist and a life in the world of camp clothes, pomp and excess was impossible.

❛ They want to be someone in life, unlike their mothers ❜

Joining us half a day after the train rolled into town, Tigran met me in a Novosibirsk café. We were in his world, which bore a stark difference to the homes of the young models I'd got to know. The café was a modern feat of architecture standing out among the surrounding dowdy Soviet buildings. It was shiny and screamed new money as young, trendy and wealthy types sipped expensive coffee.

Pulling no punches explaining the Communist way, Tigran opened up about what he felt he was saving these young women from. The Communist system essentially planned a life for its citizens. Money was small but guaranteed. Life was stable but boring. Sounding confident in the attitude of his models, Tigran asserted, 'Younger girls, they don't want that.' Things had changed especially when it came to the aims of young women. He continued, 'They want to be someone in life, unlike their mothers.'

Was he right? Had there been such a shift in just the one generation? Anya and her mother were worlds apart in their ambition, but was that individual grit and determination, or simply the generational gap showing itself in the outlook of two women from different times?

Agency Elite Stars were in town and the international scouts were too. I met Irina, a former model who'd been on the cover of several high fashion magazines and fronted campaigns for some of the biggest French fashion houses. She'd seen success and was now guiding the next wave of wannabees.

Running a class, the impossibly high-cheekboned Irina walked through poses encouraging a new move on cue shouting, 'Three, two, one, fashion.' It was brilliant. I was a little disappointed there wasn't an awful house track playing and she was being totally serious, because I was seconds away from camping it up and doing my impression of RuPaul's voice.

Her neck was impossibly long and swan-like, while her posture showed years of being fully aware of how she stood. Irina believed a good model was a good businesswoman. She maintained, 'You can have a beautiful face and a great body, but if you have nothing in your head, forget it.'

It's always awkward going to talent searches of any kind, as I dread the moment where you see the kids full of hope perform, and you know that a disproportionate number of students won't make it, compared to the few who have 'it' – whatever that is – and shine undeniably.

To my novice eyes, it was obvious who stood out based on height and bone structure alone. Both factors I assumed were essential for success in the industry, but the girls could naturally change neither. This spoke to the fact that Elite agency had 5,000 girls on their books but had only seventy working in the international industry.

One of the girls in Irina's class was Vika. She was polite and giggly. Her focus made her seem a lot older but the minute she started talking, the sweet kid who just wanted to be liked showed up. Vika invited me to her family home, which was a one-bedroom flat where she slept in the living room. It was a case of different day, same sugar-based dilemma as, just like Anya's mother, Vika's mum put on a huge spread of tea and cake. We spoke over the crazy selection of sweet things but this time I managed to remain focused. I'd grown a little. Be proud of me.

Vika was determined and wanted her career in fashion to happen but almost right away – 'You'll hear about me, I will be famous.' I loved her ambition, but quietly felt that her chances weren't great due to things beyond her control. She was sixteen and, granted, she still had time to grow but she just didn't look tall or thin enough for the scout's ideals. I'd stood with them, listened to their debates and didn't see myself as an expert by any means, but had learnt enough about what they saw as a definite no that I could now see some of those red flags in Vika.

The kid was obsessed with her weight and knew her measurements as she was constantly checking herself. Deciding that a 3cm loss from her waist would help her chances, Vika's diet consisted of buckwheat, green tea and water.

A staple of Soviet cuisine, I tried a bowl of buckwheat and it was tasteless. It smelt like a hot bowl of my least favourite cereal Weetabix. Say what you want, it might be good for you, but it never had any sugar on it, fruit in the packet, or toys in the box, so how could five-year-old me ever be a fan of Weetabix? Exactly. Rant over.

Eaten without any seasoning or sauce, Vika described the warm buckwheat as tasty, while I could only describe it as a bowl of edible depression.

❝ *Maybe I was born for this* ❞

On the twenty-second floor of a shopping mall, I found myself in another casting. This was make or break for so many young hopefuls, including Vika. By this point, I thought I might have been more comfortable in a room full of girls in their underwear but I was noticeably awkward again.

I couldn't get over how young they were. Nothing was untoward about the environment or questions and photos being taken, but my big brother reflex was on ten and my paranoia about where some of these girls might end up was all I could think about. During my time with Tigran in the swish coffee spot, he quietly touched on the horror stories of girls ending up in the sex trade or becoming escorts. He described the girls choosing to have 'older boyfriends' as young models struggling to find work, settling for careers as escorts.

It was a passing comment he didn't dwell on but it stayed with me. With all of his scouted girls working abroad and alone, how many would fall through the net? This no longer was about paranoia; there were very real dangers even if Tigran was confident his girls wouldn't fall prey to such situations.

With all of my worries shared quietly with the camera, I was the only person not excited. I was stood in a room full of hope, which threw an undeniable energy into the air. Going through so many casting calls myself, also as a kid, I knew only some of the people in the room would taste the career they were all dreaming of.

Lionel was a new face and instantly stood out. The French casting agent was looking for models for the top French fashion houses. Givenchy, Saint Laurent and Dior were just some of the fashion houses girls chosen by him could go on to work with. He was the gateway to walking at Paris fashion week and for a young girl from a small Siberian village, this was a huge opportunity.

While the younger faces and smaller frames were a high priority for the scouts from the Asian market, Lionel's criteria to walk in shows in New York, London and Paris included a minimum height of 177cm (about 5ft 7in). Apollinariya was one of the girls in Irina's posing class who'd stood out as having all of the natural attributes of a high fashion model.

She was on Lionel's radar and he had lots of questions about the young model straight away. News to me was that she'd already been to the Philippines to work and had a portfolio that was both vast and professional. In the last year, the fifteen-year-old had built a body of work that put her head and shoulders above most of the other girls in the room. Looking like a different person in every shot, her portfolio was exactly as Anna described. She was capable of being transformed into any age or style.

Smiling knowingly while stood shoulder to shoulder with visibly crushed competition, Apollinariya beamed confidence and displayed something I hadn't seen in any of the other girls. I felt like I was already beginning to sound like the casting agents as I wanted to slap myself in a moment off camera with Lionel when I couldn't help myself describe her as having 'it'. Ugh.

I pulled Apollinariya to one side and found out in a quiet chat that she'd gained a tonne of experience in her time away. When pressed on the money earned, she smiled but wouldn't reveal just how much she'd made. With the East conquered, she had her sights fixed firmly on the West, and Lionel looked like the man who could very easily make it happen. Describing herself as a natural-born leader who liked to stand out, Apollinariya knew she had something special. 'Maybe I was born for this.'

It was during this chat that I noticed that stood not too far away, watching quietly, was Vika. This casting was a day filled with potential for her and a chance to snag her big break, but all eyes were on Apollinariya. Clearly nervous, her moment came in front of the scouts. One of many faces in a line-up, she held her card at her chest shooting looks from scout to scout hoping to catch some sort of signal that they might be interested in her.

In a matter of minutes her casting was over and a new line of girls were called forward. Vika didn't receive any international interest, only advice. She was instructed to lose weight and told that her hips were a centimetre too wide, while, close to tears, the sixteen-year-old girl stood awkwardly in a white underwear set and a pair of heels she hadn't quite learned how to walk in yet.

Suffering from back condition osteochondrosis, Vika had serious pain issues and a stay in hospital had caused her to gain weight. She claimed the heels she stood in at that moment were only making the problem worse, and it was obvious that her optimism had totally gone. I asked her to take her heels off to give her back the break it deserved, and in a moment the drop in height and posture made the glassy-eyed girl look like a kid again.

One of the 90 per cent who didn't get picked, Vika left early as her time in the running was over.

For Anya, that same night presented a huge opportunity. She'd made it to the finals of reality TV show *Siberia's Next Top Model*. Tyra, you've got a lot to answer for!

I was back in another shopping centre as the final episode was being filmed in front of a live audience. I'd been invited to be a judge by Tigran, who wasn't massively clear about his involvement, or what I would have to do, but judging by the way in which everyone shook his hand, he had a lot to do with the show.

Anya was announced on stage and came strutting out to the end of the catwalk with a strong hair flick and confident smile. As one of twenty-eight finalists, she'd made it through twelve knock-out rounds already. This was a real competition but felt more like a beauty pageant than a model search. Considering the cold business-like reality of the castings, I was left wondering how much of the event was just for the TV cameras and not the industry.

Sat next to Tigran on the judging panel, I tried my best not to be distracted by the huge embroidered rose on his ice white shirt and focus on the task at hand. I was actually being given a real vote and I wanted to vote honestly. I was handed a stack of paper with photos and short biographies of all the finalists. Thankfully it was in English but I was still totally lost. I wasn't a bloody expert. Who the hell was I to have a say on who'd actually have a career as a model?

I tried to be as objective as possible but I couldn't help but feel biased towards Anya. I felt like I knew her and how much winning would mean. So much of the competition was about theatrics, but the international scouts were all in attendance too and their ongoing search offered a second chance to the TV show finalists who might have been overlooked at the castings. I had no choice; I selected Anya in every category. If my one vote meant anything, it might have helped her get closer to achieving what she so badly wanted.

It was finally the moment where winners were announced

and, unlike the TV shows I'd seen, literal contracts for work in Europe and Asia were being handed to the lucky winners one by one. Tigran stepped up to the stage to announce some of the bigger prizes, one of which was a contract to work in America.

Anya's name was announced and a huge electric guitar sting kicked out of the speakers as she walked up to collect her prize. The applause was loud but furious from her mother who watched on full of tears. I found her amid the chaos backstage to discover she'd been offered work in both India and California. Anya was understandably over the moon.

What's a parent to do in this situation? With no clue as to what awaits them, grant their child the wish to try for a better life and fantastic career while waving them off alone and on a plane to China aged fifteen? Or refuse to let them go and risk killing their dream knowing they'll resent you for life? It's not a decision that I envied them having to make.

Watching the film back, I couldn't help but see so much of my own journey in that of the young girls with huge dreams at the beginning stage of their careers.

My passion for what I was doing obviously played a huge part in my drive and focus even at a young age. My desire to make it in TV wasn't just about doing something I loved and definitely wasn't ever about being famous. It has always been about helping my family. I came from humble beginnings, and embarked on a career where nothing is guaranteed, but I only truly understand the inevitable fears my parents had as I become more mature myself.

It might not happen for Anya or Vika, but based on what I'd seen in Siberia I could understand why so many young girls stood in those endless queues to fight for their dreams.

CHAPTER 8
MAKINGS OF A MAN

I've never seen myself as particularly macho. In fact, overthinking just how manly I may or may not be has, in the past, sent me down a wormhole of incredibly harsh self-evaluation. Should I spend so much time exfoliating? Does that one time I considered eyebrow shaping make me soft? Thankfully, cutting myself some slack allowed me to realise that what it means to be a man today is dramatically different from what was once expected.

With synonyms like strapping, powerful and robust, the word masculine feels like a hell of a lot to live up to. From a young age I was told I had to be tough. Boys don't cry and being encouraged to 'man up' was a consistent instruction contradicted weekly in drama class. In that environment, I was outnumbered by girls and what I felt was just as important as what I thought. In school, or under the watchful eye of my stepfather at home, showing emotion was a sign of weakness, whereas in drama class, I'd be commended the more I'd give.

Thinking about it, I'm embarrassingly jealous of today's ten-year-old boy. The kid has no idea how broad the examples of manhood he'll experience actually are. The influences on his formative years won't be one note, and he has no clue how lucky that makes him. I say this, as I grew up an era where being a man was more about brawn than anything else.

I'd go as far as saying you could argue the shift in looking at our movie stars alone. My action heroes were monosyllabic and all muscle; today the world's biggest action hero said publicly, 'The most important thing I can do with my daughter is lead our life with love.' Ladies and gentlemen, Dwayne 'The Rock' Johnson.

Yes, there has been progression in the mainstream when it comes to attitudes towards gender roles; masculinity and femininity. But online, the unfortunate rise of outrage culture can sometimes puncture holes in behaviour we all denounce. When a famous billionaire TV star is publicly calling women he doesn't like fat pigs, dogs, slobs – and let's not forget his 'grabbing them by the pussy' – have we become so desensitised to the objectification of women that a man can say all of the above and still become the leader of the free world?

In talking to friends – some fathers, others single and dating – what became clear was that being a man today could mean so many things. In every conversation had, the broad spectrum of definitions came from the men themselves, not gender norms.

In a time when the average bloke can manscape his fuzzy boy bits, watch football down the pub and discuss the best place to buy skinny jeans at half time, how men define themselves is without doubt in a new place. But where are we when it comes to how men see women?

Upon news that *Extreme UK* had been commissioned, I was selfishly excited about the prospect of making another series but this time not having to leave the country. I'd get to sleep in my own bed for the majority of the shoot and have my nearest and dearest close by to help make sense of those more difficult days on camera.

The *Men at War* film would prove to require lots of pots of tea, as almost every night after filming, I found I wanted to talk though some of the most infuriating conversations I'd had with contributors and have some healthy conversation with real people.

Shot fifty years after women began marching towards equal rights, the film aimed to cover the battle of sexes moving into entirely new territory. The idea that so many young men had begun to feel overlooked and judged was my in. I was blissfully unaware of the can of worms I'd open the minute I ventured online, as endless links to websites from around the world were just the beginning. There was a new generation of young guys my age and younger who believed that the true victims of sexual discrimination were now men.

❛ British girls look old, they look like they've been working in a factory or coal mine ❜

It was a sunny Sunday in London and I was due to shoot all of twenty minutes from my place in the south west of the city. My barber Mark was over the moon as he knew I'd be on screen with a fresh trim, unlike the international shoots where my grown-out mess would result in him getting told off for allowing me to look so unkempt. Yes, my relationship with my barber features just as much nagging as my relationship with my mum. Only I see him more. Sorry mum.

I was in a black cab on my way to a lecture in Kensington; I was apprehensive, as I was sure there'd be elements of the day ahead I'd find funny, but I was equally as sure about my presence stirring up paranoia in some of the attendees. Shooting in the UK had its bonuses but as with anything good, there's always the small print. It was 2015 and at this point, anyone who'd followed (or Googled) my career had seen a huge gearshift as I was suddenly connected to documentary as opposed to music and entertainment.

I'd probably just found my way onto the radar of most of the room as my documentaries were premiered on the BBC's youth channel BBC Three, but were also being repeated on their biggest platform with the biggest audiences, BBC One. To those who were new to me on screen, I only made documentaries, and my Russia series had recently aired. My worry was a presumption being made that I was there to tell a similar story starring them as the bad guys.

Unsure of what to expect, I bounded up the stairs and into the grand building. American author and blogger Roosh V was holding the lecture for his growing UK fan base. Making his name as a pick-up artist writing detailed how-to books on getting laid, Roosh had self-published several books. These included gems like *Bang Ukraine*, *Bang Iceland*, *Bang Poland*, *Bang Lithuania*, *30 Bangs* and, my personal favourite, *Don't Bang Denmark*.

Outside of wanting to ask why Denmark wasn't worth banging, I needed to see for myself why so many people saw the man as hateful and misogynistic. Saying things online like 'British girls look old, they look like they've been working in a factory or coal mine,' I understood the outrage, but he wouldn't say such things out loud in public. Surely?

❛ Women are no longer trained to submit ❜

The London lecture was one of many stops on a world tour but, if his website was to believed, the guru wasn't expecting the event to be particularly straightforward. Roosh's website advertised the talks, but failed to detail any venue addresses. Openly explained as a precaution, the aim of revealing a venue last minute was to prevent feminists protesting outside. With the London talk titled 'The State of Man' covering what

Roosh described as 'The paradox of modern women', I got the impression what was to be discussed could have more depth than simply pick-up lines.

Once inside, my fears of paranoia were proven justified, as almost every man in the audience was nervous about the camera. I experienced a first with the entire room declining permission to appear on camera, leaving us with a room full of blurred faces when the final cut went out on TV.

Roosh arrived and a queue of fans quickly formed. One by one they shook his hand as he engaged, got close and answered questions. Forgetting my manners, I completely jumped the line and went in for a hello. Roosh was tall, dark and very hairy. The man had a full beard greying in parts and wore an intense stare shadowed by dense eyebrows. He was watching me closely, but warmed as my tone was conversational and my genuine interest at what he would cover was obvious.

I was intrigued by his world, what the day might hold and who Roosh V was outside of the sexual exploits I'd read about in *Bang Ukraine*. Admittedly, my interest was possibly higher than it should have been as, in 2005, like most of my mates I'd snapped up a copy of a book that would apparently change the life of any horny young man. That book was *The Game* by Neil Strauss. Advertised as a non-fiction romp through a Hollywood-based society of pick-up artists, investigative reporter Strauss exposed a world every young man wanted to be a part of.

I was fascinated by the pick-up tips shared on every page.

Stories of Hollywood actresses and models falling into bed with normal guys blew my mind. Of course I was excited, I was a man-child who didn't know any better. The pursuit of another bedpost notch helped by a book of shortcuts seemed like the ultimate cheat code. Thankfully I quickly grew out of emulating Strauss and the characters I'd read about.

My balloon of enthusiasm once pumped with the expectation that Roosh could deliver a lecture as entertaining as Neil Strauss's book was slowly deflating. Today wouldn't be that kind of party. It was a decade since *The Game* was published and Roosh V may have begun his journey as a pick-up artist, but a few minutes in his presence and it was clear he'd developed into something else entirely.

Roosh explained why he had such a large British following and I couldn't help listening closer than normal. As he spoke, it became clear he occasionally had to mask a minor speech impediment. He'd stammer the occasional word and my mind whirred. The pop psychology diagnosis would quickly point to a ridiculed, stammering child out to get his revenge on the girls who once laughed at him. I hoped there was more to his motivations than the obvious and the more he spoke, the clearer the picture became.

Roosh believed it was his job as an outsider to deliver the truth to his British following, as hate speech laws in the UK were something he was unafraid of. That following had packed out the room and were now jammed shoulder-to-shoulder, row after row in the large conference space. Men of every race, aged from their early twenties to a few in their fifties filled the plastic seats. This wasn't a room of angry nutters, they all appeared to be normal guys. The waiting crowd filled the air with excitement as our conversation ended and Roosh took to the stage.

Speaking slowly and softly, he was measured and thoughtful. Every word was considered and delivered with a calm confidence. He jumped right into men's rights and laws that hinder the modern guy. Dropping gems like 'Women and gays are seen as superior to straight men', and 'All of you here are seen as rapists', one after the other, the entire room nodded in agreeance and I wondered if I was the crazy one.

Then Roosh opened the talk out to the floor, and things quickly got weirder. The mic was passed around with everything from long-winded statements to praise directed at Roosh. It landed in the hands of a concerned father, a quietly spoken man in his forties who took the mic to ask for advice on the daughter he was raising. Worried about the examples she was surrounded by, he asked, 'What am I gonna do to stop her becoming the worst of what we see today?'

Quickly responding, Roosh took things in a direction I wasn't expecting: 'You should give her a man to marry at a young age. Eighteen. At least when she's thirty, you'll have three or four grandkids. Or she's gonna work in a job, one bad boy after another ... Many of you are going to use her ...' Roosh laughed and pointed at his audience who laughed too, while the concerned father sat in silence.

I couldn't believe what was being said. The talk couldn't be further from dating tips; the lecture and Q&A seemed to be driven by the shared belief that for long-suffering men, feminism is the root of all modern evils. 'Women are no longer trained to submit' and 'Women are being applauded and encouraged to look like fat outer space cyborgs' were just some of the other nuggets of wisdom that fell from Roosh's lips without a flinch.

The mic found its way into the hands of a young Asian man who asked about my thoughts on what had been discussed. The room was silent and every word I was about to say I knew would be dissected. I could feel the tension in the room, but it quickly disappeared the moment I spoke with a conversational tone. I didn't shy from my feelings, and was forthcoming with my pick-up trick expectations, versus the cold reality of a couple of hours spent solely on masculinity.

Roosh was more interested in my minor level of TV fame being the perfect leverage to sleep with as many women as I want. The room exploded into laughter as that appeared to be a huge interest for them also.

Roosh was in control of websites that touched over one million people monthly: his message was out and his audience was growing. Talking to a couple of men in the audience once the talk had ended, similar themes kept coming up. The idea that men were 'losing ground' was a genuine fear, with feminism described as a fashionable cause. For a room full of men who wanted to meet women, what seemed consistent was how little they trusted them.

Leaving the group, my biggest worry was due to the spread

of men I'd seen. What was clear was that there was no particular type who subscribed to the views of a man like Roosh V. I met men who were frustrated and felt powerless in a world where women were apparently superior. I walked away thrown by how unaware I was; men of all ages and backgrounds saw the world through the same lens as Roosh and what he believed was much more commonplace than I could ever have imagined.

❝ My mum's not been offended by anything I've put out there ❞

In my early twenties I wasn't a million miles away from the majority of the audience I'd met at the talk. I'd wanted to meet women and I'd wanted guidance, but what I'd seen was something else entirely. So where does being the quintessential lad end and misogyny begin?

I ventured to a south-west London comedy club to watch funny man Daniel O'Reilly perform as his popular 'lad humour' character, Dapper Laughs. It was all blow jobs and boobs and the crowd of young men and women lapped it up.

O'Reilly had lost his TV show after being filmed at a similar gig making a joke about rape: the character was dropped by the mainstream channels, forcing the comedian onto DVD and to earn a living on the live circuit. Supported by hours of at times offensive lad humour, the character was branded a misogynist and TV wouldn't touch him with a barge pole.

'If I say something on stage and someone goes out and does

it, they're screwed in the head not me.' Fully aware of where his brand of humour sat, O'Reilly saw his act as being the comedy equivalent of normal blokes on a building site. He didn't see the female fans as a surprise, citing the media as responsible for any outrage he'd dealt with. 'My mum's not been offended by anything I've put out there, because she knows I'm taking the piss out of men.'

As uncomfortable as it might have been for O'Reilly to admit, he was voicing offensive, misogynistic ideas to thousands of impressionable followers. They might have been presented as jokes, but given the age of his following, the 'Dapper' character freed them to do the same.

This was a man telling jokes while separating himself from the attitude behind the punch lines. But what happens when the man with a mic isn't a comedian, but is publicly saying things that might cause utter disgust?

❛ Women's issues are being dealt with; men's, not so much ❜

Speakers' Corner in London's Hyde Park is famous for bringing out the crazies. It's an amazing afternoon worth spending walking through the soapbox-mounted shouty types exercising their rights to freedom of speech. A crowd was forming around what looked like a very different kind of speaker. The guy barking at the crowd might be wearing a suit and tie, but he looked like a kid.

Eighteen-year-old Josh from Essex was a blogger and You-Tuber throwing up content on gender politics and men's issues. Motivated by a feeling of there not being enough young voices speaking up for men, Josh claimed, 'People don't know what men's issues are.' The guy spoke a million miles a minute and was difficult at times to keep up with.

Josh felt like someone with so many facts and stats stored in his clearly vast brain, he almost couldn't get them out quickly enough. His rapid delivery coupled with his 'kid wearing his banker dad's get-up for a laugh' outfit made Josh fascinating to watch. He looked like the eighties US TV cartoon version of Dennis the Menace. But his baby face was at odds with him sounding like he'd done speed after swallowing Wikipedia for breakfast.

Josh rattled, 'We've got the minister for women and equalities here in the UK, we've got the European Parliament Committee on Women's Rights and we've got UN Women. We have no comparative organisations for men. So I'm pretty confident women's issues are being dealt with; men's, not so much.'

❝ For the love of god please don't show your faces! ❞

Roosh V and his world tour of talks and seminars had rolled on to Canada, where his visit had become quite the news story. He was berated online by Canadian opposition and faced vocal opposition wherever he went. I wanted to explore those that supported him further but ended up coming across something called the Manosphere.

Described as an informal network of blogs and websites, the Manosphere focused on issues relating to men and masculinity, often in opposition to feminism. This network covered sites dedicated to those interested in pick-up tips, men's rights activism and a group I'd never heard of, referring to themselves as Men Going Their Own Way, or MGTOW for short.

At Roosh's seminar, feminism continually came up but was never presented in a positive light. I've always seen feminism as something only ever intended to help women, and for so many young men online to vehemently oppose it seemed bizarre. With practically every commentator or content creator operating under a fake name, it grew testing to unpick the online personas as I went in search of a broader picture.

One man didn't seem scared to put himself out there at all, he was internet famous and appeared to be some sort of a hero in almost every chat room or blog. His name was Milo Yiannopoulos.

We met at a time when he was slowly working his way up the controversy ladder here in the UK. Now famous for being the alt-right shit stirrer that fell from grace, I met a different Milo to the man who today is both loved and hated by millions around the world. This was before the gig at Breitbart and before the million-dollar lawsuits.

I was excited to finally have a conversation with someone

happy to appear on camera and explain what the Manosphere actually was.

Describing the group of men as dissatisfied with the way the world is headed, he believed a great motivator for so many was the idea of a man's role as provider becoming diluted. Boiling down the glut of information online, Milo was able to humanise the Manosphere. As far as he was concerned, this was fundamentally a group of men opposing far left politics that had somehow become tied up with feminism. Leaving the conversation feeling that little bit clearer, the last thing I expected was the louder voices from the community to have branded me as an enemy.

'For the love of god please don't show your faces,' rung out from one of the video blogs urging others not to appear on camera. The belief was that I was out to throw MGTOW and everything it stands for under the bus. I hadn't even been shooting for a week! Totally out of my depth and in an entirely new world, I decided to make a YouTube video of my own. The idea was to record a call-out to anyone in the community who felt comfortable to educate me on what the group was truly about.

Staying online, I decided to take a look at Josh's video blogs and wasn't entirely surprised by the speed he was able to crash through sentences. The bombshell in his video feed was that he started so young. In some of the earlier vlogs he was notice-ably younger and with his mouth fenced in braces while moving at light speed, the light catching his choppers was a sight to behold. The more recent clips were stunningly extreme in nature and in comparison with the measured, fact-based Josh I met on his stepladder wearing a terrible tie, this was someone else.

'The best way to discuss rape and the chances of it happening is to take the emotional element out of the question, 'cos that's why feminists are shitty at discussing rape.' Online, Josh pulled no punches, but what was the reasoning behind such deep-seated views?

He still lived with his mum and dad in a suburban cul-de-sac that was a perfect snapshot of middle-class Britain. Josh greeted me at the door in a crisp blue shirt looking more like a politician than the spotty teenager I was at his age. Walking me up to his room, the loft space held all the tells of a teenager in residence. A busy bookshelf and band posters were supported by the expected half-made bed. Publicly he was a middle-aged man in a teenage shell, behind closed doors he appeared to be every bit the average kid.

Perfect hair and teeth to match, Josh (minus his braces) was camera ready and talked me through his set-up of a camcorder, tripod and script. Prepped to record part one of his 'Drunk Sex Series', Josh walked me to the spare room which doubled as his studio. It was one of those moments where I tried not to take the piss and failed miserably, as the family who'd owned the property previously had made the room up for their baby girl. The pink butterfly wallpaper and a flower-covered lampshade felt like a total mismatch for the type of content he created.

Josh had set up to record a video on how men could be unfairly accused of rape. The whole thing was made even more surreal by the fact I was sat watching on a shiny pink cushion. The drunk sex vlog was driven by a think piece he'd read online. An instant red flag, I called into question his motivations.

Unafraid to speak out, Josh had all the issues clearly explained in his script but in conversation failed to have any real reasoning as to why he needed to share his views globally. Having spent the best part of a decade speaking to activists all over the world, meeting one so young and active was refreshing. What I wrestled with was his inability to articulate a genuine motivation.

Describing the majority of faces in the men's movement as those who'd suffered a trauma such as painful divorce or sexual violence, Josh was aware he was unlike most other men making their voices heard online. His ambition was to become a men's issues speaker or join a think tank, but I wasn't sure if he was being entirely honest with me or himself. Talking over a cup of tea, Josh explained he had an upper hand over most of his older peers as his lack of personal experience meant he wasn't coming at an issue from an emotional standpoint.

His arguments were grounded in logic, but he was battling for reasons he couldn't articulate making no sense to me. He had everything to say on an issue, but couldn't tell me why. Considering he could be a medallist in the Can't Shut Up Championships, it felt as if he was playing with important themes because they fascinated him. But should his interest fold, it sounded like he'd move on to something else entirely.

I liked Josh and saw the eighteen-year-old come to the fore the minute we stopped rolling. Meeting a few of his mates at a local pub, he sipped beer and made bad jokes. He knew how to unplug and, in so doing, I grew to believe the Josh I'd seen online was a performance.

His beliefs as to how women behave were based almost entirely on the experiences of other men he'd read about online. To form such strong opinions without living even some of his adult life felt like a waste, regardless of how much he professed to know what he was doing.

Back online, my video calling for someone from MGTOW to come forward was receiving an incredible response, only one I wasn't hoping for. It was an active comments section with people attempting to one up each other on how creative they could be while insulting yours truly. My favourite from the highlight reel was 'Fuck off you BBC poodle' which did make me laugh, but unfortunately the comments weren't just ridiculous, they were also racial.

'Now I get why Queen Victoria got rid of slavery before America did' stood out as pretty uncalled for, but the real message was loud and clear. I wasn't going to get to anyone from the MGTOW community and they'd made sure I knew about it. I'd said nothing negative about the group publicly and had just made one video calling for interaction. If this was the response I was getting, what would happen to someone calling out the Manosphere experience, especially if that someone was female?

Journalists like Laurie Penny have endured attacks online that bordered on the criminal. Given what I'd learned and that she has published two books on feminism, it's not surprising she'd been targeted. Bomb threats and pornography with her face pasted into hard-core scenes were just two examples of what Laurie had been sent since writing about the Manosphere. Penny believed she was targeted online along with any other woman who writes negatively about the community to silence and shut her down.

Putting it down to frustration and emotion powering some of the more offensive behaviour, Laurie saw their feelings as valid but not their actions. The darker end of the spectrum was responsible for some of the harassment Laurie had dealt with. That dark corner of the Manosphere was apparently patrolled by trolls.

In 2013, a campaign to commemorate Jane Austen by adding her likeness to the ten-pound note resulted in a Twitter onslaught directed at the female campaign leaders. Becoming front-page news, the story went national and some of the culprits ended up behind bars.

The amount of hate online had to be coming from somewhere, and the where-and what-fors were perfect questions for

Milo. Meeting for a coffee by the Thames, looking back on what was (I'm sure even he'd agree) a badly dressed opinion machine that couldn't stop smiling, I can't believe what he'd go on to become. *New Statesman* would go on to call Yiannopoulos 'flashy, provocative and steeped in misogyny'. The man I met held some challenging views but came across as at least having the ability to appear objective.

Milo found it ridiculous that people could be jailed merely for tweeting. It made him laugh. Fobbing off the threats Laurie had received online as typical journalistic bait and switch, he saw her reaction as uncalled for. 'The extent to which free speech has evaporated in this country is amazing.' But I'd never seen violent threats as free speech; to me a threat is a threat.

Believing men now couldn't engage in an argument in the public sphere without fearing the loss of their jobs, Milo saw men as becoming increasingly terrified to speak out.

❛ *No means no, until it means yes* ❜

With Milo's words still fresh in my mind and so much more experienced within the Manosphere, I tracked down Roosh V who had moved to Poland as he'd had enough with American women. 'They cut their hair short. They're so lazy to maintain long hair they make themselves ugly on purpose.' Roosh now called a small Polish university town home. It was quiet, cheap and full of female students.

Flicking through some of his writing, Roosh's books weren't just a 'how to' on picking up women, they read like a guide to getting arrested for sexual assault. 'No means no, until it means yes' jumped off the page as I stared in horror. These paperback books were available globally and thousands were buying them. Thinking about the young men who might read his stories and be inspired, I found myself getting angry.

On his website, Roosh had written a piece titled 'How to Stop Rape', which caused outrage around the world. His million visitors a month had shared his blog but when mainstream media discovered his writing, the universal reaction was disgust.

Writing that those in charge should 'Make rape legal if done on private property'. Roosh doubled down, 'I propose the violent taking of a woman not punishable by law when done off of public grounds.' I was repulsed. This was no longer bravado or a pick-up artist throwing around crude clues to get women into bed, this was a man with a huge platform and an audience apparently justifying rape.

The more I read of his work, the more books like *30 Bangs* and others in the collection felt as though they were fulfilling some other darker need. His work wasn't about making young men feel more confident or encouraging a sense of value, his work was essentially saying that women had none.

During the turbulent Canadian leg of his tour, the mayors of Montreal and Toronto had attempted to ban Roosh as his article on legalising rape went viral. Tour complete, he'd returned home and agreed to have me over for one final conversation.

I was greeted warmly at the door to his apartment. The first stop on my tour of his flat was the bedroom where he excitedly pointed out the 'Your face will be blurred in any video production' laminated sign he'd taken from the entrance to his talk from our first shoot day. The sign was now stuck above his bed's headboard. Classy.

The apartment was large, containing only essentials, screaming single life. The fridge was half empty but a mini bottle of supermarket Champagne was on stand-by should a lady make an appearance.

❛ How dare you come to Canada ❜

Describing himself as still recovering from the drama that was the Canadian leg, Roosh knew his article was the main cause of the resistance he faced, but described the piece as satirical. Explaining away his proposed new rape legalisation as an absurd notion, he claimed the piece was intended to encourage women to take care of themselves more. I didn't for one second believe that was his intent, and I think even Roosh was surprised at just how offended people were and how many people ended up reading the piece.

He saw himself as a victim of a smear campaign, saying the media painted him as a rape advocate. Resentful of his situation, Roosh didn't take any ownership in the way the piece was taken; he was more excited to show me a video of an attack he'd experienced in Canada.

'This is what happens when you give females choice, they choose to do this.' A busy bar filled the screen and a woman threw her drink over the head of Roosh V who was wearing a longhaired wig for some reason. Other girls followed suit as he disappeared out the bar and into the street. Screams of 'How dare you come to Canada' were backed with various insults hurled in his direction. Following him all the way to his hotel, the pack in the video had grown and Roosh was facing the real-world reaction to his writing.

Making the disappointingly predictable censorship and freedom of speech argument, he saw the Canadian reaction as hypocritical. 'My goal as a writer is to make sure that my ideas spread far and wide.' Despite the global uniformity of outrage, Roosh saw himself as persecuted, showing no ownership in the dangers of sharing with his huge following frightening ideas regarding rape. Totally disconnected from just how offensive his writing was, I worried his lack of responsibility would only lead to more of the same.

Given the short space of time I'd spent with the man, I doubted his message could progress, as unlike Josh this wasn't an act. This was who Roosh V was and that wasn't going to change.

As a teenager I was hungry for someone to follow even if I didn't realise at times I'd look in the worst of places. That desire for leadership wasn't unique to me, it's something innate in us as young men. The Manosphere in all of its permutations was providing role models, albeit an entirely different kind to the ones I might agree with.

Leaving Poland, my worry was that a growing army of young men were desperately searching for something and finding it in a mess of websites and dangerous leaders. I felt that, in reality, they needed someone to show them that being defensive and angry could do nothing beyond hindering their lives, particularly when it came to their relationships with women.

I survived the challenges of navigating that change from youth to adult life because I was surrounded by healthy examples of adulthood. Everything from women to work made more sense because of the men I chose to look up to. To go through those testing years of change and growth with a guide whose worldview was massively skewed due to his own inadequacies or issues, chances are I might have wound up with a few of my own.

That isn't to say I don't have my fair share of 'stuff', we all do, but I can say with total confidence I own mine and, more importantly, I know who's responsible for it. Me.

CHAPTER 9
CLOSE TO HOME

Pretty much every day people who want to talk to me stop me in the street. Unfortunately, more than I'd care to admit, their first question can be, 'Which one are you again?' Once answered, they're often keen to talk about my work. I'm usually asked about the on-screen moments that proved challenging, quickly followed by 'How do you choose the films you make?'

When an idea isn't originated by me or created in a brainstorm, incoming ideas trigger the same two questions every time. Firstly, is it good? And secondly, why me? If the idea passes this two-tier system, we're in business. When it came to making the *Extreme UK* series, I pushed to make a film about being a British ethnic minority and gay, as so many people in my life had endured the same struggles without a voice that could travel like mine.

By the time I was a teenager, the only example of gay London I'd experienced was the couple I'd worked with – Ant and Claude. My circle of friends was small and we'd always spend our time and what little money we had on the same thing. Girls. I was in and out of what was a buzzing London club scene, wing-manning my oldest mate Dan who I'd known since the age of four. Our time was spent going to the same places and doing the same thing: trying to out-funny each other in the presence of women.

Occasionally, we'd head out with a school friend of his, who for the purposes of this book we'll call Benny. Now Benny was the kind of teenager who looked like an adult in school uniform. He was massive. Put it this way, there was no question who got pubes first as Benny was shaving way before we were sixteen. Raised in an affluent north London suburb, Benny was from a wealthy family and was the first one out of our little gang to get a car.

Occasionally, we'd play a game (I'm actually ashamed to admit in hindsight) we called 'Pizza Drive By' where rich Benny would order way too many pizzas and the leftover untouched boxes would become ammunition. We'd hop in his jeep, drive the streets of north London and lean out of the convertible roof throwing entire pizzas at passers-by for no reason other than we found it funny. We were dicks.

Obviously, rich Benny had a pool, so regardless of the weather we'd have pool parties. The reason they stand out so much more than playing Pizza Drive By, is down to a game big Benny always wanted to play, specifically with me for some reason. In a time before they changed their name and long before the Rock became a star, my friends and I would watch WWF, the shiny American wrestling, on satellite TV. For some reason, Benny would always scream 'WWF' and grab at me for a wrestle in the pool. At first it was funny as I was never going to win that fight, but the more he'd grab at only me, the weirder it got.

By the time we were in our early twenties and Benny still hadn't introduced us to a single girl, Dan and I were thinking the same thing and, as it turns out, had been for years. The day finally came when Benny showed up with a girl out of the blue, introducing her as his girlfriend. As soon as they'd left, Dan and I had the 'Isn't he gay?' conversation, going over all of the moments we'd thought the same thing but said nothing. Unsurprisingly, Dan took the opportunity to piss himself laughing at all the times Benny had roped me into rough and tumble, or as he called it, the WWF game. Cheers Dan.

I'd spent my entire teens around a young gay man, but I'd never asked about what he was clearly internalising even though I saw myself as a friend. I wasn't avoiding the obvious; I was simply doing as I'd been taught. The environment I'd been raised in ensured that anything relating to homosexuality wasn't even a conversation. My stepfather had always told me that if I would ever 'decide' to be a gay, I'd be disowned.

For the record, my family isn't made up of mindless homophobes, but as West Africans born and raised in an extremely conservative Ghana, there was no conversation to be had when it came to sexuality. The culture I refer to was built on values established in the religious element of our lives. I'd never spoken to my parents about sex and my awkward teenage self definitely wasn't capable of managing a chat with a mate about his sexual preference.

I was given a second chance to be a better friend in my mid-twenties, when I saw Benny's struggle repeating itself but this time with a family member. As his story isn't mine to tell, I'll jump to the end and most important part of our journey as family. The 'he' let's call Charlie and the 'when' was 2012 in Ibiza. It was a boys' holiday and a huge group of us were staying in a villa, with every night dominated by long, impassioned debates over dinner. During a discussion about truth and transparency, Charlie decided to come out. The table of ten burst into tears and applause, embracing him in an incredible moment of support and love.

What made the moment so special was that everyone at the table bar one of us was entirely non-white, and Charlie being embraced so ardently went against everything the entire group had been taught.

Charlie and I didn't have a relationship until my early twenties and, as we'd grown closer, I'd been pretty confident he wasn't straight, but I never imposed my assumptions. That dinner table in Ibiza offered a moment where Charlie felt safe enough to share who he'd always been with a group he knew wouldn't reject him. Charlie wasn't coming out, he was coming out to us.

Returning from the holiday, I found myself coming back to what Charlie must have been going through for years. He would wear a mask to appease the people around him for fear of being cast out and he wasn't alone. The internal conflict he'd experienced I knew was happening up and down the country and I became desperate to have uncomfortable conversations pertaining to my journey and his. Culture, religion and family were at the core of so many black British homes; it had taken me a while, but I'd begun to understand the platform I now had and just how many people I could reach with subject matter I believed in.

I asked Charlie to appear in a film I wanted to make. I saw it as an incredible opportunity to share his story and potentially help so many in the process. He declined to be involved and I was disappointed but understood his reasoning. Aware of my usual audience size and demographic, Charlie knew appearing would impact his anonymity and he was right. He didn't want to be known as the gay one, he just wanted to be Charlie. I couldn't argue. I got it.

So, inspired by Charlie, Benny and all the other friends and family members I'd seen wrestle with the same issues, I went head first into filming *Extreme UK: Gay and Under Attack*. Making the film felt timely as gay parenthood, rights and marriage were all legal in the UK for the first time in history. And yet, some Brits still saw homosexuality as a decision, and as a black British man, I knew a large chunk of the community I belonged to held that view. But despite gay marriage being legalised in the UK, being black British and gay retains a stigma rendering conversation at best awkward, but more commonly, a taboo.

Now, I'm the first to call myself a massive tart as I love to get dressed up and a huge part of feeling good comes from my weekly haircut. Think of it as the make-up some can't leave home without applying. Before I go on, yes, I did just compare getting a haircut to a full face of slap. It changes the way you look in exactly the same way! We can debate this later, but I'm sure a disproportionate amount of you are thinking – weekly cuts are a little excessive? Well, in the black community that is normal. If you've ever been in or driven past a black barber-shop on a Friday night you'll see customers literally queuing out the door. Why? Because for a black man, a fresh cut for the weekend is as much a part of the weekly routine as a car wash or visit to the launderette.

Let it be known, I'm fully aware I've fallen into the trap of not feeling fresh without a crisp trim. That being said, a huge draw to the chair and those clippers on a weekly basis comes from the unrelenting banter and debates usually led by my barber Mark 'Slider Cuts' Maciver. Anything goes and every-thing is said, as the barber shop has always been a place black men can go to vent. The quintessential British pub was never a massively welcoming environment for me growing up, but the barbershop always offered a safe space to talk trash and talk loud.

So with my love for the swivel chair and the honesty it

encouraged, I headed to south London. South of the river has eternally been seen as a whole other country to those living on the other side of the water, but as someone who made the north to south jump at the tender age of fourteen, my allegiances are city wide. Moving south-east so young was a huge culture shock as the minute I settled in, I began to notice things looked a little different down south.

The largest population of black men in the UK live in south London, including me, so my desire to start a healthy conversation felt best-placed southside. With barbershops on every corner, the bustling, predominantly black area of Peckham was where I'd start.

I was meeting Max in Jowas, a black barbershop on Peckham High Street. Regardless of the fact that it was a weekday afternoon, the place was packed. Music and conversation was ear-splitting, as debates about football quickly became arguments. It felt like exactly the sort of place I should be starting. Max was in the chair getting a cut as we spoke and the evil eye his barber kept throwing my way was cold but understandable. I was distracting his customer and the haircut he was giving might suffer. He wasn't particularly happy but I pursued.

Max's parents were born in West Africa just like mine, and the life he'd led having being born and raised in London was dramatically different to theirs. Always knowing his sexuality, Max only began to accept it at eighteen. While at church, Max decided to share his situation with the pastor who subsequently outed him to his father. Once news hit, Max was kicked out of the family home and didn't speak to his dad for three years. We both found a way to smile through what was clearly a difficult story to tell, but our similar backgrounds helped a level of understanding. Max had been raised by a typical African authoritarian and stood no chance in attempting to have a conversation that wasn't one way.

Clearly having made peace with the situation, Max was balanced and open about what had happened, putting a large part of the blame on religion. I'd always felt that religious beliefs could be a block for an entire generation of parents when it came to so many modern issues. The immigrant need to maintain traditions from back home were a constant. To be of god and maintain cultural norms while desperately trying to assimilate, I saw become a conflict for so many of my friends' parents.

I'd always felt frustrated when I saw so many immigrant parents look down on anything resembling change. For the ardent set, embracing the progressive nature of their children was seen as abandoning their culture.

Max jumped out of the chair as the silent but no longer frowning barber waved over a young kid from the couch. His waiting mother had been in London for sixteen years and had roots in Liberia and Sierra Leone. I asked how she'd react should her son come out as gay, something which she admitted not fully understanding. Her first question to her child wouldn't be 'Have you always known?', and she didn't envision an outpouring of support either; her reaction would be one word. 'Why?'

Quietly listening on a nearby chair, a young guy in a thobe and kufi wore the signs of a man committed to his Islamic faith. Ibrahim's parents were born in the West Indies and between his background and religion, a stereotypical picture could easily be painted.

I hoped to be surprised by his outlook, but was quickly deflated as he explained why homosexuality was something he didn't agree with. He was respectful to Max and took his time to gently explain his feelings. 'A lot of good comes from men and women being together. Even the animals, they are like this. Even the plants . . .'

He saw sexuality as a choice and Max looked like he was about to explode, but somehow, he eloquently made a brilliant point. 'It's probably the most ridiculous thing saying that someone would choose to be gay. If you look at the world we live in, being gay has never been easy so why would anyone at any age say – I wanna be a homosexual?'

Ibrahim was a British-born, thirty-year-old black man holding views in total contradiction to his broad cultural experience growing up in the UK. I couldn't hide my surprise at some of his views. I'd always assumed that there was a gulf between the generations in terms of attitudes towards the LGBTQ community. What my time in the barbershop had clarified was that I had a lot to learn.

The attitudes held by Ibrahim were informed largely by his

faith, but I'd always been taught religion was about acceptance and love. Seven out of ten black Britons come from Christian homes and over a quarter of all churchgoers in London are black. If my personal beliefs held any truth, attending Sunday service should have been the place for answers. I arrived at a south-west London Seventh Day Adventist church, ready to listen and learn.

❝ My sermons are just me, like it or leave it ❞

All that I knew about the Seventh Day church was that they followed a literal interpretation of the Bible. Followers of the faith believed smoking, gambling and drinking were all vices, even when consumed in moderation. That was all I had in my locker when I arrived at the church, so I was open to an entirely new experience.

I was quickly introduced to Pastor Andrew Fuller, a beard-sporting, suit-wearing young black guy with an undeniable warmth about him. My bald man-child face may have given away my instant jealousy of his ability to grow a real man's beard. Even if it did, I wouldn't have known, as his smile was huge.

Preaching since the age of sixteen, Andrew had briefly abandoned the church, returning after a short hiatus packed with girls and drugs. By his own account, he had fallen into sin, only to return to god.

The brief history lesson left me desperate to know more about the man but Andrew had slightly bigger fish to fry in the shape of a packed church waiting for his sermon. I found a seat at the back and enjoyed the choir while doing the embarrassing dad thing of not fully committing to a full-on stood-up dance. Shuffling around in my seat to the beat, their voices were so soulful I almost forgot I was in the UK.

The scale, atmosphere and polish were very American and reminded me of churches I'd visited across the pond. My time in Pentecostal Ghanaian church did not look or feel like this. Where were the sweaty old ladies waving white hankies? Why wasn't anyone speaking in tongues or catching the Holy Ghost? This church was something else entirely and, as Pastor Andrew got the room warmed up, I noticed just how broad his audience was. Lots of young men and women had come to worship without their parents, almost matching in number the older couples and families. This was a young church, and Pastor Andrew's candour definitely had a lot to do with it.

Controlling the room, Andrew was all arms. His massive suit sleeves flapped with every wiggle and wave during his impassioned statements. He was straight-talking, and felt like a typical young guy being passionate and honest. 'My sermons are just me, like it or leave it,' he announced off the back of rapturous applause. He made every point with the kindly concern of a wise big brother, and had the younger congregation members in the palm of his hand.

I couldn't help but feel that he had chosen the topic of tolerance and acceptance to fit in with the documentary I was about to interview him for. Explaining that he too had fallen from grace, he couldn't look down on anyone. Andrew was speaking in a way I'd never heard from a pastor. The spectrum of ages nodded in agreement and once the service was over, I had to wait in line as everyone wanted to shake his hand.

He was clearly tired from the energy he'd not only given on stage but to every person who cornered him for conversation as they left, but I needed to bend his ear about his interpretation of scripture. We grew up in the same part of London and were similar ages, surely his attitude would be closer to mine than his older religious equivalent?

Pastor Andrew believed only heterosexual parents could raise a child successfully as he saw both parents vital to a child's growth. Andrew was without doubt progressive and with his difficult past behind him, his understanding of that next group of worshippers placed him perfectly to draw in a whole new generation. That said, the difference in his delivery may have made him different, but fundamentally his beliefs were the same. Essentially, if you were gay the message was loud and clear. There would be no place for you in their church.

I'm as tolerant as the next man, and given my experiences hopefully more so, but it's not enough to tolerate a person's lifestyle through gritted teeth. Really, that's just pretence. The church sticking to their guns could be seen as laudable, but to me, excluding people in this way was judgemental.

❛ I won't get with you now because you've got a dick ❜

I left the big smoke and headed to Burton on Trent, a small town just south of Derby. My loud outfit and uncapped belly laugh while bantering with the crew saw a generous helping of side eye aimed my way on the train journey. But as I walked the quiet streets wrapped in terraced housing as far as the eye could see, the strangely oppressive nature of the place began to creep in.

I'd braved the long train journey in an effort to meet Tallulah, a mixed-raced twenty-something with Caribbean and English roots. Her Jamaican dad and local mum separated when she was just three years old, so she was living with her mother and gran from the white side of her family. Arriving at the house, the door swung open to reveal a glamorous young woman in a crop top and tight jeans. Her hair was flowing down her back and framing her full face of make-up. Her huge eyes pinged open, her smile was broad and she threw out a hand to shake mine.

Her voice totally betrayed her appearance. Tallulah's deep vocal timbre as we shook hands explained her story, and why I was so keen to talk to her. Tiny in frame and feminine in manner, she had a deep voice that somehow magnified her strong jaw and Adam's apple. Tallulah was transgender and in the earliest months of her transition.

Tallulah lived with her grandmother, who hadn't got used to the change just yet and still referred to her as him. On some level, it felt as though there was a battle to let go of the grandson she loved, exemplified by the collection of framed pictures on display. Several school pictures crowded a shelf, the most recent showing a fifteen-year-old boy smiling uncomfortably. Still referring to the boy as 'me', Tallulah explained that this was just before she'd come out.

Then known as Aaron, Tallulah came out as gay believing family and friends would find that easier to digest than the full truth of her need to transition. 'I had to come out as gay just so people would get off my back.' Having always had an attraction to men, Tallulah explained that she'd always been a straight woman internally. As she gained more confidence in her late teens, she left school knowing that to be true to herself, she had to live as a woman.

This was the first time I'd spent an extended period of time with a person in transition and her struggle with acceptance helped me understand her journey so much better. She knew her gender to be one thing, while her body and the wider world was telling her something completely different.

Coming out as trans was a totally public affair as Tallulah chose to do so in the national press. As one of five women filling a double page spread in one of the UK's biggest tabloid newspapers, Tallulah was featured in a piece with the headline 'guess our biggest secret?' The unfortunately low-rent write-up also featured the awful subheading, 'Our five striking beauties are not what they seem . . .'

It was a pretty impersonal way to share her change with everyone she knew, but I guess she saved a shitload of money on her phone bill. Definitely better than a group text. We laughed about just how much of a shock the story must have been to so many people in her life. I saw it as opening herself up to local ridicule and a journalist's interpretation of her reasoning. She saw it as an opportunity to circumvent conversations she didn't want to have.

Finally away from her grandmother and in the garden, I had the opportunity to ask some of the more personal questions I could only really cover in private. Obviously, I was curious about sex and relationships. She was young and sexually active but with who? Fumbling my way through a series of questions, my slightly sweaty uncomfortable delivery wasn't a million miles off a dad breaking down the birds and the bees to his kid.

I mean, you tell me. How exactly do you ask someone you just met about the specifics of their breasts and vagina?

Wearing a tight top, she appeared to have breasts but I wanted to know if they were real. Describing her chest as 'that area' I was an embarrassing mess, but Tallulah laughed with me, helping the conversation become less awkward. She was on hormones encouraging some growth, but added size by wearing small 'chicken fillet' breast enhancers in her bra.

Approached more by black men, she only dated white guys as the stigma of, as she put it, 'Dating a chick with a dick' would always become an issue.

She laughed while explaining how often she'd hear the same thing from men of colour: 'I'd go there with you in four years' time, once you've had surgery, but I won't get with you now because you've got a dick.' Her light and breezy tone stood out, as what she was saying sounded so painful. I'm without doubt so much more emotional than I probably should be at my age. I've already accepted I'm most likely going to be the dad that cries at everything his kid does, so I would have expected Tallulah to be more affected by what she regularly experiences in relationships. The more her flippant attitude showed itself, the more it became increasingly obvious that it was a defence mechanism. I couldn't begin to imagine just some of the pain she'd experienced denying her true self and dealing with conflict every time she left the house.

The small town Tallulah called home had a small black community but a large and growing South Asian one.

Predominantly Muslim and Sikh, the religious communities didn't approve of her and weren't shy in making it known. Tallulah had had verbal abuse and death threats to her face, and bottles thrown at her head. 'Batty man go and die' was a regular slur, but she'd got to a point of not ever reacting for fear of beatings.

Tallulah displayed an incredible resilience but had clearly been affected by her decision to openly be her true self.

Fearing total strangers felt like the worst way to live; that was, until I met a man who ended up fearing his own family.

Back in east London, I was set to hear a story that would challenge everything I held dear. In London, I've always lived in a happy bubble of lefty-liberal tolerance and progressive attitudes, but I was about to realise I had no idea about grotesque things that were happening on my own doorstep. London may be a melting pot, but cultures live happily side-by-side even if they don't always mix. I had never encountered Sohail Ahmed's world, but the minute I learned of its existence it was a real wake-up call.

At twenty-two, Sohail Ahmed came out to himself. This process had taken years, as his faith had taught him that what he felt deep down wasn't real. Raised in a home that followed a strict version of Islam, his beliefs bordered on the extreme. At his most radical, he saw homosexual people as evil, and he subscribed to the harshest sharia laws. He had believed in punishing anyone LGBTQ and felt that throwing sinners off bridges or stoning them to death was just.

No longer practising any religion, Sohail moved to a flat in east London keeping his location a secret from his former friends and family. Isolated from the community to which he once belonged, he was thrown out of the family home when his parent's suspicions were vindicated in checking his internet browsing history.

While sharing the story, Sohail was able to laugh in hindsight at the websites he'd visited, which had confirmed any doubts his mother and father might have had about his sexuality. His browsing history was, shall we say, colourful. Rainbow levels of colourful. Sohail was confronted by his dad, who said 'I know the secret you're keeping from us,' and that conversation was the beginning of the end.

Bounding over and greeting me with a huge hug, Sohail was smiley, warm and happy to see me. Now, I'm not saying when I meet people for the first time they usually give me a healthy dose of the stink eye, but given the difficult nature of his situation I didn't expect anywhere near as much confidence.

The son of Pakistani immigrants, Sohail was raised in the UK, but in a home devoid of British influence. With honour and shame the biggest issues constantly causing cross-generational conflict in Pakistani homes, his sexuality caused a fracture in the family.

His parents saw his homosexuality as an illness, and had attempted to 'cure' it via exorcism – saying prayers over his body, and bathing him in 'holy' water. His mother felt so strongly that she cast him out. 'If you murdered someone, I'll still accept you, but you being gay; I can't accept you for that.'

So broken by the process, Sohail nearly took his own life. Knowing he needed to get out, he escaped and hadn't spoken to his family in over a year. Now openly gay, he was sharing his story online but still hadn't found himself confident enough to be physical with another man. Sex had become scary for Sohail and the idea of two men kissing made him feel repulsed, as he was still unable to shake the homophobia indoctrinated during his more fundamentalist days.

I couldn't believe that this was happening in London. I found it surreal that my life and home all of a few miles away could be so different. His parents were disgusted by his nature, but losing family was the most painful thing for Sohail, especially as the cause for the split was him being his true self.

𝟔 Homosexuality is an unnatural manifestation of a natural desire 𝟗

At the time of shooting, there were 1.5 million Muslims under the age of twenty-five in the UK. Finding out this stat mid-shoot emphasised the importance and power of imams for the Islamic community. We approached 200 mosques to ask an imam to discuss Islamic attitudes towards homosexuality, and they all said no. Finally, an imam in Edinburgh agreed to do it.

We met outside Whitechapel station in London in the heart of one of the biggest London Muslim communities. Agreeing to feature in the film against the will of his mosque, the young imam was difficult to engage. His nervous demeanour and suspicious tone made the chat less conversational and more of a back and forth.

At this point in my progression as a filmmaker, I'd learnt the hard way how not to make difficult conversations about me. I'd become better at separating myself from the issues I'd encounter on screen, allowing my personal beliefs to drive my questions, rather than my emotions force me to end conversations early. I'd had a solo pep talk in a bathroom mirror about not getting angry at anything offensive he might say. Unfortunately he hadn't.

From the jump he wore a heavy frown and eyed me closely. I cautiously asked my first question and his answer was a brilliant indication of what was to come. 'Homosexuality is an unnatural manifestation of a natural desire.' In my head rung out 'Here we go again', but I persevered. Surely he'd had young Muslim men come to him for advice about issues pertaining to sex or sexuality, I thought, and he had. 'You can tackle it,' was his instant response.

So sure of his methods, he went on to explain that he'd received emails from younger men at the mosque who'd experienced gay feelings. His take was that it's not justified following such emotions. He had instructed the young men to live a celibate life if they couldn't quieten their homosexual urges.

I feared the young imam's literal interpretation of scripture wouldn't make him much use to anybody who came to him for help. His advice was unrealistic and not grounded in anything resembling reality.

I've always made a point of not only seeking advice from my peers but also going out of my way to consult elders when I've encountered those tougher to manage and understand moments in my life.

Religion has never been a major influence on my value

system, but regardless I've always felt that respecting and learning from faith is far more important than criticising it. That being said, learning from the teachings, mistakes and successes of the past I see as just as important as questioning them. In meeting Sohail and talking to the imam, I was getting a clearer picture of how difficult that could become should scripture be a major part of your life.

As much as I'd like to believe you might know me by now, I was raised to believe you should never assume. I say that as I'd hate for any of you to be reading this thinking I'm staring down my nose at any one religion or its followers. My history with faith has had me living almost a third of my life with two different religious books under my pillow. I explained earlier, Islam and Christianity were the schools of thought I belonged to and so I know from personal experience that not all Christians reject homosexuality and not all Muslims hold extreme views.

I feel annoyed that I had to type that, but it has to be said. Making films covering particularly sensitive subject matter means trying hard to ensure I'd never offend anyone watching, or more importantly my loved ones. My sister is born again, my mother is Muslim and how they feel about what I say publicly matters.

With this in mind, presenting a broad section of views was paramount and thankfully the team had decided to send me to speak to the man on the street. Back in Whitechapel I was grabbing men and women leaving prayer outside the local mosque, as I wasn't allowed in with the cameras. Some declined, but those who did speak to me were honest and had a thankfully varied set of opinions.

One man saw homosexuality as a major sin, but didn't see sexual preference as taking one out of the fold of Islam. His belief was that you could be Muslim and gay. While some men I spoke to were adamant that following a religion meant you were to follow everything the scripture dictated.

In my lifetime alone, Britain has become far more accepting and tolerant and the signs are everywhere from pop culture to the stuffiest of political institutions. At the time of filming the episode, 60 per cent of the UK backed gay marriage, but support was lowest with Asian and black men.

❛ Homosexuality is a white man's disease ❜

Max's story of being disowned by his father painted a sad picture of losing family in an effort to find happiness. But Max had found acceptance in the city outside of the family bubble and surrounded by like-minded revellers at a popular club night.

Urban World Pride is a massive club night held at legendary gig venue in London. Max described it as a safe space where young gay people of colour can feel comfortable. Offering a surrogate family of men and women in the same or similar situations, the party was packed with people

of colour. Coming out and being disowned or remaining clos-
eted with a life totally separate from one's family was, Max
explained, going to be the reality for the lion's share of the
thousand-plus party goers.

As I walked in I had a strange moment of seeing a venue I
knew so well in a totally different light. Young black and
Asian guys were walking in with hoods on and full tracksuits
and trainers looking every bit the archetypal rudeboys. But
they were paying to enter a gay party and were desperate to
get in as quickly as possible without being seen. Some even
ran the minute they clocked the camera and my stupid face
off the telly.

The camp, over-the-top few were definitely in attendance,
but the majority of the room had that roadman look and attitude synonymous with straight street guys. Black girls with
skin fade haircuts just like mine hugged their gorgeous girlfriends in tight dresses as I watched in silent awe. The room
represented a world I'd never even known existed and I felt so
stupid. Of course this had always been here, of course my gay
equivalent had places to go in London, just like I did.

I'd been going to this place since my teens for club nights
and to watch live music, it was somewhere I knew well, but not
like this. Bashment and dancehall was the predominant sound
of the night and the hypersexual dance moves that went along
with it were in full swing. The only difference was that the
dance floor was rammed with men dancing with men.

Huge muscular Rasta men daggered sweaty guys in the

centre of the dance floor. For the unaware few of you about to Google daggering, I implore you to do so as it's both the most insane thing to watch, but takes on a whole new level of surreal when it's two men doing it. I wasn't judging or disapproving; I was having a great time! My eyes were wider than they'd ever been as every few minutes presented a picture I'd genuinely never seen before.

I spotted a turban in among the melee and followed the man into a separate room labelled 'Desi Room'. I walked in on a room thumping with Bangra music where gay Sikh and Muslim men were having the time of their lives. As soon as the camera followed me in, everyone ran in different directions, as, unlike Sohail, they clearly hadn't shared their true sexuality yet.

In classic house party fashion, I ended up having a long chat with a friendly woman on the staircase. Nicole was a twenty-one-year-old gay woman who'd only recently come out. Pretty and friendly, she explained how her Jamaican roots and up-bringing saw her have at times confusingly conflicting feelings.

Convinced that it was harder to be black, gay and male, she was raised by a father who taught her that being a gay man was both immoral and wrong. She was raised to believe homosexuality was 'A white man's disease', as in Jamaica that was what was taught. Admitting an ongoing conflict, Nicole spoke about not ever wanting to see gay men kiss or hear about gay men having sex, regardless of her being gay herself. She was fully aware of how contradictory her feelings were, and admitted to not being able to help the way she felt. Her struggle with her own ideas about homophobia seemed, in some ways, not too dissimilar to Sohail's.

When I'd met Tallulah, however, I'd realised that this was a woman on the other end of the spectrum. She was proud of who she was and even more proud that she's become that person, given the difficulties she'd faced.

I was back in Burton on Trent, and in a local wig shop with Tallulah where she was trying out different looks. With every new blond bob or shoulder length, floppy thing, she looked like an entirely different person. If you know black women, you'll know just how important hair can be. In the case of Tallulah it was of paramount importance as it was a small detail that not only helped her look and feel more feminine, it hid elements making her look distinctly more male.

Throwing on a dark wig cropped into a bob, I joked that she looked like the Posh Spice era Victoria Beckham. Loving the look but quickly taking it off, Tallulah rejected the wig as it drew attention to her Adam's apple. Conscious of her features, especially those that accentuated her previous life as Aaron, she did everything she could to hide her jaw and neckline. The shop was small and busy with black women shopping for weaves and wigs. Tallulah would occasionally deal with looks and louder than intended whispers of 'Oh my god, that's a man.'

Tallulah was at the beginnings of her transition, and had a

further four years to go on the National Health Service waiting list. Excited about the distant but important operation,
she explained the intimate details of the scariest procedure,
the Vaginoplasty.

Building a vagina after removing the penis, according to
Tallulah, a patient would have to spend up to six months in
recovery sleeping with a dildo inserted to prevent the open
wound from healing shut. That was an insane amount of time
in what sounded like a pretty uncomfortable position.

Giggling like a little girl, Tallulah had somehow managed
to make me regress and become an old man simultaneously,
not quite knowing how to deal with such an intimate conversation. Battling to fill the silence, I went for the stumbled,
'Well, that's a long time . . . some might enjoy it I suppose,' to
which she replied, 'At least it will be quite . . . deep.'

Tallulah's father Simon had been in and out of her life but
was building a strong bond with his daughter since coming out
of prison. He invited us round to the home he shared with his
new partner and their children. Simon was huge but made me
instantly feel at home with an abundance of charm and
warmth. Having missed a large chunk of his child's life, Simon
wondered if being raised by women, and having no male influence around, had been a factor in Aaron becoming Tallulah. I
guess in a way, he felt responsible.

The newspaper Tallulah showed me when we first met was
how her father found out about the transition, during a heated
debate of 'which one's a bloke' while in jail. Pointing out

Tallulah in total shock, Simon described staring at the paper surrounded by other inmates and saying, 'That's my kid.'

Unlike her grandmother, Simon had accepted Tallulah as a woman, making no reference to Aaron and never missing a beat in referring to her as female. He was warm and accepting and protective of his blood. Simon told me about his background of being one of the only black kids in his middle-England school life. He explained identifying with his daughter's struggle of standing out due to who she was while being chastised for it. Expecting her ex-con father to judge her, I felt better about my presumptions ahead of meeting Simon and was pleasantly surprised by Simon's progressive attitude.

I left excited for Tallulah and her future knowing she might have had a long journey ahead, but her support system was clearly growing and stronger than ever.

I stayed in the Midlands as Derby Pride was fast approaching and I invited Sohail to join me at what would also be my first gay pride. He was still coming to terms with his sexuality and I saw the event being much smaller than its London equivalent as the perfect opportunity to be a part of the majority on a much more manageable scale. Travelling to the event I checked in via text, then calls, but the agreement to join me from Sohail felt increasingly less likely the longer the day went on.

The day rolled on and my first pride was much more sombre than I'd expected after seeing so many images and videos from the hectic London affair. Derby Pride was very white and very middle class, with a brass band and middle-aged women handing out pink ribbons. Although totally coming from the right place, the event was predominantly made up of older people attending in an effort to show support, rather than a celebration by and for the people in question.

Sohail hadn't arrived and I'd given up on his attendance; I was disappointed as I'd wanted to see the day through his fresh eyes not just my own. As we walked the town centre, I was one of four faces of colour in the crowd watched by passing shoppers who stopped and stared trying to work out what was going on. The walk ended at a small park populated with a stage and marquees. As the event started to fill up, it began to feel younger. It wasn't a huge Pride celebration, but there wasn't any opposition or anti-gay sentiment in the air.

I'd waited for hours and there still wasn't any sign of Sohail. I went to leave and as I made my way towards the exit, a smiling nervous Sohail wandered in. Emerging from the crowd in a tracksuit, he broke into a huge smile and I threw my arm around him, spun him on the spot and walked him towards the main stage.

He'd never been around so many openly gay men and women and worried about standing out as he felt out of place. He was the only young Asian at the whole event and he explained that he probably wouldn't have stayed long if I hadn't been with him. Convinced he was seen as an Asian Muslim first and a gay man second, his paranoia was screaming he wouldn't be accepted. I worried I'd made a mistake and stepped away with the team to have a quiet word about leaving early with him as he felt so out of place.

My conversation with my producer and director lasted all of five minutes, but by the time I returned, he'd found a small group of dancing men in front of the main stage and joined them. It took less than a few minutes before Sohail was pogoing with the pack at the front to some horrific dance record. The music was assaulting my ears but my focus was on just how beside himself he looked. Sohail was having the time of his life and seemed to be finally letting everything go for the first time ever.

My train home beckoned and I took on the role of embarrassing guardian trying to pull him away, asking him to follow me out. Sohail politely declined with a smile as he'd decided to stay and have a night out in Derby with the guys he'd met.

Sohail's internal conflicts and residual homophobia I'd witnessed on first meeting him seemed to have evaporated. He was suddenly surrounded by what he used to look upon with utter disgust. It was his first Gay Pride and he was finally embracing who he truly was.

The *Extreme UK* series was difficult to make on so many levels. Behind the scenes with the production team, the edit was long and complicated. I understood that having my name in the series title opened me up to a level of criticism that would go on to be unavoidably personal. I pushed back on a few things, but it quickly got to the point where I'd pick my battles, regrettably letting some issues go.

Being frank, I found this film in particular was a struggle as we were dealing with sensitive subject matter and my team was made up almost entirely of new faces. Being front and centre of a documentary while belonging to a team can be a difficult balancing act, even if the film is supposed to be your baby.

I felt disappointed that the film wasn't perfect, but I'd learnt a valuable lesson in not allowing the runaway train to end up out of my control, especially if the film had my name on it.

In my mind, the final film just didn't create the moment I was hoping for. I moaned to friends and family ahead of the airing, and was encouraged to, what was it again? Oh yeah, 'Stop being a bitch and trust in your performance.' Cheers bro. My brother Cobbie never fails to keep it raw, real and unpolished.

But then the film went out on BBC Three and all disappointments connected to not realising the subject matter's potential were alleviated. As the credits rolled, I did my usual fear-fuelled scroll through all of my social channels. Twitter was very positive, Instagram was glowing and Snapchat held lots of thumbs up videos and the occasional erect penis. God bless social media.

Unexpectedly, venturing into my direct messages made me emotional. I'd received several messages essentially saying the same thing. There were young guys and girls across the country reaching out to tell me that they had watched the film with their parents. A totally deliberate act, they'd wanted to see their folks react to the stories on screen in an effort to start a scary conversation. Several of my followers on social media had watched the film with their families and come out as the credits rolled. The film gave them the confidence to share with their parents what had become their biggest secret.

I sat staring at my phone totally flummoxed, suddenly seeing the power of what had been achieved. In my programme-maker's arrogance, I'd put my ideals for the perfect film above the potential of what we actually had to affect change, regardless of my personal ambitions.

It ended up being a decent documentary that might not have changed the world but, as I learned from my grateful personal messages on social media, had maybe changed something huge in the lives of a lot of British men and women – and perhaps even given them that vital voice they lacked.

CHAPTER 10
RACE RIOTS AND ME

Race isn't something most kids think about, but due to my surroundings I had no choice but to be aware. The food, colour and culture of my heritage were unavoidable. My parents and pretty much every adult in my family shared the same West African heritage and, until recently, I had no idea how proud of that I was as a child.

Thinking back, my favourite teacher during my primary school years was Nikki. She had that perfect teacher balance of someone you'd have fun with, but also had the ability to shoot you a look. The kind mum would throw if we were visiting relatives and I was acting up. The kind that rendered you silent in seconds and probably meant you'd be getting a smack when you got home. Now, I'm fully aware it might sound odd that I'm referring to my teacher by her given name, but in the school I attended we didn't call our teachers sir or miss.

As part of filming a piece about the relationships between children and their teachers, I went back to school and had an amazing catch up with Nikki, who I hadn't seen in decades. She remembered how an afternoon of show and tell filled with goldfish and a pocket watch from the war had a sudden spike of excitement as I jumped up to perform a traditional tribal dance. I apparently wore a dashiki and explained its origins while sharing the history of the Ashanti tribe I belonged to. I was six.

From as far back as I can remember I never saw my race as a hindrance. According to Nikki, even as a child I was proud of what made me culturally different to my classmates. That pride remains to this day, but in my early teens I quickly learned how the wider world would see me and just how different perception could be from my reality.

The drama class I attended on Friday nights and Saturday afternoons made me feel as though I was part of a special club. The Anna Scher Theatre in Islington started my career on screen and represents the only form of training (outside of doing the job itself) I've ever received. The group of young actors I belonged to was made up entirely of kids just like me. We'd grown up together and we became teenagers with acting careers thanks to Anna.

Anna was tough, encouraging, eccentric and inspirational. She was the kind of leader you wanted to impress and she knew it. She placed so much value on her favourite word, *ubuntu*, that she'd learned from close friend Archbishop Desmond Tutu. It meant community care and collectiveness and hearing her drum on about it every week eventually instilled a sense of *ubuntu* in us.

The class was special in so many ways, but the conversations we were encouraged to have on race, class and current affairs always stick out in my mind. We were so young, yet being asked to really think about what was in the news and find a way to apply it to our improvised plays and performances.

One of the biggest news stories of the mid-nineties was the racially motivated killing of black teenager Stephen Lawrence, and the subsequent police investigation. We discussed the story during a class, but felt the impact of the murder much more personally when the killing was dramatised by ITV. The TV film starred our classmate Leon Black as Stephen, and watching Leon be attacked, stabbed and killed, albeit on screen, hit home in an unnervingly real way. The case became the biggest story at the time, and my mum, the news, everyone was talking about race. So to learn as a teenager that Stephen died because of racism and was targeted because of his skin colour forced me to accept that for some people, my colour would be a problem.

Throughout my teens, I had constant reminders that not everybody in this world shared my desire to take people as they found them. By the time I was in my late twenties, I'd grown an unhealthily thick skin to news of stabbings or shoot-ings as it had touched my life through friends and family members continually.

So when the death of Mark Duggan at the hands of the Metropolitan police sparked riots across the entire country in 2011, I felt for his family but my experiences of race, class, police and violence didn't reflect the shock I'd go on to see in the newspapers and on TV.

There was a strange feeling in London during the summer of 2011, it was almost as if something was about to explode. Every teenager who stopped me in the street seemed to be angry, frustrated and struggling with something. They were asking for help, guidance, a job or any kind of opportunity, and whatever was going on in the capital would go on to be the same feelings reflected across the country.

Young people in particular were angry and had every right to be. Those in charge were showing themselves to be untrust-worthy in every way possible. Stop and search powers were being abused; bankers had become thieves, yet millennials were increasingly labelled as a lost generation.

I was at Dan's house and no, 'Benny' wasn't dragging me to the carpet for a WWF wrestle. We were hanging out, eating badly and flicking through the TV when his Blackberry began to explode. His teenage cousin Sonny was less than a mile away in Camden and was forwarding instant messages he'd received. He had up-to-the-minute updates of the next tar-gets for looting that were being shared. We switched channels and watched in shock what was happening across the country unfold live on TV.

Despite the monologues from disconnected politicians and the tabloid press, the 2011 riots in England weren't fuelled by a generation rife with entitlement burning down their own manors to steal trainers and tracksuits. In my opinion, they were about distrust of the police, economic disparity and the death of a young black man.

If the news was to be believed, the scary kids in hoods from the tower blocks were having a party in the streets. The press filled pages and screen time with stories of teenagers running into sports stores to carry home as many pairs of trainers as they could stuff in their school bags. What was neglected, however, was the large number of kids stealing eggs and milk to take home to empty fridges. Poverty and frustration were overshadowed by criminality, seeing all focus placed on acts of crime while totally ignoring the cause.

This was the first time I'd witnessed riots and had never imagined the events of Brixton in 1981 could repeat themselves in my lifetime. Back in '81, a young black man had been stabbed in a bar fight and in his attempts to escape ran into a police officer. According to the watching community, the bleeding kid was thrown into a police van and arrested rather than helped or taken to the hospital. This incident on Brixton's famous Railton Road would be the beginnings of rioting and clashes with the police that lasted for days.

Just a couple of years before I was born, Brixton (at the

time, the capital of black Britain) was a warning for what could happen when a community feels targeted because of its culture, or the colour of its skin. Only a few years later in Tottenham, 1985 saw the Broadwater Farm riots. A resident died during a police raid; days later an officer died in the resulting unrest. Police presence was increased as were arrests and riots erupted on the estate.

To see history repeat itself in almost exact detail, gave the view that race relations in the capital were as bad as they'd ever been a level of credence. In the eighties, both Tottenham and Brixton riots saw the Metropolitan police blame a lawless minority rather than admitting their tactics with the community had been ill judged.

Then, two years after the riots in Tottenham, 2013 saw the beginnings of a movement across the pond that would become embroiled in the same stages of protest to unrest as seen in the UK. A simple hashtag used on social network Twitter would grow into a force debated, supported and resented. #BlackLivesMatter or #BLM began in response to the acquittal of George Zimmerman, a man arrested for shooting and killing African-American teenager Trayvon Martin in Sanford, Florida.

As the movement grew, street demonstrations became a natural progression and inevitable response, particularly following two further highly publicised deaths, this time at the hands of the police. African-Americans Michael Brown and Eric Garner lost their lives to police bullets and choke holds, sparking countrywide demonstrations and global outrage. Racial bias and violence committed by the American police force was no longer fobbed off as an unfounded claim by African-Americans. The frequency and extreme nature of police behaviour usually exerted by white officers was now being caught on camera and the world was watching.

As a black man, I was affected by watching what seemed to be an endless stream of imagery showing African-American men and women harassed, killed and assaulted by law enforcement. Aggressors cloaked as those employed to protect and serve became a dreaded subject matter between friends and me. What became daily stories of black lives being lost, twinned with the apparent minimal chances of change, even talking about the latest death or assault became painful. And yet, when the opportunity arose to front a film discussing the issue through the eyes of the community in Ferguson, where protests and riots had followed the police killing of young black man Michael Brown, the fact it was such nuanced material that I found personally affecting made getting on the flight a no brainer. This was a film I needed to front.

❛ He was a kid . . . he was a kid ❜

Young voices had become galvanised by the untimely deaths of countless African-American men and women. I felt privileged in being given the opportunity to attempt to see the world through their eyes. Growing up, I had a love affair with the US and first travelled to America at eighteen with one of my closest friends at the time.

Dev was in my drama class at the Anna Scher Theatre and even though he was younger than Dan and I, we hung out as friends. By the time we were in our late teens we were thick as thieves and took our first trip to New York together.

We were totally naïve to the ID requirements and 21 age minimum for bars in the States. Between my provisional driver's licence clearly stating my age and Dev's best 'I'm eighteen too' face, most doormen just laughed and sent us on our way. We couldn't get into any clubs or bars and as a result spent the entire trip buying trainers. We'd walk around Brooklyn and Harlem trying to sample the culture we'd idolised from afar for years. We believed we were seeing the life of real New Yorkers, but ended most days watching Dave Chappelle's show in our hotel room.

What a pair of tits. Regardless of our stupidity, we had an incredible time and returned to the UK with suitcases full of mixtapes, New Era Caps and sneakers. We were teenagers, what else were we going to spend our money on? We arrived home a week later with our heads held high believing we'd seen and been a part of black America.

I grew up immersed in the pop culture churned out by America and for a time idolised the black American experience as one that us black Brits could only dream of. Black American TV and sports stars were superheroes to me. Like the rest of the world, the graphic reality of black men and women dying

at the hands of the law shared online and picked up by newspapers and TV left me rocked.

Black America was about so much more than the pile of
crap I'd filled my suitcase with as a teenager. The obvious
oppression seen in countless videos of killings and protests
showed pain and struggle. It was now unavoidable to see what
it really meant to be African-American in all of its beautiful
and painful entirety. This was the other side of black America.
I had the gut-wrenching feeling that if I had lived there, I could
have become a victim, just like Trayvon Martin.

❛ You could see the blood flowing ❜

I arrived in Ferguson, Missouri, a northern suburb of St
Louis and was promptly ferried to a gigantic soulless hotel
minutes from the airport. The place was huge, characterless
and full of business types busy with conferences for people in
bad suits. This would serve as home for the fortnight I'd spend
in town. But I was still excited to be somewhere totally new
and so jumped in the crew car and headed out for a drive.
Every turn delivered another street I'd seen on the news, only
now the fires were out, the National Guard had gone and the
sidewalks were empty.

The sun was out but the streets were silent and the air felt
eerily still. This was sleepy, small-town America and regardless of the countless USA immigration stamps I had in my
passport, I'd never experienced this version of the States.

It wore its clichés with pride as I couldn't move for American flags and churches. The single police and fire stations were outnumbered by over thirty Christian places of worship.

The dust had settled, at face value at least. My drive through town painted a picture of calm and small-town charm, but some streets were still blotted with signs of what had happened a year prior. A row of manicured businesses would occasionally be broken by a burnt or boarded-up property. Most things seemed to be back as they'd always been, but was that for the better of the town or not?

At the time of Michael Brown's death, young black men in America were twenty-one times more likely to be killed by police officers as white men of the same age. Brown, an unarmed black teenager, lost his life to a police bullet fired from a white officer's gun and Ferguson found itself on the world's radar.

Eighteen-year-old Clifton Kinnie was a friend of Brown's from the neighbourhood and one of the many young men who found themselves in the centre of the furore following the shooting. We met in a black-owned restaurant clearly proud of the town it belonged to that had become famous for staying open during the protests. Ferguson Burger bar was a 'blink and you'll miss it' eatery hidden in a typically American strip mall. Owner Charles Davis greeted me with a stoic hello, as Clifton polished off his sandwich eager to show me what he called ground zero.

We walked the street now famously known as the site

where a year ago clashes between demonstrators and police boiled over into something else entirely. It was this street that Brown was caught on camera allegedly stealing cigars from a gas station. Minutes later Brown and his friend Dorian Johnson were spotted by officer Darren Wilson and an altercation led to Wilson firing repeatedly.

Six bullets hit Brown in the chest, forehead and arm. Dorian Johnson went on to claim that Brown had his hands up when officer Wilson discharged his weapon, but according to the official enquiry no other witnesses could verify his statement. With there being no video evidence, what actually happened continues to be debated, but the one thing that everyone agrees on, is that Michael Brown was unarmed.

Clifton talked me through the moment he spotted Michael Brown's body in the street. His first-hand account took what I'd heard described countless times by reporters and experts on the news and made it so much more personal. Clifton was seventeen at the time of the incident and what he saw had undoubtedly scarred him.

Clifton parked his car, walked the sidewalk and spotted (as he called him) 'Mike Mike' lying still, face down in the middle of the road. 'You could see the blood flowing,' he explained. At this point, the police had taped off the area holding a growing crowd back. Clifton glazed over as he spoke about the way Mike Mike's mother cried and screamed for her bleeding and lifeless son.

He explained just how angry, confused and frustrated

everyone was. The crowd was made up almost entirely of neighbours and people who knew Brown. The body was in plain view of the surrounding houses, pulling families outside and bringing kids to tears as they tried to work out why Mike Mike wouldn't get up.

The police responded by coming at the watching distressed crowd with dogs. Pushed back by cops and held in place by tape, the aggressive tactics riled the crowd, especially as at this point hours had passed and the body hadn't been covered or moved. Michael Brown was lying dead on the tarmac for over four hours, uncovered and in full view of the crying women and children who knew and loved him.

I stood on the side of Canfield Drive with Clifton, silenced by the vivid picture he painted, which no longer felt like the news footage I'd seen a million times. His pained and personal connection to Brown humanised what I knew to be a horrific story. Clifton was able to describe a character I'd built a picture of based entirely on news clippings and photos released by his family. He made Michael Brown just another teenager on the block, he made him real. Suddenly, I was being told the story of Mike Mike not the kid from the news.

We stood in silence staring at the large dark square in the road where new tarmac had been laid. The exact spot of Mike Mike's death would forever be visible, a landmark that no one asked for. 'He was a kid, he was a kid . . .'

Clifton was eighteen and about to go to college, and at the time of his death so was Mike Mike. Devastated and fighting to manage his emotions, he didn't understand why a life was lost and why there were still no answers.

❝ There is a dangerous dynamic in the night ❞

The story of the shooting went from local to national news overnight and, as word of the shooting spread, people outside of Brown's neighbourhood took to the streets. Armed with placards, Clifton and his school friends joined the protests living the odd duality of student by day, activist by night.

Black celebrities started to arrive bringing their fame to the issue and one of the first to do so was rapper Nelly. During my time presenting weekly live music show *Top of the Pops*, I'd usually open my script apprehensively during rehearsal. My biggest hope was that we'd finally feature an act I actually listened to. At the time, black music rarely found its way onto the pop charts so when it did it was special.

Nelly was one of the few rap acts that crossed over internationally and I was probably the only person on the studio floor who knew who he was. As he performed one of his first big hits 'E.I', I rapped along like a right fan boy as I'd obsessed over the music video in the weeks leading up to his appearance. Between his first few promos and lyrical content, this was the first time I'd ever have a picture painted of St Louis, Missouri from a black perspective. To see Nelly walking through Ferguson on the news brought my education on the area full circle.

I'd never heard an African-American with an accent like Nelly's until I'd heard his music. My impression of his hometown was entirely dictated by his first album until Mike Brown lost his life. Nelly's corner of St Louis would no longer be as connected to his story of the American dream, it would now be remembered for the loss of a black life in what could only be described as an African-American nightmare. The death of Brown would hit close to home as Nelly also called Cranfield Drive home for two years of his life before making it big in music. His cries for peace as protests shifted in tone only added to the growing swell of interest online.

As the days went on, the protests grew in size and predictably the police presence reflected this rise in numbers. Clifton described what became a stand-off, as lines from both sides would advance and retreat. As reports of looting began to find their way into the press, it was no longer a local news story. Heavy reinforcements arrived and local police unexpectedly appeared militarised. The streets looked very different as thousands were out in force refusing to go home.

Flares lit the sky red as the more aggressive contingent began covering their faces with masks. Then some cars were set alight and tear gas fired into crowds became a tactic used by police now fitted with shields and riot masks. Highway Patrol Captain Ron Johnson called for calm and made a point of separating the peaceful protesters and those heavily featured on the news committing crimes and physically challenging the police.

'There is a dangerous dynamic in the night,' he announced, surrounded by mics during a press briefing. Captain Johnson blamed outsiders for coming into town in an attempt to get what they could through looting. Johnson warned, 'Violent agitators hide in the crowd and create chaos.' Unfortunately, his assessment of who the trouble makers actually were wouldn't be widely reported.

As police tried to control the crowd, Clifton experienced that chaos first-hand at the butt of a rubber bullet. He explained how difficult it was to keep going with the constant threat of tear gas. Unaware of how to protect himself, Clifton was still confused as to why his peaceful protest was met with such force. 'Not only am I seventeen, it shouldn't happen.'

Two thousand National Guard soldiers flooded the streets of Ferguson in an effort to subdue the protests. 'Hands Up, Don't Shoot' became the rallying cry against the use of excessive force used on African-Americans across the country. Protests were now happening countrywide and the same chant could be heard everywhere.

❝ Society can only take so much pressure and tension before things unravel ❞

So much of what I knew about the protests was being challenged as Clifton had made everything feel so real. I'd arrived almost a year to the day after the shooting, but there were still protests happening outside the local police station. To my surprise, the cluster of men and women stood outside the grand building were there waving their signs and flags in support of the police and Officer Darren Wilson.

Several of the demonstrators waved the same sign announcing 'We support our LEO' (law enforcement officers), a shorthand used by their supporters. The crowd was predominantly middle-aged white men and women with a few exceptions.

A woman in her fifties showed me a 'We support our LEO' magnet made for her truck, proudly placed on her driver's door. She spoke with a husky, cigarette-stained voice and handled a large tray of cupcakes with long pink nails as I tried not to stare at the two-inch wide streaks of blue jumping out from her icy blond hair.

She saw their presence on the roadside as a show of support for the officers. Thankful for their service, she was adamant their protest had nothing to do with race. She believed the demonstration was about standing up for what they believe. I wanted to believe her but in my short stay I'd already accepted it would be impossible to ignore race in a town like Ferguson. It was a town dominated by its 70 per cent black population, but at the time of Michael Brown's death was being policed by fifty-three officers, only three of whom were black.

The cupcakes were decorated with blue icing which also spelt out the words 'We support our LEO'. Paying for the treats herself, she explained she usually spent between $250 and

$300 on signage and goods to give away. 'It's worth it – money can't buy that.'

I was given a rubber bracelet wrapped with the name Darren Wilson in white ink. A slightly older and much more vocal demonstrator was handing them out and insisted I too wore one. She explained that usually the keepsake would be sold at bigger rallies. She saw them as a small but important part of supporting an officer they believed to be innocent. She'd made close to $7,000 selling the bands alone, and that money was a tiny part of how much had been raised by the unassuming group stood in the street.

At the demonstrations they'd organised over the last year, the group had sold everything from caps to T-shirts. Every penny was going to Darren Wilson and his family, who they believed had been unfairly forced to retire. They'd raised over a million dollars for Wilson, which sounded to me like one hell of a retirement fund.

The woman selling the bands wore a blue T-shirt bearing a large printed police badge. A date jumped out as being of some importance. I asked what the story behind the shirt was, only to find out it was a bestseller. As she proudly explained the date, I could see a look of sudden apprehension flash across her face. In fact, she then stopped and took a massive gulp during the explanation, which made the older woman look a little ashamed and very awkward. The date on the badge was that of Michael Brown's death.

With an acrimonious debate still raging over the details

and motivations behind the shooting, it scared me that so much money was being handed to a man who might have taken a life for reasons outside of his job description. At the time and to this day, it's impossible to defend the killing of Brown with total confidence as proof and detail is thin on the ground.

The woman's logic boiled down to good people helping an ex-officer feed his family, yet I couldn't help but walk away feeling unsettled. Whichever way you sliced it, Wilson had killed a kid and as a result become a millionaire.

The people waving flags and placards were clearly trying to protect a way of life and clinging to it with both hands. I spotted one of the younger men talking to his cell phone at the end of a selfie stick. He was live streaming to an audience of eighty viewers from around the globe. I interrupted his broadcast and asked him about the nearby sign announcing the war on police officers must end now.

He too believed there was a war on the police, citing the radical left as leading the charge to bring down America. He included supporters of Mike Brown in that group and saw himself as a defender of the constitution. The more we spoke, the more he struggled to articulate himself. He feared being branded as a racist because of his views and struggled to open up about race. He awkwardly dodged question after question refusing to answer most, until he finally opened up. 'Society can only take so much pressure and tension before things unravel.' Finally, he'd made a point we both agreed on.

I'd been jumping between protesters at the rally for an hour when I spotted Chris. He seemed to want to talk to me, and I knew I had to talk to him. Chris really stood out, and not because of his behaviour. Chris really stood out because he was black.

He explained that 'Not all of them see the truth that I do,' which made me immediately both fascinated by and furious at him. My first stop on the 'what the fuck express' was what did he mean by THEM? Chris continued, 'This whole thing ain't about race, it's about right and wrong,' which was a sentiment I'd heard a few times on the news, only this belief was usually spouted by older white people.

I couldn't help but get annoyed, as Chris spoke with such passion and believed every word. To hear such a statement from a black man was just weird, as to really believe what he'd said required totally ignoring the racially charged history of America.

Chris went on to explain that he couldn't support Michael Brown as he'd robbed a gas station. With a shrug he described Brown's death as unfortunate, but okayed the shooting as Officer Wilson did what he had to do. He shifted a lump on his hip, forcing my confused stare to fall from his face to his waist. 'That's my .45, I take it everywhere I go.' Chris had a handgun clipped to his belt and wasn't the only one.

The lady with the commemoration T-shirt joined and clarified that they'd previously come up against aggressive counter protests. Apparently just about everybody who attended would now turn up with loaded weapons. As Chris and the older lady spoke, an undercurrent of Us versus Them buoyed every statement they'd make as fact.

She pulled her small, embroidered purse from her bag, popped it open and revealed she too was carrying a loaded gun. Clearly, I'm not a gun person, so the best way to describe her .380 pistol was as the kind of thing beautiful women with accents carry strapped to their thigh in Bond films. She definitely didn't remind me of a Bond girl, but the weapon did.

Every conversation allowed a further insight into the minds of the small town's white residents, but what did the predominantly black local community make of such a demonstration? Two young African-American men crossed the street; one filming everything on two mobile phones with a stoney-faced expression, ignoring my questions until he mumbled a response. Without any interest in speaking to me, he was at least filming someone who seemed much more approachable.

Smiling and shaking my hand, the man on camera introduced himself as Frankie Edwards. He lived locally and wanted to find out what was going on when he saw the flags. Frankie was being totally ignored by every protester, irrespective of the fact he wore a long white T-shirt bearing the wording 'In peace and solidarity' surrounding a clenched fist displaying every skin shade imaginable. He literally wore his beliefs even if no one wanted to have a conversation about them.

Activist Frankie explained that, so far, he'd given 7,000 of the T-shirts away in an effort to see his community unite. Unsurprisingly, the reception he was receiving didn't bode well for his efforts. 'We need to come together as a people, not just this race and this race but as a whole.' Determined to be heard, Frankie was disappointed that a year had passed yet the community made up of blacks and whites living side by side still didn't speak. The growing distance between our conversation and the protest exemplified his frustrations.

As he continued to describe a growing segregation in Ferguson, another older lady wrapped in a flag bearing the stars and stripes approached and listened quietly. Frankie was warm and desperate to engage but the only person willing to do so was me. Clearly feeling a little embarrassed, the lady recognised Frankie's desire to begin a dialogue and slipped into a long monologue explaining her support of the police. She wanted to see respect shown to residents of all colours including the police. She barked, 'If you don't like black people, don't like white people, move out of Ferguson.'

For some, the protest might not have been about race, but what was obvious was the expectation to pick a side. There was an annoying repetition in every conversation as everybody said a version of the same thing. Most recognised a desperate need for dialogue, but even with Frankie right there, they didn't take the opportunity.

❝ *If you do not walk down my streets, then you do not know what happens on my streets* ❞

A fifteen-minute drive from the city centre buzzing with business and the picture of multiculturalism saw me hit the dense suburbs. Filled with all-black neighbourhoods, at the time we were there, one in five households were living below the poverty line. Home ownership was half that of the white community, helping me to understand how the relentless layers of inequality could play a part in what was bubbling beneath the surface. The unavoidable disparity in quality of life I could see played a huge part in what exploded when the riots began.

Fixing the battered image of Ferguson had become a mission for some; none more so than the group of older white women who ran the 'I Heart Ferguson' shop on the main strip. T-shirts and posters bearing the heart branding filled the windows and shelves. Walking into the small store, a smiling white woman in her eighties warmly greeted me from her chair.

I introduced myself to Dorothy Kaiser, a volunteer with a smile almost as perfect as her impossibly ice white hair. Starting out with a couple of T-shirts, the store opened after the incident and took off. A small pile of yard signs were propped up against the wall, Dorothy explained that was all they had left after already giving out 10,000 to local homeowners.

As she quietly described how she'd watched the aftermath of the riots, another volunteer joined Dorothy. They both expressed their anger about what had happened in their town, believing Brown's death and subsequent protests encouraged chancers from over thirty nearby towns to travel in, loot, riot and cause as much chaos as possible.

The volunteers were still angered by the amount of destruction caused during the riots and rightly so. It was impossible to ignore the visible evidence in building shells still black with ash on the main and most prestigious streets. That being said, their feelings were based entirely on the version of Ferguson they knew. Their take on Brown's shooting and the resulting protests unknowingly exposed a lack of empathy. A total lack of understanding for the kind of interactions with the police their black equivalents might have spoke volumes.

When you're my colour that isn't a choice. The level of suspicion placed on people of African-American descent by the police is a reality totally foreign to the likes of Dorothy. Both her and her co-workers take on why there was still so much anger in Ferguson reflected that.

Literally across the road from I Heart Ferguson was Cathy's Kitchen. A black-owned business, it stayed open during the riots providing refuge for protesters not wanting any part of the increasingly dangerous rioting. As I wolfed down several shrimp-heavy snacks, head chef James and I got talking. He believed that if another innocent black man was to lose his life at the hands of a police officer due to excessive use of force, things could only become worse in the country. 'If you do not live in my community – if you do not walk down my streets, then you do not know what happens on my streets.'

A constant stream of assaults and deaths of African-Americans at the hands of the police were being caught on camera. Shared on social media and quickly going viral, each video pushed the country further into tense territory. When Baltimore resident Freddie Grey lost his life while in custody, Baltimore erupted.

Protests quickly graduated to riots overnight and it didn't take long before the entire world was watching. The National Guard was once more called in and a six-day curfew was enforced. Riots and violence made the headlines but, frustratingly, I watched as the stats didn't. At the time of filming and in that year alone, 176 had died at the hands of American police officers. Five of them had been in Missouri alone.

With so many eyes on the police force, I couldn't quite believe my luck when the police agreed to have me sit in on a training day. I was driving a stupidly huge American SUV and kept making a dog's dinner of parking. Definitely not starting the day in the smartest way, I nearly crashed the thing while doing illegal manoeuvres in the police car park but somehow made it into a bay.

My biggest ambition for the day was to get some sort of an idea as to what the local police force might be up against. The pack of rookies looked a lot younger than I'd expected, which was probably down to the rabbit-in-the-headlights expression they all seemed to share. This tiny local force was under a national spotlight making the importance of training all the more of a priority.

The young men and women donned newly starched brown uniforms. They were in their final weeks of training, and the exercise I'd be observing pitted them against their instructors in a simulated scenario. The cops were suiting up with heavy amounts of paint-loaded firepower which felt fitting for a hostage scenario, but that wasn't the day's test. The rookies were being tested in a traffic stop simulation.

My British naivety saw me forget that America has that added danger of civilians with guns. The constitution of course enshrines the right to bear arms, and for a police officer, that right could mean their lives. I down sat to watch beside a lieutenant who talked through what they'd be tested on. The amount of artillery both the rookies and their civilian-playing superiors packed for the simulation felt like a lot, the lieutenant felt otherwise and delivered a jaw-dropping comment about his officers: 'In the back of their mind, they have a back-up plan to kill everybody in the car if need be. Nobody else has to think that way.'

The first simulation was a routine stop. Being deliberately difficult, the 'civilians' quickly escalate the stop into something else entirely. Guns are fired and officers are hit. Knowing when to use one's weapon as opposed to allowing intimidation or fear to dictate the pulling of a trigger was the point of the test.

I watched uncomfortably as the superior officers played average Joes doing exactly what I've done in the past when stopped. Questioning authority, answering back and being a smart arse were my go-to reactions.

Watching such behaviour play out from the perspective of an officer, I could see how paranoia and fear from either the cop or civilian might escalate a situation in a matter of seconds. These young officers would be stopping cars for the rest of their careers, so to be reminded of that good old second amendment (the right to bear arms) and the chances of routine spiralling into a fire fight made sense. I left hoping the focus of the lesson ultimately wouldn't be how to handle gunfire, but more how to manage conflict.

In theory, the training should make officers' interactions with the predominantly black community better. Right? Well, in 2014, the city of Ferguson spent four times more money on police uniforms than police training. In one year alone, of the reported 11,000 traffic violations, nine out of ten were involving African-Americans. If the cops made the assumption that who they stop will be armed and dangerous, what would that realistically mean for the average black man or woman in Ferguson?

The continued hostility and anger in the community wouldn't make the jobs of the newly graduated officers easy, but would they be ready? Just how possible is it to be new to policing and do your job without bias in an environment where divisions are so visible?

I had hope for the rookies as they were on the verge of a career. My hope was tied to them using their power on the street properly, but given the licence to be whoever you choose when walking with a badge and a gun, who knew who they might become?

❝ That's why I don't sag ❞

I had an appointment booked with a young and white political activist and human rights lawyer Brendan Roediger. His building and offices felt incredibly corporate, but this was a young guy who put his beliefs front and centre, joining the Ferguson protests and helping those who ended up behind bars.

Lean and baby-faced, his oversized suit made him look a little like a kid playing dress-up, but the minute he got going it was clear Brendan wasn't for the games. A firm handshake and warm greeting set the tone for what would be a friendly and informal chat, bowed by an unrelenting weight of heart-breaking facts. It was unnerving being sat in the uncomfortable client chair, but Brendan quickly showed himself to be quite the opposite of the quintessential suit, not just in his instant short hand, but also his attitude.

Describing the relationship between the police and African-Americans as one of distrust, his belief was the relationship couldn't be anything but. He explained that his experience had proven that the police were looking for ways to begin interactions leading to citations. Brendan believed that money played an unhealthy part in the equation: 'The police operate for profit.' This was an entirely new concept, and my motor mouth was suddenly out of order as I listened utterly stunned.

At the time of filming, St Louis based many of its municipal budgets on fining the residents of the municipality. Up to 60 per cent of any one area's budget would come from fines, primarily those issued for traffic violations. Brendan went on to explain that increasingly new laws were being created with an indisputable racial bias.

There was a sagging pants violation (wearing one's trousers below the waist line), a manner of walking violation and recently walking in a group had become a finable offence also. These new laws carried a $200 fine and felt like an unbelievably obvious attempt to specifically punish young black men. With such laws in place, distrust between black neighbourhoods and the predominantly white police force were at an all-time high.

As a legal aid worker, Brendan spent the lion's share of his time defending poor people on minor offences in court. He allowed me to ride along to see exactly what he did and who he'd be defending. As we walked from the office block to his car, I noticed my jeans were sagging a little low. I didn't have a belt on that day and was a fair bit heavier in 2014, so wearing my clothes baggy was my best tactic. Sue me.

I raised my T-shirt to show Brendon just how low my denim had dropped and he confirmed a watching police officer probably would have stopped and fined me.

Things became all the more serious as soon as he explained

what would happen to me as a consequence. 'If you missed your court date because you didn't have enough money to make the payment, you'd go to jail.' I checked my pockets and I didn't have enough to buy my way out of jail. Brendan found it hilarious, dropping a very dry 'That's why I don't sag.'

Brendan believed the system in place took advantage of African-Americans, intentionally. Describing systemic racism as being a fixture since the country's inception, he believed the lawmakers were continually finding new ways to execute bias. In St Louis County there were ninety municipalities, some of which shared their services. So for the ninety small boroughs – if you will – according to Brendan, there were a whopping fifty-six different police departments.

Depending on the time of year, the majority of those municipalities would hold their own part-time court. This meant a judge would come out once or twice a month for a giant docket to work through a long list of minor cases. With there being so many cases and so few courts, the venue would be determined by availability, meaning court could take place anywhere from an official building to a school gym.

Cases like unkempt lawns with high grass, speeding tickets and sagging pants would dominate the cases heard. For Brendan, it was common to go to a 90-per-cent African-American town where judge, prosecutor, clerk and police officers in court were white and every defendant would be black. In terms of optics, he described it as looking like Apartheid South Africa.

We arrived and I couldn't help but be saddened by the

jammed parking lot. There were few spaces as so many people had already arrived to face the judge. The venue for court was a middle-school gym and the queue to be seen ended in the entrance. Brendan was representing a young black man who had traffic violations to clear.

Many people had showed up without legal representation. According to Brendan, that, by and large, would be because they couldn't afford one. We said our goodbyes as Brendan went in; I decided to stick around in the parking lot to take everything in. So much of what he'd delivered so matter of fact was only really hitting home as I had a moment of calm to take it all in. Slouched against the crew car, my moment of quiet was repeatedly interrupted by cars pulling up to park as residents hopped out to see the judge. In the half an hour I waited, every single person I saw arriving for court was black.

With the majority of the older white community in Ferguson subscribing to the 'you commit the crime, you deserve the punishment' ideal, if what I was seeing first-hand at the court was to be believed, the only people committing crimes were black.

This was America with a black president, but also with a systemic racial bias. To see an entire law enforcement system weighted heavily against its black citizens left me pondering a core question, how possible is it for a predominantly black community to be policed by a predominantly white police force?

❝ *When race and power collide, you have an issue* ❞

I reconnected with Clifton who answered my cries for help as I was in desperate need of a haircut. Walking me into a popular local barbershop, we could have been with Max in Jowas barbershop in Peckham. As expected, chat was constant and debate was rife. A chair was dusted down and my inner tart was praying I wouldn't get butchered by hair clippers on camera. It didn't take long for the chatty barbers to find out exactly what it was I was shooting and quickly the entire shop was involved in the conversation.

Clifton spoke of a desire for change at an operational level. He wanted the police to change the way they did things: 'When race and power collide, you have an issue.' I asked the entire shop if ever they found themselves in trouble would they call the police? A resounding and powerful 'NO!' came back from barbers, customers, fathers and sons.

Quietly listening while making a good job of my trim, my barber interjected to provide a little context: 'Not all police officers are bad, but a lot of them do abuse their authority.' Citing a diminished feeling of safety around the police, she continued, 'I can show you thirty, forty kids with guns.' Clifton spoke to the bigger issue of guns in the neighbourhood. He explained how much easier it was to acquire a gun than it was to register to vote or have access to higher education.

Another barber brought up guns and opened the can of worms that was the second amendment. I'm not a fan of guns at all but if I were living in America, I honestly don't know what I'd do. 'Somebody come in your house with a gun – would you lay down or fight?' I hadn't thought about the realities of living in an environment where it was almost a given that the bad guys would carry weapons. He asserted a final time, 'You need a gun in your house,' and as far as he was concerned, that was the end of the conversation.

At the time we were filming, over 280 million guns were in circulation across the States, which worked out as almost one for every American. Driving to the next location, I couldn't help but express just how much the numbers scared me. Our American driver and sound guy had very different takes.

Our sound guy wasn't an owner, but our crew driver had two shotguns. Sound guy Matt explained that, to Americans, guns were always presented as cool. Agreeing that philosophic- ally they definitely weren't, he saw guns presented in a cultural context in the same way a motorcycle would be. They were cool, powerful AND legal, so why not have one? Given that logic, I started to see just how polar opposite the American attitude was to my British one.

As far as I was concerned, to the average man in the UK guns weren't real. They were plastic toys we'd run around with making 'pee yaw' noises. For most British kids, toy guns were cool to play with, but rarely would that cool sustain into adulthood.

Growing up I had toy guns in crazy colours made of cheap plastic. At no point did I ever think 'Wouldn't it be great if this was real?' Talking to Matt, it became clear that, for many Yanks, guns had a level of cool no different to a motorbike or fast car.

In an effort to understand guns, I figured I should fire one. I met up with reserve cop Paul and was shown around his firing range and retail business, which carried over 400 guns in stock. His cheapest handgun came in around the $200 mark, which unbelievably was cheaper than the sneakers I had on.

I stood staring at a huge wall filled with handguns, Paul span me on the spot gesturing toward the 'best bits' behind glass. The bits he referred to were the bigger weapons for sale, some of which didn't even look real. With extending this and snapping on that, most of the shotguns looked like props from *Robocop*.

One of his bestsellers was the .12 gauge shotgun, and Paul referred to it as a 'home defence specialty'. The hunk of metal looked like it'd fallen from the pages of a Judge Dredd comic and the very grey, very white customer base filling his shop all looked very excitedly at the weapon.

Paul explained that, during the protests, all law enforcement was pulled into the busiest areas leaving huge chunks of residential roads un-policed. As a result, he saw a huge spike in gun purchases as people wanted to protect their homes, property and themselves. In the four months post-riots, gun sales in Paul's shop were up 84 per cent compared to the previous year. According to Paul, four in five of his customers were white.

His white, middle-aged customers feared the rioting black faces they had seen on the news. The irony was that statistically, these African-Americans were far more likely to be killed by firearms carried by police or civilians.

As a reserve officer, Paul wanted me to understand the danger all officers were putting themselves in, but more importantly, how easy it would be to make a life-changing snap decision when under pressure and holding a weapon. His team created an artificial scenario and suddenly I found myself in the exact same position I'd seen the training rookie cops subjected to.

Paul attempted to make me feel just some of what he'd experience while on duty. He'd constantly find himself alone in testing situations knowing the nearest backup could be seven to ten minutes away. He handed me a blue replica gun that was the exact same size and weight as his on-duty weapon. I was armed with paint pellets and sent towards a doorway for a training exercise intended to test reaction to and management of a dangerous scenario. I wasn't told what would meet me on the other side and the closer I got, the heavier the gun became.

The room was massive and two masked men argued loudly. Noticing me, they advanced as I pathetically attempted to take control. My meek voice was doing a shit job of sounding butch and then, as if from nowhere, one of the two men produced a knife and came right at me. I was literally back to the wall at this point and pulled my gun shooting a single paint pellet in his stomach.

I had to make a decision quickly and ended up making a

bad one . . . But I wasn't an officer and I hadn't been trained. Getting it wrong as a civilian wasn't in any way the same as doing so as an officer of the law. But what would it take to minimise police officers making life-ending bad decisions?

❛ They changed the law; they made it better for everyone else ❜

Only fifty years had passed since African-Americans marched for civil rights and equality. With modern times marred by mounting incidents of police brutality, a new generation has become politicised. Demanding a change in the police treatment and media portrayal, this younger, louder, internet savvy wave of voices forced the country to confront the uncomfortable truth that racism still runs deep in America.

Since Michael Brown lost his life, Ferguson has seen some positive changes. In 2014, three out of the six city councillors were now black, offering a perspective that reflected the majority of the constituency. There was a new police chief with a whole new attitude beginning his tenure making a call for help from the community. A new bill was passed capping the amount of revenue the city could collect from traffic violations. But Clifton felt there was still more to do.

It was his high-school graduation party and I'd been invited to join the barbecue. Graduating and becoming the pride of his family, Clifton was heading to Washington State University to read African-American and Political Studies. In search of a little more insight into who he was at home, I asked him if he'd show me his bedroom.

Full of the expected teenage mess but weighed down with trophies, Clifton talked me through his favourite sneakers, hats and books. Flicking through what most inspired him, Clifton pulled out a Martin Luther King quote. 'Riots are the language of the unheard,' he said with a smile; the relevance to all we'd discussed felt incredibly fitting.

Clifton felt his generation was being labelled as something it wasn't, constantly dismissed en masse or stereotyped. Protesters were not the same as rioters and Black Lives Matter was certainly not the same thing as looters. Seeing his generation of activists as 'continuing the work, but in a different way', Clifton felt a part of something bigger than him.

Comparing the modern-day African-American struggle to the battles fought by the same people but in a different time, Clifton reminded me of the threats made to those who stood up to segregation. Judged and treated as criminals, the supposedly radical civil rights movement changed America for good. Clifton proudly proclaimed, 'They changed the law, they made it better for everyone else.'

In his fatal contact with Michael Brown, officer Darren Wilson apparently didn't break any law or protocol but what cannot be denied was the racist system crawling with corruption to which he belonged.

For the white minority in Ferguson, the police department represented safety and security. For the black majority living lives of constant harassment at the sharp end of institutional racism, their relationship with the law was riddled with resentment. The lack of understanding troubled me, as there wasn't anything I'd seen that came close to some semblance of progress.

Agreeing to front a film about race in America meant I'd need to confront the reality that the flight home might not be one filled with optimism. Unfortunately, my instincts were right as the greater issue wasn't individual acts of violence, but the system that allowed history to continually repeat itself.

Any hope I felt was placed not in some miraculous policy changes on every level, but in individuals like Clifton Kinnie, who had experienced the dark side of modern America. Historically, it had been the young idealists and dreamers like Clifton who had changed the country for the good. Maybe, just maybe, it could happen again.

CHAPTER 11
SOUTH SIDE

In 1996, aged thirteen, I had a special bond with the city of Chicago. I'd never been to the United States, let alone the Windy City, but from the comfort of my smelly teenage bedroom, I'd transport to Chicago weekly. Channel 4's short-lived basketball show *NBA Live* fronted by Mark Webster and living legend Scoop Jackson afforded me a virtual court-side seat to witness arguably the greatest starting five of all time.

Longley, Pippen, Harper, Rodman and, of course, Michael Jordan were gods among men. I watched the legendary '95/'96 season in awe, claiming 'the Chi' as if I'd been born and raised there. It was Jordan's returning season after a year out playing Minor League baseball and every game was an event. He led the team to a record seventy wins and an NBA Championship all while wearing the now classic Jordan XI shoe.

I coveted those bloody sneakers but didn't have the money or opportunity to buy myself a pair until a whole five years later. May god bless the year 2001 and the flawless reissued 'Bred' colourway that nearly brought me to tears the moment I held the box in my arms.

Just so you're aware, I'm doing everything in my power not to have a massive rant about how sneaker culture has deteriorated into a money grab for the internet generation. My love for footwear stretches back to my childhood where I'd sit silently for hours drawing sneakers I'd seen in catalogues and magazines but couldn't afford. To me, those shoes, that team, that season, that city – Chicago meant Jordan and an amazing moment in time.

Outside the Jordan years, there wasn't much pulling my tiny attention span back towards Chicago. Oprah Winfrey emerged as juggernaut of media but didn't feel connected to the city in the way those five men in red did. A few years passed and staying up late to watch a live basketball game happening on the other side of the Atlantic no longer spoke to my hunger for connection in the same way.

I was now in my mid-teens and every thinking moment away from scripts and girls I didn't have the balls to speak to was dedicated to hip-hop. *The Source* magazine became my bible and my favourite MC was a man who not only had one of the most distinctive raspy tones, but through his words I rediscovered Chicago. In the year 2000, *Like Water for Chocolate* was released. This was the fourth studio album from the rapper and Chicago native Common.

Orchestrated by one of the greatest producers of all time, J Dilla, the album tackled race, love and poverty – themes I'd wrestled with for the entirety of my teens. I explored his entire back catalogue, and with lyrics like 'I'm comin' from the South Side, where roughnecks reign; If you can't stand it, don't go outside', his Chicago was a world apart from the sneakers and slam-dunks I knew. It was angst peppered with the realities of a life on the fringes of society.

Drugs and gangs ran the South Side, and Common's music became a vivid window into the lives of those who'd never make it to the stands to cheer on The Bulls. By 2004, Common had joined forces with fellow Chicago rapper Kanye West's G.O.O.D. music label. Kanye went on to become . . . Well, Kanye, a man whose influence has gone global.

Kanye Omari West would go on to produce the entirety of Common's 2005 album *Be* and the two musicians would continue to collaborate for years. With their hometown a regular theme in their collaborative efforts, it wasn't until Kanye shone a light on a young rapper from the Windy City that my understanding of Chicago would change yet again.

On 2011's *Watch the Throne*, Kanye rapped 'I feel the pain in my city wherever I go, 314 soldiers died in Iraq, 509 died in Chicago.' This track, 'Murder to Excellence', didn't pull any punches about what was happening on the city's South Side. I was now in my late twenties and stories of loss of life suddenly held so much more weight. This wasn't just music any more, the lyrics spoke to a bloody epidemic claiming young black men. Kanye doubled down: 'The old pastor closed the cold casket and said the church ain't got enough room for all the tombs.'

A year later, a teenager by the name of Chief Keef saw his fame skyrocket when Kanye remixed his biggest hit 'I Don't Like'. The power of West's influence threw the then 16-year-old (already huge online) into the speakers of out of touch hip-hop fans in their late twenties and early thirties . . . like me. Under house arrest for UUW, or Unlawful Use of a Weapon, Keef wrote and recorded his verse for the remix in his grand-mother's lounge. Rapping, 'I got tats up on my arm 'cause this shit is life', Keef openly referenced his gang affiliation.

I was totally side-swiped by the teenager and fell into a wormhole of videos and think pieces online. The kid already had a loyal localised following, but going viral meant mainstream and global interest. Video after video of Keef and his shirtless teenage friends mugging at the camera clocked up millions of views online. They waved gang signs, tattoos and guns and their audience seemed to eat it up. To the Sonics of local teenage producer Young Chop, they had their own sound in Drill Music, and a growing audience declaring them as rap's newest superstars.

Once again, music would be the catalyst to a new level of understanding Chicago. These kids were rapping about a gang-infested, segregated city with the highest murder rate in the country. The South Side had such an unrelenting body count that it earned itself the unwanted nickname Chiraq. It was Chicago's own Middle East. While Keef's mix tapes and You-Tube fame netted him a record deal with Interscope records worth $6 million, there were thousands of other kids just like him who didn't make music but were just as young, living just as dangerous a life.

What were the chances of escaping such an environment, and surviving the double whammy of police brutality and black-on-black crime?

It was 2016 and I'd experienced what I thought could be every kind of on-camera challenge possible. My twenty-fifth year on screen was my thirty-third year on the planet and my desire to grow on a personal level had been fast-tracked after I'd invested in more regular therapy. The transparency I was willing to deliver would only help the film and my relationship with an entirely new team.

A few months earlier, I'd found myself in one of my favourite restaurants on Soho's Dean Street sat opposite Toby Trackman. He is a director and the production company had suggested I meet him for the yet to be commissioned Chicago film. Quickly bonding over his musical Bristol roots we chewed each other's ears off about club nights and B-sides spiralling into the depths of geekdom.

But just how hard would I be pushed? He made a point of wanting to challenge me in some of my moments of reflection. The best work I'd delivered outside of conversation with contributors had continually come from discourse with my director. Through so much shared experience, my usual collaborator Sam and I found a short hand and fluidity. But what would the new outlook of Toby's bring to the conversation and more importantly, what would he expect from me?

I knew Chicago had recently seen an increase in gun violence and I was heading right into the thick of it. To read about lives being lost was eternally different to being surrounded by it. I honestly didn't know how I'd manage, but knew whatever reaction might find its way to the surface I was ready to examine it on camera.

❦ *Those of us who have been kissed by the sun, there appears to be a target on our backs* ❧

Once again, I'd arrived in the US knowing I'd be making a film about the black experience. Unlike Ferguson, however, there wasn't currently a media spotlight shining on Chicago and my relationship with this city was a constantly changing love affair that had lasted years.

America was at a crossroads; what had for so long been the plight of some was now fighting for the attention of many. The country was gripped by allegations of police brutality and an increase in gun crime was tearing the country apart. But I started my journey knowing that, in this city, police violence was only part of the story.

The national outrage towards police shootings was the big story, but in Chicago, gun violence was also out of control. As the city struggled to cope with the carnage, who was responsible?

It was our first day filming and our drive wasn't long but gave us enough time to establish a healthy rhythm of name-calling and playing music loudly. Toby made the mistake of mentioning that his friends had sometimes likened him to Bart Simpson's best mate, Milhouse. Well, I could see their point: he had the glasses, the haircut and, now and then, the geek-like demeanour. It seemed like it would almost be rude not to call him that.

We arrived and Millhouse, sorry, I mean Toby, had me dive right in the deep end, starting the shoot with a small demonstration outside a local police station. Three young black men stood silently holding stop signs in front of the police building. All three signs were tagged with words below the bold STOP in white. I found myself fixed on the youngest of the three, whose sign read 'STOP KILLING US'.

As well as the silent stop sign protest, a mass of sullen faces stood before news cameras. The demonstrators were holding a banner filled with the faces of African-American victims of police violence. 'The police are killing our women and children,' said a man in an immaculate suit. He had the air of a community leader elected to speak for the families, but his linen and matching fedora contradicted his plea, as he looked less like a community leader and more like a 1950s Harlem dandy. He continued, 'Those of us who have been kissed by the sun, there appears to be a target on our backs.'

Outrage at black deaths at the hands of white cops was rising across the country and Chicago was no different. Emotions were at boiling point. In 2015, police in America killed 306 African-Americans, eight in Chicago alone. The well-dressed spokesperson was almost pleading with cameras begging for change. His tone was a conscious and deliberate whine, not too unlike a preacher begging for his followers' agreement: 'The Chicago police do not get to be judge, jury and executioner of our children.'

Sadly, his content and delivery were so familiar that they felt like clichés. I'd heard men speak on behalf of black communities in America this way my entire life. It felt reminiscent of some of the loudest voices from a bygone era where change was pleaded for. When a young guy in a baseball cap and hoodie got on the mic, his measured, no-nonsense style didn't ask for, but demanded change.

One of the two men had lived through the civil rights era; the other was a millennial with a totally different level of expectation from the country he called home. Speaking to the cameras with pure confidence and clarity, he took aim not just at police brutality, but also at gang violence. He didn't shy away from problems in his community, but insisted on accountability from the people supposedly protecting them.

I attended the monthly police review board, a forum giving locals the chance to air their grievances. With frustrations already articulated to the waiting media, I was expecting things to only get louder once we'd headed inside. The board took place in a conference hall-like space and was packed with concerned locals. A media line-up stood at the back of the room, waiting to cover what would unfold. Their presence was more than justified as the tension in the room was palpable.

Those who'd arrived were not only impassioned but clearly connected to the issues. Many were wearing funeral-style tribute T-shirts displaying the names and faces of lost loved ones. This certainly wasn't a room of weekend warriors, they'd been personally affected and, by the looks of things, directly galvanised to do something.

One after another, bereaved mothers stepped up to the mic berating the police. 'And you all don't give no fucks because he wasn't one of your kids,' rang out of the speakers as the tearful parent let loose on those she saw as responsible. I could hardly watch as the board of police and city officials silently sat and listened with no apparent show of emotion. A few flashed signs of empathy, but most sat blank-faced and could easily have been wondering what to have for their dinner that night.

The more scathing the comments made by grieving

parents, the louder the reception from the audience became. Claps and cheers filled the room every time furious parents dismantled the system and its mute representatives. It must have been cathartic for them, but would it really change anything?

As the board wound down, I got talking to a twenty-two-year-old father of one whose son was fast asleep on his shoulder. Ja'mal Green was a local man and activist who'd attended hoping to hear or see something different, but was about to leave unimpressed. He smiled, admitting the sessions always get heated but 'No solutions ever come out of it, that's the problem.' Ja'mal continued, 'When you see our neighbourhoods looking like third-world countries with no resources, no opportunities and no jobs, its regular.' For someone so young, I was surprised by his lack of optimism:

'You live in it so long there is no hope.'

I got talking to Antoine Hudson, a polite thirteen-year-old who was there with his mother Tambrasha. Antoine's brother Pierre had been shot dead by police at just sixteen years of age. As Tambrasha spoke passionately, the room erupted into applause. Antoine watched proudly with an air of maturity I'd never before seen in one so young.

'Black young males are dying left and right every day in Chicago,' he told me. He was matter of fact and didn't flinch at what was more than a statement; he was describing his own situation. Antoine wore a look of acceptance, seeing the environment he'd grown up in as broken but constant. He knew no different and as a result had decided that crying wouldn't help. Holding everything in, he'd chosen to put his feelings aside in an effort to support his mother who he described as not being as strong. His tone was adult but his baby face made the whole conversation surreal as I kept forgetting I was talking with a child.

Tambrasha was wearing a t-shirt bearing the name and face of her beloved late son, Pierre. She'd made some kind of peace with losing one child but had become increasingly protective of Antoine, insisting he wasn't safe. 'I pray for him every day.'

Her eyes glassed with tears as she explained the forces she'd battle against were gang related. Until the incident, what ultimately took her son was the least of her concerns. 'I always prayed about the gangs and the violence, but now it's sad that I have to cover my kids and pray for them against police shootings.' Antoine comforted his mother as she began to cry again. He was being strong for her but who was being strong for him?

'What do we want? Justice! When do we want it? Now!' rang out. The young, straight-talking activist I'd watched speak to the cameras led the crowd out, chanting in unison. Grieving mothers hugged each other as the review board shook off the weight of the last hour of being shouted at. It was strange watching the community desperate to be heard leave through one door, while those with all the power to change things quietly exited through another. Those with the power to help and those in need may have been in the same room, but they felt worlds apart.

I'd spent years learning about the city through the verses of some of my favourite rap records; now I was finally here but I hadn't emotionally prepared myself at all. During the review board I looked around the room to see people that looked just like my family members tearfully recounting the most horrific of stories. I couldn't help but imagine the faces of my loved ones at the podium, or worse yet on a T-shirt. The unmistakable pain and levels of violence I'd just heard about made everything I'd read and heard in the music aggressively immediate and suddenly very real.

❝ So-called black on black crime; we call it state-sponsored crime ❞

African-Americans make up one-third of the city's residents, yet in 2016 Chicago police killed nine people and all but one were black. The drive from where I was staying to where the majority of filming would happen gave a visual to the disparity in the city. North of the river and surrounded by a bustling city centre, the financial district lead to the tourist hubs and hotels I returned to every night. South and west of the city were predominantly black and had the highest levels poverty.

One such area was Gresham, where in 2013 Pastor Catherine Brown was aggressively arrested in front of her children. Ironically, Brown was a volunteer working with the police to help improve interactions with the black community. Her children, aged eight and one, screamed as a police cruiser deliberately crashed into their car. Threatened at gunpoint, Brown was then pulled from the driver's seat, dragged across the bonnet of the car, tearing her skirt off, and then beaten in her underwear. Laughing, the officers silenced her screaming kids by spraying them with pepper spray.

Pastor Brown talked me through the incident, as she'd obtained police dashboard video showing the entirety of the ordeal. It was a sickening watch and an experience which has left her eight-year-old daughter wanting out of Chicago, and with a newfound hatred of the police.

Pastor Brown referred to her role as a police liaison and community volunteer in the past tense. Her days of trying to help the black community and local police get along were over. Following the incident, Catherine was prosecuted on charges including aggravated battery, assault and two counts of attempted murder. She was eventually found guilty of reckless conduct, a misdemeanour for driving in reverse, while all other charges were dropped.

She still works with the neighbourhood, but Catherine had taken a step back, minimising her interactions with the law while doubling down on her relationship with local community leaders. She regularly hosted a group of elders who'd discuss their corners of Gresham and what could be done. I was invited to join the round table and felt instantly welcome the moment I arrived.

Catherine Brown's house was a real family home and she was clearly a pillar of the community. Family pictures filled the walls, the stove was always on the go, and the fridge held enough food to feed the whole of St Louis. She was a great hostess, but I knew if I ate much of the wholesome food she offered me, I could soon be falling asleep.

The table was made up of older men all itching to unload their issues with the current state of Chicago. The minute I saw the older brother in a dashiki, I knew we were bound to hear some home truths: 'So-called black on black crime, we call it state-sponsored crime.' The belief at the table was that the system had created an environment in which no African-American could truly prosper. They said violence wasn't just about guns – having their schools, day centres and mental health facilities closed down constituted violence on their communities. I had never heard the word used in that way, but it was impossible to disagree.

Englewood had long streets filled with beautiful homes; the majority of which were unfortunately in a state of disre-pair. Fish and chicken spots sat on most corners filling the sticky air with that oil stench that's impossible to get out of your clothes. However, I'd been in town for around a week and as the South Side became more familiar, it began to feel much more appealing then north of the water where I was staying. There, the perfect streets and global chains filling every com-mercial space gave the area a homogenised numbness. There were no defining characteristics to the skyscraper-heavy city centre. I could have been anywhere in the world, but not when I was South Side. The energy on the streets you could feel, the people sat in front of their homes made life in Englewood tangible, immediate and vital.

I didn't expect residents on the south and west sides of the city to stop living their lives because of the frightening numbers relating to violence. But I was surprised at just how much I was drawn to the forgotten and separate side of Chicago life just on the other side of the water.

❛ They don't go to work and think, today I'm gonna shoot somebody ❜

Cases of police brutality dominated the front pages of local papers and countless hours of screen time. We put in an official request for an interview to the Chicago police department but they declined to be a part of the documentary. However, Toby and my producer Becky Reid had an idea how to get around that.

Hungry and super-smart, Becky spoke quicker than I did and had so many ideas about how to make the film even stronger than the pitch the channel had already commissioned. Totally genuine in her opinions of my previous work, Becky was straight up about what she thought I could do better and I bloody loved it. A sign that things would go well with any team I worked with usually came in the god-given ability to give and take insults using profanity with poetic flair. Becky was from

Croydon; she could hold a master class on insults. Quickly realising we'd probably attended the same club nights in our younger years, my tight shoes and loud Moschino shirt combination matched by an admission of her flat cap and Chinese patterned slippers gave us no choice but to click in our embarrassment. Becky and Toby quickly felt like old mates. Like Diana, Becky had a talent to get anyone on side and her way with people would go on to prove invaluable.

Becky had learned about an event called The Blessing of the Bikes and we drove out to one of Chicago's nicer suburbs to see it. It was a huge motorcycle meet and ride out, which excited me as I'd been taking motorbike lessons at home and had my test set for when we got back. However, the closer we got, the more my excitement faded. As I rolled the car past a churchyard packed with hundreds of gleaming motorcycles and massive blokes with beards, leather vests and patches, I realised that these weren't Hells Angels. They were off-duty cops.

Growing up, I didn't have the best experiences with London's police. Getting pulled over in my car on a regular basis wasn't fun but it almost became an expected part of being on the road. It sounds incredibly clichéd, but my interactions with the law have been either cordial or the total opposite. The fact that I'd left home, had a mortgage and a decent lifestyle by the age of eighteen didn't prevent me being stopped and asked, 'Why are YOU in this car?' nearly every time I got behind the wheel.

Arriving at the Blessing of the Bikes I didn't feel particularly comfortable. A welcoming committee most likely wasn't on the cards and with personal experience teaching me that healthy interaction would be thin on the ground, I was apprehensive. I was essentially ambushing a sensitive off-duty event attended by hundreds of officers. I look at that in hindsight and think how easily things could really have gone left. Cheers Becky.

The church's surrounding streets and its own parking lot were lined with motorbikes. Predominantly Harley Davidson hogs, the sun pinging off of polished chrome was almost as difficult to compete with the sounds of the engines.

Wives sat and scrolled social media while their husbands ogled each other's machines. We were unannounced and the off-duty cops weren't pleased. I started to try to talk to some of the guys regardless and the few that didn't walk away were friendly and chatty. Sat on a huge Harley in a leather vest peppered with badges commemorating fellow officers who'd lost their lives, Al Francis opened up about the dangers of their job.

Al was the president of Wild Pig, a police-only motorcycle club. He described policing Chicago as being dangerous depending on the area. We were sat in a beautifully manicured neighbourhood where a lot of officers lived but Al was adamant that bad guys were everywhere.

We started to discuss the criticism the force was facing regarding the police shootings, but were promptly shut down.

A stern-looking biker in wrap-around shades approached, shook my hand firmly and warned Toby not to point his camera at him. My time at the event was clocking no more than ten minutes and already it was looking like we were done. The organising officers wanted to know what we were shooting and, more importantly, our angle. Becky clicked into full charm offensive mode and assured him the film we were making was grounded, bound to my journey and aspired to a balanced view.

Granting permission to continue, Mr Wrap Around Shades pulled Becky to one side to ensure she understood our continued access was dependent upon steering clear of sensitive subject matter. By that he meant everything I instinctively wanted to ask the officers about.

The Blessing of the Bikes event was a memorial gathering and ride out for cops killed in the line of duty as, in the last decade, nine officers had been fatally shot. A priest walked the street and car park splashing holy water on the motorbikes from a bucket using a large broom. Yes, it was as strange as it sounds, but I seemed to be the only one who found the whole thing a little odd.

One attendee who was happy to speak didn't come on a bike; she was with her son and wanted to pay her respects. Sandy Wright lost her father in the line of duty to a bullet from a young African-American man. Sandy's father had been a neighbourhood officer on the South Side who would always stop and chat to local shop owners, kids and passers-by. One day, as he talked to a young gang member, he was hit by bullets fired by two kids from a rival gang who had just been to a friend's funeral and were seeking revenge.

Having lost her dad, Sandy's feelings on policing would never be the same. Sandy believed no one was supporting the police, and she saw their efforts as misrepresented: 'They don't go to work saying, today I'm gonna shoot somebody.' Growing more emotional with every statement, she went on, 'The police are outgunned right now' – referring to the amount of weapons officers encountered on the streets.

Then the lot fell silent as a mic was handed to a young woman. From a piece of paper she read a list of officers who'd lost their lives on duty. A bundle of blue balloons were released and Sandy started to cry.

As the loud and endless queue of motorcycles lined up and rolled out, the buildings either side of the street felt like they were about to collapse with the noise. I watched them leave while digesting Sandy's frustrations. But with Catherine Brown and that table of elders from the South Side still fresh in my mind, I couldn't help but see the similarities. People were dying on both sides of the debate yet everybody believed they were the victims. The biggest problem I could see was that no one was asking what role they played in the problem?

Police brutality was rightfully a huge story and in the national spotlight, but the overall numbers of shootings showed a much bigger problem. In 2015, twenty-three people were shot by the police, nine fatally. At the same time there were almost 2,500 black-on-black shootings, of which over 350 were fatal.

The body count in the city since 2001 has surpassed that of soldiers killed fighting in Iraq and Afghanistan, yet attitudes towards death in the two dramatically different scenarios had become similar. Chicago residents were chalking up loss of life on a weekly basis but outrage was minimal. The people dying weren't soldiers who knew what they were signing up for; these victims were predominantly kids sold a dream by gangs that ended in caskets.

In 2016, someone was shot in Chicago on average every two hours. This frightening statistic delivered a continual stream of content filling column inches and TV reports, but how could somebody report this relentless stream of misery and not be damaged by it?

❝ *Responsibility? Where do you begin?* ❞

I threw Becky and Toby around the back seats of our cheap rental SUV. Empty water bottles and half-eaten cereal bars rattled around the foot wells while Becky told me off for my shit driving. We were in a typically enormous car park for a local supermarket waiting to meet a young journalist who was taking me out on his night shift.

Peter arrived shortly after I parked the tank and everything about the man was non-descript. He drove one of the most popular cars in America, a black sedan, and dressed and spoke in a way that didn't encourage attention. This was a man who didn't want to stand out and considering the environments and people he reported on, I totally understood why. Peter was a journalist who spent his evenings searching for the story, looking specifically for gun crime. Essentially, Peter made a living diving head first into the kind of situations any sane person would run from.

That night he had no plan outside of reacting to what he heard and following the story. He used police scanners and Twitter to stay on top of stories as they happened. His set-up was simple: a hand-held radio that looked like a walkie-talkie allowed him to listen in to police and fire services. As they used public airwaves, it wasn't illegal to hear their interactions. Talking in plain English, not the ten codes you'd hear on TV, Peter would listen for shootings. Should one occur, he'd know about it as it happened.

The sun began to set and I was rolling with Peter so I jumped in his car as he spun us out of the parking lot. Toby was in the back desperately trying to get balanced and comfy with his camera, but the increasingly crappy roads the further south we went didn't help. Peter pointed out previous crime scenes on almost every corner, as we drove deeper into Englewood.

The amazing irony is that Chicago has some of the strictest gun laws in America. There are no gun shops in the city at all, they're not allowed. Yet in 2015 the police seized over 6,000 illegal guns smuggled in from neighbouring states.

We were driving for a few minutes when the scanner sprung to life. 'Shots fired!' A panicked officer called for an ambulance and Peter put his foot down. We were off and headed to the crime scene at speed. I was worried about getting arrested before we'd even arrived as he drove as if we had blue flashing lights on the roof. We broke several laws on the journey over I'm sure, but this was his business and getting there while there was still a story to report was a skill he'd perfected.

The code 'Fire Rollin' was repeated over the radio, explained by Peter as shorthand for sending paramedics to the scene. A young man had been shot in an alley between some residential buildings and the train tracks. We arrived at a busy police scene as ambulances and police lights painted the dark street a glowing blue and red. A group of officers separated from us by yellow tape stood together quietly talking. The victim had been rushed to hospital in critical condition while several men in blue combed a nearby grassy area looking for something.

The yellow police tape protected the scene and Peter and I could only get so close, but the little access we had was reduced even further as an officer moved us further back extending the area covered by tape even more. Peter pulled a cop to one side fishing for information while the detectives tried to wrap up the crime scene and get away as quickly as possible.

Back in the car, the police radio carried reports of shootings all over Chicago. Peter wrote off those cases too far to get to, knowing something would eventually pop up that night on his patch.

We pulled into a twenty-four-hour diner after some sort of sustenance post-adrenaline burnout from the crime scene. As Peter brought the car to a stop, the radio announced that the victim of the shooting we'd got to had just died. He was eighteen.

The yellowing walls and ceiling of the diner could have been put together for some sort of American crime drama. The crabby, hairnet-wearing older waitress and cigarette-smoking chef went about their jobs as we flopped into an empty booth.

It was the first time in hours I'd seen Peter in full light and I noticed just how tired he looked. He carried dark circles around his eyes and stubble that didn't look deliberate. It looked like his night job – consisting almost entirely of poverty and death – twinned with his day job where he'd write about it, had started to take its toll. To absorb so much pain, then be expected to articulate and share it as a written record on a daily basis would quickly break me.

Just like me, he loved the city he called home, but I wasn't sure how he could happily function in it as his mental mind map was littered with crime scenes. I'd struggle to walk certain streets or even eat at certain establishments knowing just how many people had died in or around them. 'You can't let violence define a location,' he said, which was an admirable outlook, as he'd made an effort to revisit places where incidents had occurred, in an effort to rebrand them in his mind.

Peter knew certain blocks by crime scenes or victims and

as much as he said he hadn't been majorly affected, his face told a very different story. He wanted to slow down, but the fact it was only May and there had already been over 1,400 gunshot victims that year, he knew the niche he'd carved for himself meant he wouldn't stop working.

Becky found a website tracking the deaths and shootings in Chicago which regularly updated its figures as the numbers were growing daily. It was 25 May and there had already been 54 homicides that month alone. With six days left, how many more people would lose their life before the counter reset for June?

❝ Let's take our frustrations out on him ❞

In 1933, Reverend A R Leak opened his own funeral home with $500 earned as a bathroom attendant. His aim was to help local black families who couldn't afford to bury their loved ones. Still going and bigger than ever, the Leak family business continues to provide free and heavily discounted funeral services. With so many victims of gun crime becoming their responsibility, the Leaks were seeing the effects of the city's problem with violence first-hand, so I visited the funeral home to learn how they managed the numbers.

Toby told me to walk down a long corridor and through a huge metal door at the end. He didn't tell me what was on the other side. As soon as I went through it, a sharp smell I didn't recognise hit me. It was chemical and totally foreign to me. I turned into the room and the sight of eight dead bodies covered in white sheets stopped me in my tracks.

Dressed in scrubs and a hairnet, Naidra introduced herself. I was in her place of work and her job was to get the dead ready for their families to view and then for their funerals. Explaining my confusion at the smell, she referred to it as the smell of death that she'd disturbingly become used to. I can't really explain the strange feeling of those embalming fluids mixed with bodies temporarily prevented from decomposing. Seeing so many bodies outlined by the white sheets was haunting. I'd never been around so much death.

She was working on bodies that had already been embalmed and was seeing victims shipped in from the medical exam room daily who were riddled with bullets. What she found most difficult wasn't the amount of gunshot victims; it was how they'd been shot. Naidra explained the shock she'd feel in opening the body bags to see faces broken up by huge bullet holes.

The levels of violence happening in Chicago made her fear for her son. Her three-year-old would be on her mind all day while working, as her biggest fear was to open a body bag and see his face staring back at her. Through first-hand experience, Naidra knew avoiding gang life or culture didn't always exempt you from its reach. So many of the victims she'd deal with were just in the wrong place at the wrong time. She spoke about her son getting caught up in the violence regardless of how good he grew up to be. 'It may not have been for him being in a gang, he just could be on the wrong side of town and they decide, let's take our frustrations out on him.'

I had to step out of the room as it started to become all a bit too much. I sat in the hall gathering my thoughts as the professional part of my brain began to turn off. I'd said yes to making the film months before the shoot was scheduled and as fate would usually have it, life didn't slow down around me. About a week before I boarded the flight, a good friend of mine had died and his funeral was promptly scheduled for a day in the middle of the shoot.

As a teenager, music was a huge part of my life, not just as a DJ, but as an MC as well. By the time I was in my early twenties I'd recorded close to a hundred demos with one of my best friends, producer Kevin Mcpherson, and was offered a publishing deal by living legend Guy Moot at EMI records. My music lawyer and friend was Richard Antwi whose honesty and incredible professionalism helped me walk away from the money and pursue my growing career in TV. He refused to let me damage what I'd built at that point by starting an entirely new career, even though I'd be walking away from a six-figure sum.

Richard's funeral was happening while I was in Chicago and suppressing my sadness in that moment sat in the Leaks hallway was impossible. Death was on my mind and after literally being surrounded by it while talking to Naidra, I finally cracked. Losing a friend only a few years older than me filled me with feelings of mortality. Missing the chance to say goodbye to Richard and being around so much death in the funeral parlour took the role I filled at the centre of the film and twisted it.

I stepped outside and couldn't help but let the tears out, as making sense of the loss I felt on a personal level and the unrelenting death I was talking about every day in making the documentary had reached boiling point. It had to come out and boy did it. It was a snotty ugly cry and I'm glad Toby was completely unaware, as I needed that moment on my own. I eventually got my shit together and headed back inside to carry on shooting.

❛ If I can survive Chicago, I wanna give my family a better life ❜

Most of the victims of gun violence in Chicago are under the age of thirty, and parents on the South Side were living with the very real threat that their children may not make it to adulthood. Ja'mal Green, the young father and activist I'd met at the police review board, was performing at a community peace event. He sang on stage receiving huge applause and, after his performance, I was invited to join him and his fiancée at their basement apartment.

The young couple were raising a constantly giggling baby boy and seemed far more mature than their years would suggest. Ja'mal couldn't hide his frustrations at what he called a lack of male leaders in the community. By having a son, Ja'mal believed he'd raise a man who'd give back just as he'd done. His fiancée Ayana Clark was also just as frustrated with their living conditions but didn't see their current home as one they'd be in forever. Her southern accent was broad, making the weight of her words lighter on the ear.

Ayana was scared to take their son Ja'mal Jr to the park: 'You're limited in this city about what you can do with your kids.' Ja'mal believed he didn't live in the city, he was barely surviving it: 'If I can survive Chicago, I wanna give my family a better life.' Explaining that everyone was in survival mode – from the gang bangers right the way through to normal guys like him – even if they went about their survival in different ways, he understood the motivations.

Ayana explained the gang member mentality by simply stating, 'Every dollar you make, is a dollar I don't make, so in order for me to make that dollar back, I have to kill you to ensure that I make that profit.' It was a cold reality she painted, but for her, it came down to conditioning. She blamed the mayor who'd shut down fifty schools on the South Side.

Ayana believed there were two very different Chicagos, and their home was right in the middle of the neglected side. Ja'mal believed the north was seeing all the support, forcing some parents to turn a blind eye to their kids to dealing drugs, as that had suddenly become the only way to keep the lights on.

❟ *That don't supposed to be* ❟

An average week at The Leaks funeral home would see two or three young victims of gun violence. Lee McCullum Jr was the twenty-ninth person to lose their life that month alone. He was found in his mother's car with multiple gunshot wounds to the head and I'd been invited to his funeral.

Sat at the back of the full church, I got talking to one of his mentors and close family friend Michael. We sat at the back of the packed hall and spoke quietly as friends and family members around us quietly cried. I was struck by just how many young faces were there to mourn the death of Lee, making the premature nature of his death inescapable. Michael insisted he was a good kid who just wanted to play basketball, but how does a good kid on the right path lose his life to gun violence?

Michael strongly believed Lee's loss of life was extra painful for so many, not because his life had more value, but because he was on the right path. As far as Michael was concerned, the environment was to blame: 'It's a lack of respect for human lives. It's a lack of fathers, it's a lack of standing up and being men to their child.' Michael couldn't hold in his anger and it seemed he wasn't alone in feeling that Lee's death was not only incredibly sad, but unjust.

I'd arrived in the darkest outfit I had scraped together from the blacks and blues I'd packed in my suitcase. When I arrived, I was surprised to see his entire family and closest friends head to toe in white. Michael described the choice of clothing as 'respect that he was an angel'.

Lee's father, Lee Senior, stepped up to the podium and held the room's attention with his short, clipped words. Reading from a small piece of paper, he'd planned a speech for his son but his presence alone demanded the attention of the room. Not the tallest in height but huge in stature, Lee Snr was clearly grieving quietly behind his dark shades. He looked so young himself, further emphasising the young life that had been taken.

Throughout his speech his eyes jumped from those in front of him, to the young friends of Lee trying their best to show no emotion at the back of the room, and the open casket holding his dead son. Speaking to the responsible shooters, he said, 'Ima pray for you in a different type of way,' which received a loud round of applause from the parents in the room.

The threat of a retaliation on Lee Jr's behalf felt increasingly likely as the young pack holding the wall seemed more and more enraged as the service went on. Lee Snr made no attempts to hide who he was speaking to as he raised his voice: 'Fall back, 'cos I can't do no more funerals.'

Michael left my side and stepped up to the podium. His delivery was worlds apart as every ounce of frustration and rage poured out of him. He repeatedly shouted 'That don't supposed to be', while pointing at Lee's lifeless body. Michael had been in prison for over twenty-one years and Lee Jr's death infuriated him. 'That's supposed to be me.' Like a man possessed, Michael pleaded for there to be no retaliation but with emotions running so high, I was moved but unsure if the message hit home enough for Lee's visibly emotional young friends.

As Michael stepped down, I looked to Toby and Becky who were now hiding at the back of the church. They were both bright red and tearful as the powerful speeches had affected them too.

It was a funeral service the likes of which I'd never experienced. Understandably grief swept the room, but the pleas for no further violence made the loss of life so much more painful and the message so much more vital.

The service ended and the room full of men, women and children in white filled the tall concrete steps. Outside, Michael quietly shared news he'd had of an imminent potential show of disrespect to the family. He'd heard those responsible might come by shooting from a car to further establish their strength. The family quickly said their goodbyes and left while I tried to work through everything that had just gone on. The biggest battle for me was the need so many felt to do something about Lee's death, but with the same level of force causing the same level of grief to another family in another church.

Lee McCullum Jr was the 221st victim of a fatal shooting in 2016. It was only May. Thankfully, two weeks passed and there had been no retaliation.

That night, Toby insisted we'd get out for a team dinner and Jesus did we need it. It was one of the hardest days I'd ever had on a shoot and it wasn't because of the filming conditions or the team, it was because of the weight of the subject matter.

All three of us left the church totally drained and with nothing left to give, we ended up stuffing our faces with every kind of taco on the menu while Toby and Becky smashed back a few tequilas. We needed a night off and decompressing as a team pulled us together. We ate and giggled hysterically and needed it. I've been happily teetotal for years, but that night I envied the release Toby and Becky could find in a bottle.

❛ This the law of the land of the other man . . . we just pawns ❜

Michael and Lee Snr invited us over to the McCullum family home. Occupied by Lee's grandmother, the house was the family hub crammed with food, photos and memories. We met on the street as I parked and as we walked to the house, every step Lee took let out a small noise. It was only then that I realised Lee was walking on a prosthetic leg.

Lee Snr lost his leg through no fault of his own; he was being a good Samaritan. In an attempt to break up a fight he got shot and due to circulation issues his leg was amputated. I stood in silence as Lee told the story, but it didn't stop there. He then went on to show me the large scar he had on his head where he was shot. In the head. And survived.

Picking up his son from a Halloween party, Lee turned a corner and walked into a fire fight, catching a bullet to the skull in the cross fire. Telling both stories with a quiet calm, it seemed as though the man had made peace with both incidents. Lee explained he was angry, but not any more. 'I'm angry about my son, that's what I'm angry about.'

Proud of his naturally athletic son Lee Jr, he showed me his son's massive pile of trophies and medals. In an effort to get to know who Lee was, I asked if they'd planned for sports to be a part of his future? Lee Snr walked away slowly saying 'Yes' over and over, as that possibility would be something he'd never know.

Every wood-clad wall was filled with photos and signs of the huge family. There were too many children to count, but with there being so many pictures of him, it was clear Lee Jr was a favourite. Sat on big fluffy, comfy couch, Lee Snr fell back into his seat on the kind of sofa only grandmothers have. It was impossible the amount of pattern on that one piece of furniture, yet it was unbelievably comfy.

'It hurts that he's gone . . . I feel like I failed because he lost his life.'

Michael stood in the hall watching quietly as we spoke. 'It's gon' always hurt,' Michael barked in his now familiar tone. He believed the trust between the community and the police had totally eroded. It was an atmosphere where people were taking justice into their own hands and the system was only making matters worse. 'It's broke, you can't fix something that's broke – you got to replace it.'

Lee showed me pictures of his son's graduation. In every photo the kid was beaming with pride. There were photos of

Junior hugging and kissing his girlfriend and their young romance was sweet and clearly real, but now unfulfilled.

Michael was hurt not just at losing young Lee Jr but listening to his friend speak with every word charged by so much pain. 'This the law of the land of the other man ... We just pawns.' Standing in the dark doorway, Michael was visibly upset and felt powerless in both his future and that of his community. Resigned, Michael let out an unusually quiet, 'The system been broke.'

It was a revealing but deeply painful conversation. I said my goodbyes and left quietly.

I'd spent over a week on Chicago's South Side and the place just kept smashing me with curveballs I never could have prepared for. As I left, Lee Snr called me back to the house's porch and pulled from his pocket his cell phone. Without asking, Lee thrust in my face images of his son on the autopsy table. His face was riddled with cuts and deep bullet holes. I was speechless as Lee put his phone away holding eye contact. He wanted me to understand what he was trying to live through and I wondered just how many times he had stared at that hellish photo.

I walked away to the car as kids in the wide sunny street played loudly. A boy on a pink girl's bike complete with flowery basket rode past smiling. All innocence and giggles, while the images I'd just seen of Lee Jr filled me with sadness.

Lee was a good kid but he lost his life to gang violence. If that was the case, how could you truly feel your child – just like the boy on the bike – would stay protected? What was becoming undeniable was that no matter what might be instilled in your child, their behaviour, manners and morals couldn't protect them from cross fire or a stray bullet. Just because of the street you live on, your child might not make it to their eighteenth birthday.

I drove away bouncing down a main street filled with pot-holes. Every third shop was closed down or boarded up. I couldn't help but feel I was in a place sending loud and very direct signals to its African-American residents. No one cares about the area and no one cares about you. But what might that lead to? Well if you're a child being told nothing around you and (by proxy) you don't matter, what respect will that child grow to have for their own life or worse still, someone else's?

❛ People think it's not your problem, until that problem knocks on your door ❜

So who was speaking up for the next generation? A group of fathers and college fraternity brothers were taking to the streets of Englewood in an effort to send a loud message. They marched the streets head to toe in purple, chanting, singing and clapping. Residents stopped to watch, cheered them on, or joined in and marched with them and it was incredible to witness.

They chanted, 'Stop the violence, save our youth, put the guns down.' Cars beeped their horns in support while some came to their doorways raising a single fist in support. I walked with a father who'd brought his six-year-old son along, believing the walk would be something the kid would remember for the rest of his life.

We arrived at a car park and stopped as the pack congregated. The crew of former classmates sang loudly and begun step dancing. Stamping and clapping, they used just their bodies as percussion. It was beautiful to watch the group of fathers and grandfathers so united in their mission. Then, one of the men stopped a song to make an announcement about news he'd just received. 'While we was walking, a brother just got shot.' This had happened literally minutes before as we passed. 'We have to have a greater presence,' another man shouted. 'We gotta be louder next time.'

Mike, a taller, quieter man stepped up to make a speech. The group fell silent in support as some gripped his shoulder, others his back. They were marching to send a message, but also in honour of his daughter, Tiara Parks, who at just twenty-three had lost her life as the victim of a stray bullet. 'We have to get ahead of the problem.' Rumbles of agreement floated with every statement made.

He spoke of helping others and protecting the children, forgetting mid-flow he didn't have a daughter any more when speaking about doing right by the children of others. Full of emotion, he corrected himself and was instantly embraced, just about avoiding tears.

I told Mike about attending Lee's funeral. He stopped me

talking with no more than a look. 'Lee McCullum?' he asked. 'That was the boyfriend of my daughter that was killed.' His words nearly knocked me off my feet. His daughter and her boyfriend had been shot dead just three weeks apart.

Mike was a cop and even his daughter wasn't exempt from the violence: 'People think it's not your problem, until that problem knocks on your door,' he said. Tiara just happened to be in the wrong place at the wrong time and his position as Deputy Sheriff made no difference to the safety of his child. He risked his life every day and was visibly close to break-down, as his efforts to better his community couldn't keep his child alive. He'd done everything he believed he could to keep his daughter away from the violence. She went to college, she had her life together, but the violence plaguing the city still touched his door.

Tiara and Lee were two connected lives lost, both victims of guns and segregation-fuelled tensions that continue to rip the country apart. Could it be that for many black people, the ever-elusive American dream had been replaced by a fight for survival?

I came away from the Windy City with more questions than answers, but I felt a level of pride in my willing to share every doubt, annoyance and frustration with the camera.

This film almost entirely stripped away the voiceover track, which only showed up when it was really needed. I felt trusted in my role on screen as that steered the film, but what made it were the people I'd met and their willingness to share.

All the films I've made so far have taught me amazing lessons in objectivity, listening, patience and so much more, but perhaps none more so than *Life and Death in Chicago*. For me, this project set a benchmark for the level of work I was to be a part of. There is still so much to learn, but I knew I had made something I could be proud of, and felt excited about what I would do next . . .

ACKNOWLEDGEMENTS

As things have progressed over the past few years, I couldn't be more proud of the way in which my career and outlook have developed. This growth hasn't been achieved alone – my support systems and collaborators continue to push and challenge me to do better. Finding a sweet spot between trusting my gut and accepting guidance, is the only way I can describe navigating the successes and failures of a life in TV.

With that in mind, I'm beyond grateful for my incredible management team at James Grant, who put my ideas in front of the perfect partners in BBC Books and Penguin Random House. I learned so much during this process from my genius editor Ian Gittins. (Ian, I know this project is just the beginning of an exciting new chapter!)

Without the support of the BBC and their development of me as a credible, factual face, these amazing experiences might not have happened in the first place. Danny Cohen, Charlotte Moore, Patrick Holland, Damian Kavanagh and Jamie Balment, thank you.

To the production companies Love and Sundog and every

director, producer, fixer, researcher and runner I worked with – these films wouldn't have made it to air without your belief and hard work.

Lastly, to my family. I've always seen friends as the family you choose; so to separate the two groups wouldn't be right. My mother, brothers and sisters (blood and otherwise), I hope you know exactly how much you mean to me. Your cooking, endless cups of mint tea, lend of an ear and advice, played a huge part in the book being written. Your help in managing everything I faced, both on and off camera, professional and personal, during the making of these films kept me present and focused and for that, I'll forever be thankful.

INDEX

INDEX